Analytic Activism

Oxford Studies in Digital Politics

Series Editor: Andrew Chadwick, Royal Holloway, University of London

Analytic Activism

DIGITAL LISTENING AND THE
NEW POLITICAL STRATEGY

DAVID KARPF

WITHDRAWN

OXFORD
UNIVERSITY PRESS

OXFORD
UNIVERSITY PRESS

Oxford University Press is a department of the University of Oxford. It furthers
the University's objective of excellence in research, scholarship, and education
by publishing worldwide. Oxford is a registered trade mark of Oxford University
Press in the UK and certain other countries.

Published in the United States of America by Oxford University Press
198 Madison Avenue, New York, NY 10016, United States of America.

© Oxford University Press 2016

Library of Congress Cataloging-in-Publication Data
Names: Karpf, David, 1978– author.
Title: Analytic activism : digital listening and the new political strategy /
David Karpf.
Description: New York, NY : Oxford University Press, 2016. | Series: Oxford
studies in digital politics | Includes bibliographical references and index.
Identifiers: LCCN 2016021262 (print) | LCCN 2016037349 (ebook) |
ISBN 9780190266127 (hardcover : alk. paper) | ISBN 9780190266134 (pbk. : alk. paper) |
ISBN 9780190266141 (Updf) | ISBN 9780190266158 (Epub)
Subjects: LCSH: Political participation—Technological innovations. |
Communication in politics—Technological innovations. | Political campaigns—
Data processing. | Data mining—Political aspects. | Big data—Political aspects.
Classification: LCC JA85 .K37 2016 (print) | LCC JA85 (ebook) |
DDC 332.40285/4678—dc23
LC record available at https://lccn.loc.gov/2016021262

9 8 7 6 5 4 3 2 1

Paperback printed by Sheridan Books, Inc., United States of America
Hardback printed by Bridgeport National Bindery, Inc., United States of America

For Alison, now and always

Contents

List of Figures and Tables

Figures

Tables

Preface

The inspiration for this book came from a conversation I observed at Netroots Nation in the summer of 2011. The executive directors of two major online political activist organizations were debating a television commercial that they were jointly developing, part of a broader effort to recall Wisconsin governor Scott Walker. Each director had his or her own vision of what the advertisement's central message ought to be. There was a strong argument for both ideas, and no simple means of determining which was right. A lifetime of experience—originally as an environmental organizer and trainer, and later as an academic researcher—has taught me how these conversations unfold. These decisions generally get made either through attrition or through hierarchy; either someone grows frustrated and gives up, or someone asserts authority (formal or informal) and makes a unilateral decision. The conversations are never quick. It was almost lunchtime, and I was getting hungry. I started thinking about how to politely leave them to it. And then I heard something new:

"Well, we'll test it."
"Yeah. Let's test it."

The act of testing had become a neutral arbiter of sorts for these netroots leaders. Faced with a strategic dilemma, they developed tactical responses and then looked for feedback mechanisms that would tell them if their ideas were working or not. Rather than choosing tactics because *that's what we always do*, or because *that's what our peers do*, or because *that's what the boss expects* (or, frankly, because *that's what the donors have asked for*), these netroots organizations had developed an alternative norm: when you are facing a hard choice, look to data for guidance. I immediately forgot my hunger as I became occupied by a series of questions: *How* are they going to test this? What sort of data can they gather? What can it *actually* tell them? And what are the limitations? What *can't* it tell them?

When we think about the Internet and citizen politics, strategic conversations like this one rarely enter into our field of awareness. We tend to focus on the speed of the new media environment or the radically reduced costs of participation. We are living through a moment when a video recorded on a handheld device can be posted online for free and spread virally to millions of people, igniting a movement along the way that demands a government response. The basic tools for citizen political engagement have never been more readily accessible than they are today. And the leading theories of citizen political engagement were created for an era when the basic costs of participatory acts were steeper. The disjuncture between old theories and new citizen practices has attracted a wealth of inquiry into the novel opportunities and possibilities for acts of political speech online. But I had an inkling, listening to these netroots leaders talk, that the act of listening online was equally important.

These netroots organizations were relying not on the Internet's speed or its low transaction costs; they were relying instead on digital media's *measurability*. The ability to measure online acts has given rise to a culture of testing that, in turn, has changed how organizations think about strategy, tactics, and power. This is a new style of activism—what I term *analytic activism*. At the intersection of digital listening, the culture of testing, and massive scale, advocacy and activist organizations are making decisions in different ways. But the reality of this testing and participation is much messier than it often appears to be in journalistic coverage and TED-style sales pitches. Analytics is not guiding us to a promised land of scientifically derived optimal campaign techniques. The two netroots leaders relied on testing to help them decide between competing visions for their advertisement, but this does not necessarily mean they arrived at the ideal campaign tactic. Rather, analytics are rendering new objects, themselves artifacts of public opinion that exert weight in organizational decision making, settling the tough arguments in new ways. Strategy is still messy, chaotic, and imperfect.

I had, by this point, already written and revised the bulk of my first book. As I pondered that simple phrase, "Well, we'll test it," I realized that there was still a lot left for me to figure out. How does this digital listening work? How does it change the work of political activists? How does it compare with older forms of organized listening or sentiment analysis, like polling and focus groups? Where does it work best, and when should we treat it with skepticism? As I ran through these questions, another realization settled in: "Oh, hell. I'm going to have to write a sequel."

Writing a book is a lonely pursuit, but the task is never completed in isolation. This book has been shaped by the insights and suggestions of many academic friends and colleagues. Chris W. Anderson, Kevin Collins, Nina Hall, Hahrie Han, Matt Hindman, Daniel Kreiss, Rasmus Kleis Nielsen, and Matt Powers all read and commented on every page of the manuscript and challenged me to make it better at every turn. Jesse Littlewood, Sahar Massachi, Michael Silberman, and Micah Sifry took time out of their busy lives as netroots practitioners to do the same. I also owe a debt of gratitude to Jack Balkin, Yochai Benkler, Bruce Bimber, Tosca Bruno-van Vijfeijken, Andrew Chadwick, Archon Fung, Steve Livingston, Fenwick McKelvey, Caitlin Petre, Hollie Russon-Gilman, Nikki Usher Layser, and Ariadne Vromen. Their conversations and suggestions over the past three years have heavily shaped this project.

This book could not have been written without the engagement, patience, and generosity of dozens of political practitioners who took the time to speak with me about their work and help hone my understanding of the field. I am particularly indebted to Nicole Aro, Phil Aroneanu, David Babbs, Nick Berning, Ben Brandzel, Matt Carroll, Noland Chambliss, Milan de Vries, Stefanie Faucher, Matt Fitzgerald, Anna Galland, Adam Green, Michael Grenetz, Tara Harwood, Colin Holtz, Felix Kalb, Amanda Kloer, Jesse Littlewood, Jackie Mahandra, Sahar Massachi, Sam McLean, Nicco Mele, Michelle Miller, Daniel Mintz, Hallie Montoya Tansey, Josh Nelson, Robin Priestley, Ben Rattray, David Segal, Ilya Sheyman, David Sievers, Michael Silberman, Neil Sroka, Jon Stahl, Taren Stinebrickner-Kauffman, Stephanie Taylor, Ben Wikler, and Nathan Woodhull.

Aaron Swartz and Jake Brewer also each played an important early role in this project. Aaron was a goddamn wizard at thinking through the complex issues of listening to and building an online community. Jake had an infectious hope and enthusiasm; it made everyone around him believe a little harder and work together a little better. Each of them died tragically in the past few years, long before their time. There are places in this book where I feel keenly aware of an Aaron-shaped and Jake-shaped hole—places where one of them would have corrected my analysis, or objected to an interpretation, or pushed the field in an entirely different direction. It was an honor to know both of them, and I can only hope that they would enjoy seeing what our conversations turned into. In Aaron's memory, the first three chapters of this book are available immediately under a Creative Commons Attribution-Noncommercial-No Derivative Works License (version 3.0), and the full book will be made available under a Creative Commons License two years after publication. I know he would have expected nothing less.

I began working on this book just after joining the School of Media & Public Affairs at George Washington University. I have benefited from an outstanding intellectual climate there, with colleagues and students who have supported my work and encouraged me at every turn. The early research phase was supported by a research grant from the Columbian College Facilitating Fund, and part of the writing phase was supported by a University Facilitating Fund research grant. I am truly blessed to have found myself in such a strong and supportive community. During my final year working on the book, I have also had the good fortune to work with Devan Kreisberg. Devan has been the best research assistant I could hope for. She single-handedly improved every part of this book manuscript, asking keen questions and offering thoughtful suggestions. (It is best that no one ever see the mess that chapter 2 was before Devan found a way to salvage it.) I have also had the pleasure of once again working with two excellent editors—Angela Chnapko and Andrew Chadwick—at Oxford University Press. Between the three of them, all remaining intellectual errors and impenetrable language can be attributed only to my own stubbornness.

Analytic Activism

1

Will the Revolution Be A/B-Tested?

This is a book about technology, civic associations, innovation, and power. I argue that some of the most important impacts of digital technology lie not in the capacity of disorganized masses to more easily *speak*, but in the capacity of new civil society organizations to more effectively *listen*. The book examines the organizational logic underlying key digital activist tools—distributed petition sites, automated tactical optimization systems, and online video platforms designed to promote "virality"—and the media logic that determines the power and effectiveness of these tools. It also examines the limitations of emerging technological platforms, raising a cautionary flag about the ways that putting too much faith in these new measures of online sentiment can lead us astray.

Current scholarship on digital politics often becomes mired in a pair of intellectual cul-de-sacs. Scholars either celebrate digital politics as supporting a new era of spontaneous, "bottom-up" civic engagement or bemoan the rise of "clicktivism," which supposedly degrades citizen power by encouraging worthless online acts of simple solidarity. I find that the reach of both these intellectual camps tends to exceed their grasp. In virtually every case of large-scale, long-term citizen activism (digital, offline, or a mix of the two), organized political associations continue to play a key intermediary role. The "organizational layer" of politics is often ignored by academic interlocutors with an interest in digital politics.[1] The spontaneous feel of a suddenly trending Twitter hashtag belies the organizational processes occurring just offstage, behind the scenes. Organizational concerns—fundraising, membership growth, reputation, strategy—are hidden variables that play a decisive role in how we ought to interpret the data. A "like" or retweet can be either powerful or pointless—it depends on the broader strategic context of these acts of digital communication.

---

[1] Notable exceptions include Kreiss (2012); Nielsen (2012); Karpf (2012a); Bimber, Flanagin, and Stohl (2012); Vromen and Coleman (2013); Chadwick (2013); Costanza-Chock (2014); Baldwin-Phillipi (2015); and Wells (2015). As you might notice from these publication dates, we are collectively starting to do a better job of taking organizations seriously again.

My goal in this book is not to convince you that new communications technologies are *good* or *bad* for citizen political activism. I aim instead to suggest that this is fundamentally the wrong question. All powerful social movement tactics have always been premised on a strategic analysis of what the media environment *affords*. Like it or not, the era of broadcast television has ended, just as surely as the era of broadsheets and pamphlets did. The digital era supports different tactics. The most powerful citizen activist organizations will, once again, be the ones that leverage, innovate, and adapt. This book grapples with how activist organizations employ digital communications technologies to develop and refine new tactics and strategies that help them build power and win victories in the twenty-first century.

What Is Analytic Activism?

Analytic activism is a new approach to citizen-driven politics that makes use of the affordances of digital technologies to fashion new strategic interventions in the political arena. It is a change in organizational structure, processes, and work routines.[2] Three prominent features distinguish it from other forms of activism.

First, analytic activism embraces a *culture of testing*, which guides organizational learning and shapes organizational practices. The culture of testing can be as simple as conducting A/B tests to determine which email headline is best (Karpf 2012a; Issenberg 2012; Kreiss 2012). But it can also be dizzyingly complex. Rather than relying on the way they've always done things, advocacy groups are now testing which tactics and techniques are most effective at engaging new supporters, forging deeper ties with existing supporters, and leveraging power over targeted decision makers (Han 2014). The culture of testing creates feedback loops that help analytic activists learn, innovate, adapt, and evolve within a fast-changing hybrid media system.

Second, analytic activism prioritizes *listening* through digital channels: social media, like Facebook and Twitter, or more established digital media like email and website traffic. As I discuss in chapters 2 and 6, digital listening does have its limitations; it is listening without conversation, and thus lacks many of the benefits that are derived from two-way interaction. But analytic activists place an emphasis on digital listening where many of their peers fail entirely to listen. All forms of present-day activism make use of (at least some) digital media to

---

[2] Darren Halpin (2014) raises a key point in this regard: there is a difference between treating groups as a unit of analysis and studying the structures, incentives, and pressures that shape organizations. When we treat organizational form as a black box, the impact of analytic activism is suddenly rendered invisible, left hiding in plain sight.

construct new forms of activist speech. But the distinguishing feature of analytic activism is that its practitioners are using these channels to listen in new ways, not solely for new forms of speech.

Third, analytic activism demands *scale*. As we have learned from Google, Facebook, Netflix, and Amazon, there is a tremendous digital advantage in raw numbers. These companies routinely glean valuable information about the interests, habits, and needs of their customers that smaller and/or start-up competitors simply cannot identify (Hindman forthcoming). They do so through testing and analytics, applied on a massive scale. The larger your numbers, the more precisely (and more frequently) you can turn to analytics for insights. Likewise, many of the tools and techniques of analytic activism provide substantial value to organizations with 1 million members while being virtually irrelevant to organizations with 10,000 members. Analytic activism is a tool of large, established advocacy groups.

One implication of these three features of analytic activism is that *not all digital activism is analytic activism.*[3] Individual citizens and viral social movements also benefit from the affordances of the Internet. As Lance Bennett and Alexandra Segerberg (2013) have described, the lowered costs of communication and coordination online have given rise to new forms of "connective action," in which disorganized masses of citizens can coalesce around a shared political interest without developing a stable organizational infrastructure. These connective episodes can have an important role in shaping the broader public consciousness and pressuring political elites. They draw on the new "culture of connectivity" that has become ubiquitous in our daily lives (Van Dijck 2013). But their minimal structure also limits their capacity for listening, testing, and learning. It is only the organizations with larger memberships, with their stable infrastructure and their routinized strategic practices, that are able to leverage digital media into this new style of analytic activism.

Likewise, the field of analytic activism is distinct from the radical "horizontalist" activist movements, such as Occupy Wall Street and worldwide "movements of the squares" that have captured both the public's and academia's imagination over the past few years. The horizontalist tradition has a substantial pedigree that predates the rise of digital communications networks. Radical anarchist activists,

---

[3] Throughout this book, I will switch between the terms "activism" and "advocacy." I'll also describe the organizations in this study with a variety of terms: "activist groups," "advocacy groups," "political associations," and "social movement organizations." This is meant to signal that, though each of these terms is associated with its own divergent academic literature, the boundaries between the terms are practically indistinguishable. Kenneth Andrews and Bob Edwards made this point in a 2004 article reviewing the "disconnected literatures on social movements, interest groups, and non-profit organizations" (479). I find their argument persuasive, so I treat the terms as interchangeable.

"black bloc" protesters, and the Yippies of the 1960s all preached and (to at least some degree) practiced horizontalism. Today, horizontalism is too often incorrectly treated as synonymous with digital activism. As Paolo Gerbaudo (2012) has demonstrated, leadership in these (primarily offline) movements takes the form of "activist choreography," wherein key actors within activist networks employ social media to softly help coordinate activist activity and influence the direction of their radical movements. This is an important development in digital activism, but it is distinct from what I would term analytic activism. Occupy Wall Street and similar activist movements lack the culture of testing that we see in organizations like SumOfUs.org, Change.org, and MoveOn.org. Their lack of vertical leadership structure alters how they strategize, how they listen, and how they learn.

The "hacktivist" networks like Anonymous and Lulzsec that Gabriella Coleman (2014) vibrantly describes in *Hacker, Hoaxer, Whistleblower, Spy* also represent a distinct form of digital activism that stands outside the sphere of analytic activism. Hacktivists are (obviously) engaging deeply with digital media and technology. But they are not focused on converting data and analytics into outputs that help them craft media interventions to move forward a specific political agenda. They are instead focused on directly exploiting vulnerabilities in software and hardware to create power outside the traditional boundaries of politics. Hacktivism is a distinct phenomenon that attracts different players with different skill sets, norms, beliefs, and goals. It deserves (and receives) detailed treatment and attention in its own right. Rather than attempt to shoehorn all these forms of digital activism into a single rubric, I choose to readily admit that they fall outside the scope of this study.

Analytic activism creates new *strategic objects* that can be iteratively used to develop new types of political intervention. Strategic objects are the shared reference points around which strategic conversations are constructed. Put plainly, new data *matters* only if it is presented to the right people, in the right context, and in the right format. If the only person looking at social media analytics is the communications intern, then those digital traces aren't going to make much of a difference. If, instead, an advocacy organization incorporates analytics reports and experimental results into its weekly strategy meeting, then analytics gain the capacity to alter decision makers' course of action. Strategy is about making choices, and strategists make choices on the basis of information that they have jointly agreed is relevant to the outcome. What makes analytic activism distinct from other forms of digitally enabled activism is its focus on turning new forms of digital listening into strategic inputs that, in turn, contribute to new forms of digital speech.

By digitally listening, monitoring, and testing, activist organizations are able to better define tactical success, and this pushes them to try out new strategies. This book is filled with examples of innovative activist campaigns that seized public attention and created meaningful pressure on political targets. The focus of the book is on understanding the organizational processes that shape and produce these activist campaigns.

And the strategic innovations that result have never been more necessary, because the media environment that supported old strategic assumptions has been radically reshaped. The power of social movements has always been premised on successful interventions with the dominant media of the day. As we have moved from a broadcast media system to a hybrid media system (Chadwick 2013), the most popular tactics and techniques have lost much of their bite.

A Media Theory of Movement Power

We often make two mistakes with regard to the interaction of media institutions and political activism. First, we still frequently treat "the media" as a unitary, stable, and undifferentiated system. This was a defensible assumption in 1993, when William Gamson and Gadi Wolfsfeld wrote their authoritative treatment of the subject, "Movements and Media as Interacting Systems." Gamson and Wolfsfeld demonstrated that "social movements need the media far more than the media need them" (117). They did so by tracing the interests of social movements and of industrial media organizations that typified the broadcast news era. But in the decades that have elapsed since that classic work was published, the media system has undergone a continuous series of upheavals.

We can no longer simply state that some protest actions are inherently more media-friendly or newsworthy than others. We now have to specify *which media* and *which news*. Protest tactics are made media-friendly when they align with dominant media technologies. They become newsworthy when they fit the norms, incentives, and routines of the major news organizations of the day. When we talk about the "media system," we still largely have in mind the broadcast media institutions that dominated twentieth-century American politics—the nightly news and the daily paper in particular. Today, those broadcast institutions remain relevant, but they are also facing new competitive pressures, adopting new journalistic routines, and making use of new media technologies. As Andrew Chadwick (2013) suggests, we have replaced the old media cycle with a new "political information cycle." Stories unfold differently in the political information cycle. Social media buzz helps to determine the mainstream news agenda. Partisan news sites highlight different stories to appeal to their niche audiences (Jamieson and Cappella 2008; Arceneaux and Johnson 2013). If movements and media are interacting systems, then the dramatic changes to the media system must produce ripple effects that change the opportunity structure for social movements.

Second, we treat the media as though it were a *mirror*, held up to society and reflecting back the most important or prominent issues of the day. The dominant theories of policy change in political science, in fact, have long tended to ignore the role and interests of media institutions (Kingdon 1984; Baumgartner and Jones 1993). These theories draw empirical data from newspaper coverage, equating it with evidence of public opinion and public events. Media attention serves as a stand-in for public opinion in this tradition: If a topic makes the front page of the local paper or receives four minutes of coverage on the nightly news, we treat it as evidence of public interest and public will. As Susan Herbst (1998) demonstrates in *Reading Public Opinion*, both political activists and legislators treat the daily news agenda as evidence of public opinion.[4]

But a long research tradition maintains that media has *never* been merely a reflective technology. Kurt and Gladys Lang first offered this insight in their seminal 1953 study of the MacArthur Day parades: *Media is a technology of refraction, not reflection.* Introduce television cameras into an event, and you will manufacture a public spectacle. People will behave differently, performing roles for the cameras. Place newspaper reporters or bloggers at that event, and you will reveal different elements of the same spectacle. Media coverage is not a neutral arbiter or reflection of objective reality. It documents a performance that it is helping to co-create. As Gamson and Wolfsfeld (1993, 116) put it, "A demonstration with no media coverage at all is a nonevent, unlikely to have any positive influence either on mobilizing followers or influencing the target. No news is bad news." Successful protest events are strategically designed to attract coverage from the dominant media of the day. And as the media system changes, so too must our understanding of successful protest events.

To think clearly about the opportunities that the changing media system presents to activist organizations, we must historically bracket successful movement tactics. Different media, dominant at different points in history, incentivize different forms of public spectacle. The release of a new policy report will be much more appealing to policy bloggers than to television journalists. Press conferences are an artifact of the broadcast era; bloggers see little value in a press release. The broadcast television era imparted great leverage to advocacy tactics that could make the six o'clock news. The current digital era, with its niche news programming, 24-hour cable stations, hashtag publics, and social sharing, creates leverage for a different set of tactics. The relative power of individual protest tactics—petitions and sit-ins, marches and boycotts—changes apace with the shifting media system. Whether we label these changes to the media system as indicative of changing "media regimes" (Williams and Delli Carpini 2011), "information regimes" (Bimber 2003), "hybrid media systems" (Chadwick 2013), or "civic information paradigms" (Wells 2015), the central point is that

---

[4] Indeed, as Susan Herbst (1993, 1998) has repeatedly demonstrated, media coverage often serves this role for researchers precisely because "public opinion" is so hard to define.

media technologies and media institutions play a role in determining the strategic value of various protest tactics. All movement power is, in part, premised on understanding and leveraging the interests of these changing media entities. Movement power is, in this sense, also media power.

Activism is adapting to the digital age (as are we all). Our expectations of activists, however, remain decidedly anchored in the preceding century. In particular, the era of grand US social movements (roughly the 1960s and early 1970s) often receives hagiographic treatment from scholars and practitioners alike. Those movements were powerful, their tactics successful. Present-day movements are frequently compared with movements of this era and found wanting. In making this comparison, we usually ignore how those earlier movements were strategically tailored to the emerging broadcast media environment of the day.

Let me animate this point with a celebrated example: the "Bloody Sunday" march in Selma, Alabama. Taeku Lee discusses the tremendous success of this action in his 2002 book, *Mobilizing Public Opinion*:

> The movement strategy of provoking police brutality with nonviolent direct action fit well in Selma. Sheriff Jim Clark's bigotry and short temper were notorious. . . . The activists marched uneventfully [on Bloody Sunday] through downtown Selma but barely crossed the murky Alabama River on the Edmund Pettus Bridge before they were met by a detachment of law enforcement officers. About fifty Alabama state troopers and several dozen of Sheriff Clark's posse waited on horseback, fitted with gas masks, billy clubs, and blue hard hats. . . . Newsmen on hand captured the surreal chain of events with film and camera. By sundown, scenes from Selma were broadcast in living rooms throughout the nation. One television station, ABC, interrupted their evening movie, *Judgment at Nuremberg*, to air a film report on the assault. *The raw footage ignited a firestorm of public outrage.* (2–3, emphasis added)

Lee is describing a key moment in one of the most celebrated, successful social movements of the twentieth century. It was not the sheer number of protesters (approximately 600) that made this action so powerful. Nor was it the poetry or the righteousness of their cause. Central to the protesters' strategy was a clear reading of the affordances provided by the broadcast-era media environment. If Sheriff Jim Clark had left those protesters alone, the march would have ended uneventfully. The protesters would have had tired limbs and not much else to show for it. If the cameras had not been present, Clark's brutality would have gone unheralded, another chapter in the long history of violence against African Americans in the American South. But raw footage of police brutality was piped into living rooms across the nation. To borrow a phrase from Todd

Gitlin (1980), "The whole world was watching." And since this was 1965, a time when we had only three stations, there was nothing else on television.

Against tremendous odds, civil rights movement activists proudly and stridently forged a better society. Their personal courage was coupled with great strategic acumen. There are good reasons why present-day activists and scholars seek insight from the social movements of that era. But in the search for insight, scholars, public intellectuals, and practitioners alike tend to overlook how the tactics of that era were crafted to match the media system. If the Bloody Sunday march had occurred in 2015, it would have included hashtags and retweets, mash-ups and Vine clips. But it also would have reached a smaller, niche audience through the nightly news, and it would have been immediately reinterpreted, reframed, and denounced by partisan elites. The whole world would not have been subjected to the same images, and the resulting public mobilization would have unfolded along a different path.

Another example: In 1969, during the early years of the environmental movement, two galvanizing moments came when *Time* magazine ran a story about the Cuyahoga River catching fire and when an oil spill off the coast of Santa Barbara received national news coverage. This was not the first time that a major oil spill had happened, and it was the *twelfth* time the Cuyahoga had caught fire. But because of the limited viewing options of the broadcast media environment, these images were seen in living rooms throughout the nation. Rivers catching fire make for great television footage. The early leaders of the environmental movement seized upon the public attention generated by these broadcast tragedies and used it to galvanize media-friendly actions like the first Earth Day. As Ronald Shaiko (1993, 97) put it, "One might ask, philosophically, If Greenpeace activists hold a protest rally in the woods and the media are not there to cover it, do they really make a sound?" The birth of the environmental movement and its most iconic tactical successes were rooted in the affordances of the media system of that time.

The problem, however, is that this glamorized remembrance of past social movements inappropriately shades our perceptions of modern-day social movements. Consider, for instance, Nicholas Lehmann's (2013) indictment of 2010 environmentalists' failure to pass climate legislation through the US Congress:

> "Today's big environmental groups recruit through direct mail and the media, filling their rosters with millions of people who are happy to click "Like" on clean air. What the groups lack, however, is the [1970] Earth Day organizers' ability to generate thousands of events that people actually attend – the kind of activity that creates pressure on legislators."

By Lehmann's reckoning, the environmental movement of 2010 was a failure because it did not generate the same "thousands of events that people actually attend" that the environmental movement of the broadcast era had generated. Now, in the simplest sense, Lehmann is factually incorrect: Beginning in October 2006, seven students from Middlebury College worked with their professor, Bill McKibben, to launch the Step It Up day of action on climate. After six months of organizing, facilitated mostly through the Internet, the Step It Up day of action occurred on April 15, 2007. It included 1,410 events across the country (Fisher and Boekkooi 2010). Step It Up later changed its name to 350. org, a leading climate advocacy organization that regularly plans massive global days of action that feature 4,000–5,000 simultaneous events. The youth-led Energy Action Coalition has also repeatedly planned a series of citizen lobby days that have broken records as the largest in US history, bringing 15,000 young people in face-to-face contact with their congressional representatives. Present-day movements still plan plenty of "events that people actually attend." But that attendance is no longer picked up and refracted through a broadcast-dominant media system. Without the amplifying power of the broadcast-era industrial media, the same tactics no longer produce the pressure that they once did.[5]

The difference between Step It Up and the original Earth Day was not in the quantity of simultaneous teach-ins. It was not in the power of their rhetoric or the resonance of their media frames. The difference was in how those mass protest events were refracted and amplified through the larger media apparatus (and, one might add, in the sclerotic state of US congressional politics).

The original Earth Day, like the Bloody Sunday march in Selma, was strategically tailored to take advantage of a media regime that no longer exists. The mere existence of the teach-ins was *news*. The Earth Day teach-ins attracted broadcast media attention. And the public political agenda was defined through that media attention. New media refracts at different angles. Recruitment for Step It Up/350.org actions occurs through email lists, Facebook shares, and blog posts. The fact of the 2010 day of action was hashtagged and retweeted. These digital actions defined *a* political agenda for *a* public. But they did not leave the same imprint on the broader public consciousness. The lesson gleaned from successful social movements' past cannot be to mimic exactly what they did. The leaders of the present must strategically adapt to this digital refraction, just as social movement leaders of the past adapted to the broadcast refraction.

---

[5] Incidentally, I was in Washington, DC, for the initial Step It Up day of action. Having heard a constant drumbeat about the event through listservs, discussion boards, blogs, and other niche media, I arrived at my parents' home that weekend and told them why I was in town. My mother was a welfare rights organizer in the 1970s, and my father voted for Nader. Neither of them had heard about the event. In the post-broadcast media environment, you can efficiently target your message to the niche audience you seek to mobilize. But lost in the process is the beneficial inefficiency of spillover information, wherein untargeted individuals become generically aware that a social movement is under way.

The current hybrid media environment provides opportunities for activist movements and activist moments that would have gone missing in the older industrial broadcast media environment. As James Rucker, founder of ColorOfChange.org and cofounder of Citizen Engagement Lab, argues: "The media landscape twenty years ago would have prevented the stories driving the Movement for Black Lives today from breaking through. The voices we're now hearing, reading, and seeing are all enabled by an open Internet that has largely avoided corporate or government filter. And they are shifting public dialogue, impacting culture, and building momentum to change policy" (Center for Media Justice et al. 2015). When we lionize the tactics of social movements from a bygone era, we blind ourselves to the opportunities and potential presented by current media technologies.[6]

Indeed, this appears to be a key ingredient in the success of present-day political movements. The Movement for Black Lives (a.k.a. #BlackLivesMatter) has directed national attention to the crisis of police violence against young African Americans. It has done so by adopting a distinctly hybrid media strategy, including the use of hashtags that connected the dots between a series of individual tragedies and place-based protests, which themselves became the topic of media coverage (Freelon, McIlwain, and Clark 2016). These activists are not choosing between broadcast media and social media. They are using the tools at their disposal—including social media accounts—to create leverage over their direct targets (public officials) and secondary targets (including mainstream media organizations). Broadcast media outlets sent reporters to Ferguson, Missouri, to cover protests surrounding the death of teenager Michael Brown because Twitter conversation signaled its newsworthiness (Tufekci 2014c). The presence of those same reporters then helped to co-create the unfolding political spectacle (Tau 2014). Both broadcast television cameras and cell phone cameras are technologies of refraction. Social movements of the 1960s developed their tactics for an industrial broadcast media environment. Social movements of the 2010s are modifying their tactics for a hybrid media environment.

There is no single "correct" strategy for leveraging digital media into movement power. There are, however, a set of practices that, when properly instituted, help activist organizations adapt to the rhythms of the digital age. This book is an exploration of the strengths, weaknesses, possibilities, and limitations of those new practices. In particular, the book focuses on the role that new digital listening tools have begun to play in fashioning new tactics and strategies that help

---

[6] Dan Mercea and Marco Bastos (2015, 2016) have likewise traced the role of "serial activists" in transnational social movements—people who repeatedly use social media to help publicize, support, and orchestrate protest events. And Hadas Eyal (2016) has demonstrated that, among Israeli NGOs, "digital fit" is a key determinant of traditional media coverage. Though I focus mostly on American case examples in this book, there is strong evidence for similar changes on the global scale.

large-scale political organizations create leverage in the hybrid media system. *Analytics* encompass a cluster of technologies that allow organizations to monitor online sentiment, test and refine communications, and quantify opinion and engagement. These are *backend* technologies, viewed by professional campaigners through internal "dashboards" and fashioned into strategic objects that are discussed at weekly staff meetings.

Properly harnessed, these technologies allow large organizations to engage in analytic activism. Improperly harnessed, they can send civil society organizations down a crooked path that leads to prioritizing issues, campaigns, and tactics that are more *clickable* over those that are more *important*. As I will discuss later, analytic activism supports new innovations in *tactical optimization, computational management,* and *passive democratic feedback.* It enables organizations to learn and listen in different ways and to capture the energy refracted through the hybrid media system. This book highlights leading examples of analytic activism and derives lessons about its promise, its potential, and its limitations.

The rest of this chapter delves further into the three features that distinguish analytic activism from other forms of digital activism: testing, listening, and scale. It concludes by outlining the remainder of the book.

Analytics-Based Activism and the Culture of Testing

> What I've learned at MoveOn is that anything can be tested.
> And it probably is.
> —Stefanie Faucher, MoveOn.org

> If you're not looking at your data, then you're not listening to your
> members. And that probably makes you kind of an asshole.
> —Senior analytics staffer

In the US political context, the use of analytics is commonly associated with fundraising—particularly in presidential campaigns. Michael Slaby, chief technology officer of the 2008 Obama presidential campaign, estimates that analytics-based website and email optimization netted the campaign an extra $57 million (Kreiss 2012, 145). In his 2012 book, *Taking Our Country Back,* Daniel Kreiss describes these optimization efforts as part of a broader practice of "computational management." The Obama presidential campaign tested *everything.* It used analytics to build larger email lists, raise more money, and spend that money more efficiently than any previous electoral campaign in US history. If, as Jeffrey Alexander (2010) argues, the Obama campaign was equal parts social movement and discursive performance, then Kreiss highlights that both parts emerged through a complex sociotechnical apparatus.

The simplest form of this analytics-based optimization is known as *A/B testing*. An A/B test is a simple experiment: Website visitors or email recipients are randomly assigned to two groups. Both groups interact with exactly the same message, featuring exactly one variation. The variation can be an email subject line, a suggested donation level, or different images or campaign colors. Dan Siroker, a former product manager at Google who worked for Obama's new media team and now runs a website optimization company called Optimize.ly, describes his experience on the Obama campaign thus:

> I joined what was being called the "new media" team. . . . The team had competent bloggers, designers, and email copywriters; I wondered where I might be able to make an impact.
> One thing stood out to me: a red button.
> Online donations to the campaign came from subscribers to the email newsletter; subscriptions for this came from the campaign website's signup form; and the signup form came as a result of clicking a red button that said "Sign Up." This was the gateway through which all of Obama's email supporters had to pass; it all came down to one button. So, one simple, humble question immediately became pivotal. *Is This the Right Button?* —(Siroker and Koomen 2013, 3–4, emphasis in original)

Siroker and his colleagues tested every element of the online user experience. Fiddling with the shape, size, color, and language associated with the button ("Sign Up Now" vs. "Learn More") and associated image improved their sign-up rate by an estimated 40.6% (Siroker and Koomen 2013, 7). This translated to 2.8 million additional email subscribers, 288,000 more volunteers, and $57 million in added donations. For the Obama presidential campaign, analytics-based optimization was very big business. Hallie Montoya Tansey, cofounder of Target Labs, argues that these processes can be used for a much wider range of data-driven decisions: "mailings, phone calls, field offices, any type of expensive contacts."[7] Brian Christian (2012) likewise suggests, "A/B testing is not simply a best practice—it's also a way of thinking, and for some, even a philosophy. Once initiated into the A/B ethos, it becomes a lens that starts to color just about everything—not just online—but in the offline world as well."

This picture of website and email optimization hardly seems like a step closer to anyone's vision of an ideal democratic society. Fifteen years ago, Steven Schier warned that an unhealthy mix of party polarization and new technology was

---

[7] Interview notes, Hallie Montoya Tansey, July 25, 2013.

replacing citizen *mobilization* with citizen *activation*. "Activation employs telephones, direct mail, and Internet communication in a way that allows distinctively phrased messages of maximum possible impact. It does not seek to get most potential voters to participate in an election, as does mobilization, but instead fires up a small but potentially effective segment of the public to help a particular candidate at the polls or a particular interest as it lobbies government" (Schier 2000, 9). Schier worried that emerging niche marketing techniques were rendering mass citizen participation obsolete: "Mobilization encouraged popular rule. Activation impedes it" (9). The niche marketing that caused Schier's alarm is quaint compared with the A/B testing and microtargeted segmentation performed by modern political campaigns. There is a reasonable argument to be made that A/B testing in political campaigns represents the supreme triumph of marketing in elections (Tufekci 2012).

The well-publicized work of the Obama campaign represents only *one type* of analytics, though. The Obama team's use of A/B testing was a form of *tactical optimization*—their goals were already fixed (acquire supporter names, identify volunteers, raise money), and the question they were asking was fundamentally quite simple ("Is This the Right Button?"). Digital trace data about this question helped them improve tactical performance toward these goals. The Romney campaign, with less reliance on computational management, was no closer to our democratic ideals. It also engaged in niche marketing— but niche marketing that was simply *less efficient*.

Analytics (alternatively referred to as digital trace data) can be used for a wider range of purposes than we saw in the Obama campaign, however. The Obama campaign used analytics and testing to refine individual tactics and to evaluate competing strategies.[8] But it did not use analytics to ask its members to set its priorities. The goal of an electoral campaign is simple and transparent: Win on Election Day. The goal of a social movement organization is far more complex and fluid: Build power to create a more just society. We can easily evaluate whether an electoral campaign has won or lost. But the near-term measures of activist success are indeterminate. And that creates space for activist organizations to employ digital listening for broader agenda-setting purposes. MoveOn.org, for instance, uses analytics to help gauge the will of its membership (what I termed *passive democratic feedback* in my previous book). Analytics for MoveOn is a governance input, a means of setting strategic direction and determining what the organization's goals and priorities ought to be. Table 1.1 defines these three uses of analytics and describes their scale, purpose, and

---

[8] Not all of the Obama campaign's data and experimentation were digital in nature. The campaign ran experiments to improve its phone call scripts and field contacts, for instance. The culture of testing and experimentation can be applied beyond the scope of digital media.

Table 1.1 **Three Uses of Analytics in Activism**

Uses of Analytics	Scale	Purpose	Limitations
Tactical optimization	Small	Improve efficiency/effectiveness of individual tactics	Low durability, focus on "growthiness" (chapter 5)
Computational management	Large	Evaluate competing tactics and strategies	Analytics floor (chapter 5)
Passive democratic feedback	Variable	Obtain governance feedback from supporters/members; set the organization's direction or priorities	Listening without conversation (chapter 6)

limitations. Having already described tactical optimization, let me now describe each of the additional categories.

COMPUTATIONAL MANAGEMENT

A single A/B test can change the language of an email or phone script, but it cannot transform a campaign or organization. When the culture of testing is adopted more broadly, it can have a much more expansive impact. In *Taking Our Country Back*, Kreiss offers evidence of how the data-driven culture of the Obama campaign led to a new style of "computational management," in which data and testing became key features in the big-picture strategy meetings. The Obama campaign developed new analytics tools to monitor the impact and return on investment of a variety of campaign practices. Rather than isolating A/B testing within the communications team or the fundraising team, Obama's campaign looked to measure impacts across all channels and used those quantified results to direct future resource expenditures.

Likewise, as Sasha Issenberg (2102) discusses in *The Victory Lab*, the data-driven turn in political campaigning has led many organizations to challenge old consultant-driven assumptions about what works in politics. Since the publication of Alan Gerber and Don Green's seminal 2000 paper in the *American Political Science Review* (engagingly titled "The Effects of Canvassing, Telephone Calls, and Direct Mail on Voter Turnout: A Field Experiment"), a new generation of political campaigns has begun to take social science seriously. Issenberg identifies the Analyst Institute (AI) as a central hub of the Democratic Party network for using data (online and offline) to improve campaign techniques and bring millions more citizens to the polls on Election Day. Experiments run by the AI are far more complex than the simple A/B tests used by the Obama new media team that Siroker discusses. They help answer larger questions about voter behavior and help guide serious conversations about the empirical state of citizen engagement.

The difference between computational management and tactical optimization lies in how widely experimentation and analytics are adopted. In some advocacy organizations, analytics and the culture of testing have taken root only in the online communications department. The result tends to be a "test and pray" model, in which campaign communicators routinely run A/B tests to optimize an individual tactic, but have no larger support structure for extracting useful lessons from those tests or for passing those lessons up to C-suite executives.[9] And the problem with "test and pray" is that it limits the impact that testing can have on strategy.

There is an A/B testing story that is often told and retold at trainings on digital experiments and the culture of testing. It originates from Daniel Mintz, who currently is the director of data and analytics at Upworthy.com and previously held a similar position at MoveOn.org. The story begins with a fundraising experiment. MoveOn staffers were interested in finding out whether members would respond to zip code–based donation targets. Rather than sending national email blasts that included a text box saying (for example), "We need to raise $250,000 in the next 24 hours," Mintz and his team wondered if they could more effectively motivate their members by providing a text box saying, "We need to raise $2,500 from [your city]." MoveOn tested the zip code–based donation frame and indeed found a statistically significant increase in donation rates. The group didn't know *why* this change worked—it could be that geographic frames made the issues more relevant, or that smaller funding goals made an individual donation seem more impactful, or simply that any divergence from boilerplate fundraising language results in a novelty effect. Nonetheless, the data had spoken, and the new "from your zip code" style quickly became standard within the organization.

Within six months, many of MoveOn's peer organizations had caught on to this new wrinkle and adopted the same language. Mintz and his team wondered whether the diffusion of this language had altered its impact. So they decided to run the experiment a second time, to see if the results held up. They did not. The zip code–based fundraising goals turned out to have had a short-run novelty value, and nothing more.

For analytic activist organizations like MoveOn, the null result of this retest is a small triumph rather than a disappointment. It represents the difference between short-term "test and pray" A/B testing and computational

---

[9] Interview notes, Michael Grenetz, February 19, 2014.

management. The individual outcomes of A/B tests and analytics reports are far less important than the data-driven learning routines that analytic activists use to determine how they can operate most effectively. While tactical optimization narrowly improves the performance of individual tactics, computational management allows for new organizational learning routines that are applicable to a wider range of concerns, including how an activist group identifies priorities, defines its supporter base, and builds a shared narrative and political identity. The most important thing is not the results of any one test, but the habit of testing that encourages continued learning, debate, and experimentation.

PASSIVE DEMOCRATIC FEEDBACK

I initially introduced the concept of passive democratic feedback in my previous book, *The MoveOn Effect* (2012). Particularly for civil society organizations, analytics can be used for strategic direction setting, not just for optimizing campaign communications toward a set outcome. The difference between passive democratic feedback and tactical optimization can be reduced to a simple question: "What are we trying to optimize?" The Obama campaign had a clear, fixed goal: Win a majority of the vote, in states representing a majority of the Electoral College, on November 4, 2008. By contrast, political advocacy organizations operate in a shifting environment. Their goals circle around galvanizing public support and building political power to solve some public problem or advance some issue agenda. The tactics for achieving these goals change alongside both the political system and the media system. There is no set end date for these organizations. When the McCain campaign lost in 2008, it ended. By contrast, when newly formed MomsDemandAction.org failed to pass gun legislation in the aftermath of the Sandy Hook school shooting, the organization kept working toward that goal.

One byproduct of these differences between electoral campaigns and political advocacy associations is that there is far more space within advocacy groups for legitimate debates over what they should do next. Simple tools like A/B testing and weekly member surveys can provide netroots advocacy organizations with clear indicators of member opinion on these crucial, agenda-setting questions. The process of obtaining passive democratic feedback is identical to the processes of tactical optimization. But here the organizations are using analytics tools to determine member *priorities* rather than to drive up member action rates. As I will discuss in chapter 2, passive democratic feedback may not approach our Habermasian ideal of an engaged, deliberative public. But it is a good deal better than the advocacy landscape that it is replacing.

Digital listening can also take a more sophisticated, active form through governance-related computational management practices. From a governance perspective, analytics can represent a powerful force when used as a routinized structure for rough hypothesis testing and organizational learning. I witnessed this in the summer of 2013 during a site visit to the national office of 38 Degrees in London. 38 Degrees is the UK equivalent of MoveOn in the United States (Chadwick 2013, Chadwick and Dennis 2016). Both organizations are members of the international OPEN network (Online Progressive Engagement Networks) (Karpf 2013b). With 3 million members (approximately 4.6% of the national population), 38 Degrees is one of the largest and most active civil society organizations in the United Kingdom. During my visit to its office, I made note of a whiteboard that prominently displayed the question "How can we increase active membership by 30%?" This was the "Testing Whiteboard." Every week, 38 Degrees staffers hold a brainstorming session on what questions are worth testing. They then formulate a set of rough metrics and hypotheses, spend the week running small tests, and then convene at the end of the week to summarize what they have learned.

The Testing Whiteboard does not display the same social science rigor as the experiments run by the Analyst Institute. But the quality of the research design is less important than the existence of the conversation itself. The Testing Whiteboard functions as a strategic object. It creates a space within 38 Degrees for a set of routinized strategic conversations that otherwise would not occur. It promotes a culture of testing, which leads activists to question old assumptions and try out novel strategies. Just like Mintz with his zip code–based fundraising retest, 38 Degrees has created a space for learning and experimentation that can challenge established campaign wisdom. And that learning and experimentation extends beyond political tactics to include a broader set of questions about how the organization can effectively engage with its members.

I will argue that this is an optimal adjustment to the demands of movement/ media power in the digital age. The social media giants of our day are still tinkering with their platforms, and the dominant mainstream media organizations are still learning how best to interact with these digital institutions. Under these circumstances, the capacity to experiment, learn, and retest is a critical advantage. As I have previously suggested (Karpf 2012b), political organizations and social scientists alike are currently facing a unique set of challenges posed by "Internet Time." Simply put, the Internet of 2016 is, in important respects, *different* from the Internet of 2012, or 2006, or 1996. The devices that we use to access the Internet, the sites that we frequent on the Internet, and the ways that we use those sites are all in a state of flux.[10] And this is all happening while the medium itself diffuses to broader segments of the population.

---

[10] "Internet Time" is a phenomenon that occurs primarily at the content layer of the Internet. The physical layer of the Internet (the cables and wires and fiber) and the protocol layer (computer interoperability standards) are prone to stability and even anticompetitive behavior. See Zittrain (2008, ch. 4), for a discussion of the multiple layers of the medium.

The Internet changes *fast*, and rough tools like the Testing Whiteboard promote a cultural habit of experimentation and measurement among netroots political organizations. The valuable output of the Whiteboard is not any specific lesson, but rather the weekly conversation that it invites. The Testing Whiteboard opens up new pathways for routinized organizational learning and strategic adjustment. Analytics, in this sense, become a tool that activist organizations can use to continually optimize their tactics for the current media system.

Like all tools for activism, digital listening and experimentation are imperfect. The changes I have described in this chapter represent crucial features of a new style of large-scale, reformist advocacy campaigning. It is a style that is particularly well aligned with the new hybrid media environment. But, as I will discuss, it is also a style that introduces its own biases and limitations.

"Growthiness" and the Analytics Floor

Analytic activism has its limits. Much of the final two chapters of this book is devoted to boundary conditions—to the areas and topics where digital traces can do more harm than good. It is, for instance, far easier to optimize tactics than to optimize strategy. (For instance, consider: Should the environmental movement prioritize national climate legislation, or should it focus on the state and local levels? Which option will build more power and ultimately lead to success? Arguments can be made in both directions. Digital traces won't conclusively settle the matter.) But there is also a lower boundary to consider: the *analytics floor.*

There is a good reason why all of the examples of analytics for political campaigns and activism come from large organizations. With a few noteworthy exceptions (discussed in chapter 5), small organizations simply cannot make use of internal analytics (chapter 2 discusses the difference between internal and external analytics). If you have an email list of 5 million people or a website that receives 500,000 visits per day, you can run regular A/B tests on random subsets of your list, then apply those lessons to the rest of the supporter base. If you have an email list of 500 or a website that receives 50 visits per day, then A/B testing will not provide statistically significant results within a useful time frame.[11]

---

[11] Technically, with a large enough effect size one might still observe statistically significant results with small lists. The New Organizing Institute has demonstrated this point through a small controlled experiment proving that reminder phone calls increase the response rate to online surveys. But in practice, there are very few nontrivial, nonobvious findings that an activist group can obtain with such small lists.

Three variables determine the exact dimensions of the analytics floor: (1) base-line action rate, (2) list/audience size, and (3) minimum detectable effect.[12] For the purpose of illumination, imagine that you belong to an advocacy group seeking to raise money from small donors. Baseline action rate is the rate at which your members currently respond to an average fundraising email. List/audience size is the total population that you can sample from. Minimum detectable effect (MDE) is the threshold at which you would *actually* adopt a different fundraising email. For a fundraising email from a large, US-based nonprofit, the baseline action rate is usually in the single digits, and a 1% or 0.5% change would be above the MDE. To reliably detect an effect of this size, your organization would need a testing pool of approximately 15,000 individuals.[13] For the test to be worth the effort, you would then need to apply the results to a large enough list to at least cover the costs of running the experiment itself (if your membership list is 16,000 individuals, the results of your 15,000-person test won't be worth very much!). For MoveOn or the Obama campaign, this is a routine practice. But for your neighborhood Parent Teacher Association or for a national organization devoted to a small niche issue, it is a practical impossibility. Analytics are useful for dealing with massive amounts of data. Some politics is still decidedly local, though.

It follows that analytic activism produces increasing returns to large-scale organizations. An organization with 1,000 members can barely make use of analytics. An organization with 1 million can incorporate digital feedback into its work routines. An organization with 10 million can detect even smaller effect sizes, run even more sophisticated experiments, and use these results to develop an even greater comparative advantage.

One result is that digital advocacy organizations have a powerful incentive to accumulate massive email lists. In *The MoveOn Effect*, I discussed how this change in communications technology is tied to a generational transition among advocacy organizations. Direct mail is a technology that requires narrow lists and high response rates because of the marginal cost incurred by each additional piece of mail. The marginal cost of an additional email recipient is close to zero,[14] and this permits broad lists and low response rates, enabling the rise of

---

[12] Evan Miller has developed a free online tool that provides these calculations: http://www.evanmiller.org/ab-testing/sample-size.html (accessed June 25, 2016). His 2010 essay, "How Not to Run an A/B Test," is also frequently cited by practitioners: http://www.evanmiller.org/how-not-to-run-an-ab-test.html (accessed June 25, 2016).

[13] http://www.evanmiller.org/ab-testing/sample-size.html#!5;80;5;1;0 (accessed June 25, 2016).

[14] I say "close" to zero because of two limiting factors. The first is email acquisition cost. This can be zero for organic growth, but many organizations either pay to acquire emails directly or hire staff members who are charged with list growth. The second is email deliverability. Lists with low response rates are in danger of being flagged as spammers, in which case their messages either will never reach supporters or will be automatically diverted to a spam box. Many organizations manually remove dormant email addresses specifically as a response to deliverability challenges.

multi-issue progressive generalist organizations like MoveOn and Democracy for America.

In chapter 3, I will discuss a second result of the incentive for list growth. In the past few years, we have witnessed the rise of massive distributed petition platforms like Change.org and MoveOn Petitions. Change.org is a platform where anyone can create his or her own petition, sometimes sparking successful local, national, or global campaigns for change. It is also a for-profit "B-corp," whose business model consists of generating larger email lists for existing advocacy groups through "sponsored petitions." And this business model leads Change.org to prioritize list growth–friendly petitions over petitions that are tied to the central political issues of the day. Chapter 3 offers a comparison between Change.org and MoveOn.org's distributed petition platform, MoveOn Petitions. It analyzes six months of data from these two sites, offering an indication of how their niches and business models affect what types of petitions they support and what types of campaigning they each encourage. Even though both organizations have embraced digital listening, the culture of testing, and the value of scale, we will see that they use analytics to promote entirely divergent models of political engagement. There is virtually no overlap in the petitions and issues that they feature on their sites or in the types of allies and partners that they work with. As we will see in chapter 3, analytic activism does not drive all organizations to a single homogeneous set of tactics or priorities. Analytics provide new tools for listening, experimenting, and monitoring. How an organization makes use of what it hears and learns will vary dramatically, based on its underlying mission, vision, and funding model.

Analytic Audiences and Extending Beyond Echo Chambers

It is time for a reassessment of what the Internet is good for.

We have tended for years to hold two distinct claims to be true: first, that the Internet is full of cat videos and celebrity photos—*serious* topics of public importance are ignored on the Web, while Kanye mash-ups and blooper videos go viral overnight; and second, that political talk online is composed of "echo chambers," where motivated partisans push each other to even greater extremes while avoiding any information that might challenge their worldview. These two claims are far from mutually exclusive. As Markus Prior (2007) shows in *Post-Broadcast Democracy*, when we expand the range of media choices available to the public, citizen-consumers will act on their relative entertainment preferences. Those who enjoy politics will watch more political news and will seek out partisan outlets that match their preferences. Those who don't enjoy politics will turn to SportsCenter instead of the nightly news broadcast.

In writing *The MoveOn Effect*, I postulated that these two claims represented a fundamental stumbling block for Internet-driven social change campaigns. The Internet lowers the transaction costs for citizen participation. Lower transaction costs better reveal the demand curve for political news. But they do not reshape citizen *preferences*: "If the average citizen was not thirsting for political information, they will not develop a taste for it simply because it has been rendered more easily available" (Karpf 2012a, 158). Both the abundance of cat videos and the growth of echo chambers can be easily understood as evidence of citizens enacting their underlying preferences. Cats are funny! Poverty is depressing. And political crosstalk is far less enjoyable than talking with your fellow partisans (Wojcieszak 2010). The end result is that the Internet, circa 2012, was much better for political *mobilization* than for political *persuasion*.

But the Internet, and the "social web" (e.g., Facebook, Twitter, Tumblr, and Reddit) in particular, keeps changing. And since the publication of my first book, there have been some surprising developments in the area of political persuasion. Most notable is the rise of Upworthy.com, the behemoth content curation site dedicated to sharing "stuff that matters." Founded by two former MoveOn. org staffers (one of whom, Eli Pariser, also authored *The Filter Bubble*), Upworthy is heavily invested in the culture of analytics and testing. It hires content curators who search the web for socially meaningful "seeds" of content (videos, stories, and infographics). Upworthy curators have developed a cottage industry of sorts, specializing in identifying the narrative qualities that make a story shareable (Critchfield 2013). Once a seed has been identified, those content creators then brainstorm twenty-five potential headline frames, applying A/B testing and more advanced analytics to determine which one works best. The differences can be tremendous: Upworthy's editor at large, Adam Mordecai, tells the story of a single video that he and Sara Critchfield published under competing headlines. Mordecai's best headline generated 10,000 pageviews. Critchfield's generated more than 1 million pageviews, drawing mainstream media coverage of the latest "viral video" sweeping the nation. Analytics and testing are baked into every aspect of Upworthy's business plan.

Upworthy's growth has been nothing short of astonishing. In November 2013, the site attracted more than 80 million unique viewers, most of them via Facebook newsfeed-driven social sharing. By comparison, CNN.com receives 12 million to 12 to 15 million visitors per month, and NYTimes.com receives approximately 20 million visitors per month.[15] Upworthy has become the

---

[15] Alexa.com (accessed March 26, 2014).

subject of numerous journalistic articles and parody sites. But, as I discuss in chapter 4, it has also demonstrated the very real potential for reaching beyond the online political echo chamber and attracting mass public attention to non-trivial topics.

Upworthy is representative of a broader trend in the hybrid media system in which a combination of aggressive testing and social media–based sharing has changed what types of stories reach a mass audience. Unlike the digital analytics discussed in chapter 3, which focus on advocacy groups using digital tools to listen to their members/supporters (analytics for mobilization), Upworthy applies many of the same techniques to listen, reach, and connect with the broader public (analytics for persuasion). Chapter 4 of this book discusses how advocacy organizations have, just in the past few years, begun to combine analytics and social media to reach much broader audiences than we (or at least I) previously believed to be feasible. Upworthy reaches beyond the traditional activist echo chamber specifically by optimizing its communications for network-based social media sharing. Advocacy organizations like New Era Colorado, the AFL-CIO, and the Gates Foundation have begun to partner with Upworthy to reach these wider audiences and leverage them into powerful political tactics that are augmented by increased mainstream media coverage.

Analytics for Organizing and the Analytics Frontier

> That's still the big problem we face: the places where it *matters most*
> [offline] are also the places where we have the *least data*.
> —Senior analytics staffer

If the analytics floor defines a lower boundary for the use of analytics in political campaigning, then we can also conceive of the outer boundary as comprising an *analytics frontier*. While the floor is defined by scenarios in which data is too sparse or lists are too small, the frontier is defined by questions that are too *complex* for digital measurement. Put more simply, analytic activism can certainly help you mobilize a crowd, but (at least so far) it is less useful for organizing that crowd into a movement or converting that movement energy into long-term victories.

The simplest online interactions tend to be the ones that are most amenable to analytics. Tracking clicks and shares is easy. Tracking conversations is a bit trickier. Tracking online-to-offline participation is still quite hard. Tracking impacts on elite decision makers is nearly impossible. The more complex the task, the fewer people will engage in it and the more variables you need to simultaneously account for. Think of the analytics frontier as an old map from a bygone era: It can be extended with time and effort, but until then, it defines the limits beyond which we can only scrawl *hic sunt dracones* (here be dragons).

As I discuss in chapter 5, two conceptual distinctions further complicate the analytics frontier. First is the difference between *organizing* and *mobilizing* (see Skocpol 2003; Ganz 2009; Han 2014). Mobilizing is about breadth—the number of bodies at a rally, signatures on a petition, or phone calls to a senator. Organizing is about depth—the number of volunteer leaders committed to your cause, the skills and relationships they have developed, and the hours and resources they are willing to give. Hahrie Han (2014) provides clear evidence that building deep grassroots volunteer capacity comes through time-consuming, relational work—from *organizers* rather than *mobilizers*. The organizations that invest in community organizing reap dividends in the form of a committed, engaged volunteer leadership base. But it is a steep investment and one that few advocacy groups, online or offline, have committed themselves to.

The problem is that organizing is fundamentally built on relational conversations, while analytic activism tends to rely on listening *without* conversation. Micah Sifry (2013) argues that this represents a major problem, limiting the long-term effectiveness of digital activist groups. In a 2013 article titled "You Can't A/B Test Your Response to Syria," Sifry writes, "It's really striking that a decade into the emergence of online political organizing, there is still no commonly accepted and easy-to-use tool that would enable groups to conduct large-scale debate and deliberation aimed at producing a common pro-active policy on anything—despite the fact that collectively these groups have millions of email addresses and, at least in theory, the resources to put towards the problem. (It's not for nothing, after all, that the Internet is much better at saying 'stop' than it is at saying 'go.')" As we will see in this book, analytics for mobilizing are more robust and well developed than analytics for organizing. There is a real danger that, in attempting to "listen to the data," the current wave of analytic activist organizations will become fixated on the (mobilization) data that speaks the loudest and clearest. The analytics frontier is defined by efforts to expand analytic activism into these more challenging realms of organizing, mass conversation, and deliberation.

The second key distinction complicating the analytics frontier is that between organizing and campaigning. As Taren Stinebrickner-Kauffman (2013), executive director of SumOfUs.org, explains, "Campaigners are different from organizers. The fundamental mission of an organizer is to empower other people to create change. The fundamental mission of a campaigner, though, is to set their sights on a particular change they want to create in the world, and then go out and make it happen, whatever it takes. If that happens to involve empowering people along the way, then that's great. But if you can make that change by having drinks with the nephew of a Senator, so be it." As we will see in chapters 5 and 6, the current wave of netroots political organizations is constructed mostly for campaigning, not organizing. The bias toward campaigning is not an immutable element of analytic activism, but it does help to define the shape of the current analytics frontier.

These are complex issues that Han, Sifry, and Stinebrickner-Kauffman are raising. They focus our attention on key concepts like movement power and strategy. As Stinebrickner-Kauffman puts it, "Who cares if you can get more people to make phone calls by picking the best subject line in your email if you don't even know if the phone calls have an impact?" For both the leading academics and the leadership of political associations, these questions of depth, power, and effectiveness represent a vexing frontier, the tough puzzle that they continually attempt to solve. We did not have a clear solution to building powerful social movement organizations during the era of industrial broadcast media, and we quite certainly do not have one today, either.

The challenge of the analytics frontier is that blind reliance on analytics can exert a pressure on activist organizations to prioritize those objectives that are most easily quantifiable. The solution, as I detail in chapter 6, is to *blend multiple inputs*. Social media data and A/B tests can be combined with weekly member surveys, relational organizing conversations, and tough debates among coalition partners. Analytics and the culture of testing are not leading to a perfect, optimal strategy for social movement success. They are tools that help large organizations nimbly experiment, learn, and adapt to their changing surroundings. Strategizing remains hard, messy work. Analytic activists do not have all of the answers. They are just finding better ways to ask the right questions.

Outline of the Book

The chapters that follow provide a deeper dive into the concepts and themes that I have introduced thus far.

In chapter 2, I offer a detailed discussion of what we mean when we throw around terms like "analytics," "algorithms," and "big data." These terms can mean different things when they are used by computer scientists and management gurus. Just as important, the practices of digital listening and online experimentation carry a wide range of divergent ethical implications, depending (for instance) on whether that listening is being conducted by governments, businesses, or voluntary associations. Chapter 2 helps to define these terms and places them in conversation with our traditional understanding of concepts like public opinion and revealed preferences. It also discusses five ethical considerations that help us to differentiate the types of analytics used by activist organizations and the types of analytics used by data vendors, banks, and governments. For readers who have come this far in the book and are left wondering, "What do you mean by analytics?" or "Where are the data brokers and the NSA in all of this?" I encourage you to read just a bit further.

Chapter 3 turns to the digital petition industry. After assessing the various ways that online petitions act as powerful media objects within the hybrid media system, the chapter draws on a unique comparative dataset comprising the top 10 featured petitions at Change.org and MoveOn Petitions, collected daily over a six-month period. From this dataset, it becomes remarkably clear just how different these two analytics-reliant organizations are, despite featuring massive, open petition platforms where any citizen can create a petition with the potential to reach millions and galvanize social change. This chapter both offers examples of what analytic activism looks like in practice and highlights the importance of organizational variables for understanding digital advocacy and digital activism. Different organizational logics drive each of these petition sites: these logics determine how analytic tools are deployed and what types of petitions, issues, and campaign victories are promoted as a result.

Chapter 4 then uses the case of Upworthy.com to illuminate how persuasive political information now travels in new ways. The chapter offers a rejoinder to the "echo chamber" hypothesis that has been a fixture of theories of online politics for nearly 20 years. Through a longer look at the emergence, development, and growth of Upworthy.com, we can see how the shift from an Internet of search engines to an Internet of social sharing fundamentally affects the opportunity structure for social movement organizations. Upworthy itself is not an activist organization, but it represents a change in the media system, which, in turn, alters the available routes to movement power.

Chapter 5 takes up the themes of the analytics floor and the analytics frontier in greater detail. After more thoroughly defining each of these boundary conditions, the chapter offers multiple case examples of organized efforts to push against these current limitations. These include "big listening" projects that leverage external analytics data to help small activist organizations adapt to the digital environment, as well as list-pooling efforts that help small organizations run shared experiments to help navigate the analytics floor. They also include systematic efforts to define new campaigning and organizing metrics to help activist organizations optimize for power-building instead of "vanity metrics," as well as pilot projects in *governance gamification* that represent a radical increase in the governance role that online supporters might one day play within their political associations. The purpose of chapter 5 is both to define the current limits of analytic activism and to illustrate how organizations are attempting to move beyond those limits.

In the concluding chapter, I offer a broader assessment of what analytic activism is and is not currently capable of. This chapter returns to a theme from my previous book, the *loss of beneficial inefficiencies*. Beneficial inefficiencies are important social and institutional functions that were provided in the organizational ecology of the previous media regime by virtue of its very inefficiency.[16] Analytic activism, like all digitally mediated institutions, is still in a state of becoming, and it can become better or worse over time, depending on how a constellation of practitioners and interested supporters choose to help it develop. So I conclude the book both by summarizing what we have (hopefully) learned and by highlighting the central problems that must be addressed moving forward.

---

[16] Think, for instance, of the strengthened social ties that come through operating a phone tree. The purpose of the phone tree is to distribute information. A spillover effect is that it builds relationships among neighbors. When we replace inefficient phone trees with more efficient neighborhood listservs, we lose the beneficial relationship-building that accrued through the inefficient medium.

2

Understanding Analytics, Algorithms, and Big Data

> If the twentieth century engineers of consent had magnifying glasses and
> baseball bats, those of the twenty-first century have acquired telescopes,
> microscopes and scalpels in the shape of algorithms and analytics.
> —Zeynep Tufekci (2014a), "Engineering the Public"

> We're gonna talk algorithms . . . which, you know what?
> Frankly, I don't know what the fuck those are.
> —David Carr, "Do Algorithms Dream of Viral Content?"

The basic communication process includes (1) a communicator, (2) a delivery medium, and (3) a recipient. Over the past two decades, we have lived through constant changes in delivery media. The technologies associated with communication have expanded from telephone, radio, and television to an endless array of digital gadgetry. And this has led many researchers to investigate the myriad new ways in which we can now speak. From email to text messaging, from blogs to Vines, from tweets to Snapchats, digital media provides an ever-increasing range of tools for what Manuel Castells (2009) labels "mass self-communication." The capacity for engaging in political speech has been democratized, giving rise to what Yochai Benkler (2006) terms the "networked public sphere." The necessary tools for political action have never before been so widely available.

But while the impact of new technologies has galvanized the research community to explore new forms of speech, far less attention has been directed at the other half of the equation. Digital communications leave traces that, in the aggregate, allow for new forms of listening. For the most part, this digital listening remains invisible. We become aware of it only when something goes wrong. Facebook publishes an academic study of online emotional mimicry based on experimental data it collected without the knowledge of its users (Kramer et al. 2014), prompting a public outcry over research ethics

(Tufekci 2014b). The *New York Times* publishes an exposé about chain stores like Target using predictive analytics to figure out which of its customers are pregnant (Duhigg 2012). Edward Snowden blows the whistle on bulk data collection by the National Security Administration (NSA). We have a general sense that companies and governments are tracking our online activity, but we do not encounter digital listening in the same way that we encounter digital speech, so these forms of algorithmic monitoring remain mostly out of sight, out of mind.

Digital listening can carry two very different connotations. Sometimes it implies responsive and responsible governance: "Your concerns are being heard." Other times it can sound menacing and foreboding: "They can *hear you*, even when you thought no one was listening!" One can often discern a sharp divide between those who mostly see the technological and social promise of big data and those who mostly see technological and social menace. Are we moving toward an era of responsive, nimble companies, media organizations, and governments? Or are we quietly constructing a panopticon? The potential promise of digital listening is that it can transform outdated and ineffective bureaucracies. The potential harm is that it can be used to repress political speech, enable psychological manipulation and the "engineering of consent" (Tufekci 2014a) on a massive scale, and cloak exploitative policies behind a veil of mathematical secrecy (Pasquale 2015; O'Neil 2015).

Both the potential and the risk of digital listening are equally relevant. Not all types of digital listening are threatening to democratic governance. I will argue, in fact, that some have great positive potential—within the appropriate boundaries, it is certainly better to have institutions that listen than institutions that do not. But if we are going to understand the potentials and the threats of digital listening for organized political participation, we have to begin by establishing what this phenomenon *is*. This chapter discusses analytics and its close conceptual cousins, big data, and algorithms. The chapter defines the phenomenon of digital listening and places it within broader academic debates over the nature of public opinion and citizen participation. The chapter also suggests ways to distinguish between cases where digital listening is mundane or benign and cases where it deserves heightened scrutiny and regulation. MoveOn.org's use of analytics does not engender the same ethical concerns as Facebook's use of analytics. Google's algorithmic monitoring of our email does not present the same risks as the NSA's algorithmic monitoring of our email. A political campaign's use of big data to identify potential supporters carries different risks than a government's use of big data to scrub the voter rolls (Berman 2015a). The chapter serves both to demystify terms like "analytics," "algorithms," and "big data" and to clarify some of the ethical considerations we should apply to the use and abuse of digital listening.

What Are Analytics?

In the digital economy, analytics are how we keep score. We leave digital footprints everywhere we go. Visit a website, click on a link, open an email, watch a video, like a post on Facebook: all of this online activity is being passively recorded.[1] In the aggregate, those digital traces are often referred to as "big data." But big data is *too big* to be of much use unless you have decided *which* online activities are worth paying attention to. We navigate this sea of data through a combination of analytics—reports that provide information on key digital metrics—and algorithms. An algorithm, as Nick Diakopoulos (2015, 400) explains, "can be defined as a series of steps undertaken in order to solve a particular problem or accomplish a defined outcome."[2] Algorithms are automated decision routines. As Frank Pasquale (2015, 8) writes, "Software encodes thousands of rules and instructions computed in a fraction of a second. Such automated processes . . . improve the quality of our daily lives in ways both noticeable and not." When we talk about algorithms, we are talking about automated decision processes. When we talk about analytics, we are talking about particular metrics and reports— strategic objects that capture some slice of online traffic and reproduce it in an accessible format. Algorithms and analytics are not neutral. They are developed with a specific output in mind, and their calculations encode a series of value-decisions.

Analytics capture data that otherwise would not be permanently available. It is commonly suggested that once something is online, it stays there forever (Mayer-Schonberger 2009). Helen Margetts and her coauthors (2015, 22) make the strong assertion that "every participatory act, however small, carried out on social media leaves a digital imprint." That's only approximately true, though, and at times it represents a dangerous misconception about the online environment. Blog posts may be cached by Google and remain accessible forever. Tweets may end up in the Library of Congress, and embarrassing Snapchats can be saved as a screenshot to haunt you forever. But the indicators that we monitor for digital listening tend to vanish if someone isn't actively collecting them. The data captured by an analytics report—how many people visited DailyKos.com via Facebook links in August 2014 or how many donors clicked on Elizabeth Warren's fundraising page in the hours after her campaign speech—requires a

---

[1] And as Philip N. Howard (2015) points out, the "Internet of Things" is increasingly recording our offline activity as well.

[2] Algorithms, by this definition, are not necessarily digital phenomena. I use a simple algorithm to decide who to root for when watching baseball, for instance: (1) if the Nationals are playing, root for them; (2) if the Yankees are playing, root for the other team; (3) if neither team is playing, don't choose a side.

Table 2.1 **Categories of Analytics, with Examples**

	Descriptive	*Predictive*
Internal	Obama campaign website analytics	Amazon book recommendations
External	Twitter visualization tools	Consumer profile modeling

technical intervention to gather, organize, and preserve (Karpf 2012b). Tarleton Gillespie (2014, 171) refers to this process as making data "algorithm-ready," and Lisa Gitelman (2013) has noted that " 'Raw Data' is an oxymoron." As journalist Adrianne LaFrance (2015) compellingly documents, there is even a case of Pulitzer Prize–winning digital journalism having disappeared entirely from the World Wide Web. Big data and analytics do not capture all online activity, and our digital traces are not saved online forever. Big data and analytics capture only the activity that software engineers and data scientists have endeavored to save and render accessible.

Analytics can be *internal* or *external,* and *descriptive* or *predictive* (see table 2.1). Internal analytics are first-party or second-party analytics. They monitor your own activity (how is my website doing?) or the activity of individuals you directly interact with (how often has this person visited my website, where does this person come from, and where does this person go next?). External analytics are third-party analytics (what websites do individuals of high net worth in Knoxville, Tennessee, tend to visit?). They compile data on a broader scope of social activity that you do not directly interact with. External analytics frequently operate through intermediary data brokers who act as "information fiduciaries" in gathering, storing, and supplying the data (Balkin 2016). Descriptive analytics are often rather mundane: weekly Twitter updates announce that you gained 12 followers and were retweeted 7 times, Google Analytics reports on how many people visited your website, daily Fitbit reports on how many steps you've taken and hours you've slept, and Facebook reports on how many people "liked" your page in the past week.[3] (My personal favorite is Amazon Authorcentral's weekly report, which informs me that one person in Denver bought *The MoveOn Effect* last month.) These reports gather trace data from online activity and compile that data into a user-friendly report.

In isolation, none of these simple descriptive analytics provide actionable data. Knowing that someone in Denver bought my book is not going to change how

---

[3] Keep in mind that most of these examples of internal analytics *also* become external analytics in other contexts. Fitbit provides you with first-party, internal analytics on your steps taken. But it also stores this data and can sell it as third-party, external analytics to any party with an interest in health trends.

I conduct my research. Knowing that 37 people visited my latest blog post via a link from Twitter isn't going to change my blogging or tweeting habits. What they provide is psychic gratification ("I walked 7,143 steps yesterday. I can do better than that today!"). They satisfy a basic impulse to know whether anyone is paying attention. They can also be used to measure progress, to create an incentive or reward system, or to determine the results of pilot programs or experiments ("Headline A attracted 73 clicks, and headline B attracted only 21. We have a winner, folks.").

If the analytics you and I usually encounter are simple and mundane, terms like "analytics," "big data," and "algorithms" can also be shrouded in an air of technological mysticism. As the aggregate data increases, data scientists can move from simple description to inferential prediction. In 2008, Google conducted its much-heralded "Google Flu Trends" experiment (Mayer-Schonberger and Cukier 2013; Lazer, Kennedy, King, and Vespignani 2014), which predicted regional flu outbreaks with greater speed and accuracy than the Centers for Disease Control on the basis of geolocal searches for flu symptoms. Joseph Turow (2011) writes about how banks use massive consumer profiles to separate potential customers into two categories: "targets" and "waste." Nick Diakopoulos (2015) has identified four main functions that can be performed through predictive analytics: prioritization (x before y), classification (x and y are cases of z), association (x and y are connected), and filtering (show x, remove y). The logic of these predictive algorithms is best understood in the context of their applications by Netflix and Amazon, but they can also be used to provide differential treatment to customers or identify public health threats. One common theme here is that predictive analytics require massive scale, while descriptive analytics can function at small or large scales.

The most troubling uses of predictive analytics tend to crop up where third-party intermediaries provide analytics for predictive models. When banks create target-and-waste models, for instance, they are not relying solely on the second-party interactions they are having with customers on their own site. They are purchasing consumer profiles, linked through cookies to individual web browsers, then running sophisticated analyses and using them to make decisions that can influence our future behavior. When predictive analytics are applied internally, they tend to have fewer headline-grabbing implications. Change.org, for instance, uses predictive analytics to serve up petitions to its visitors. After you have signed a petition asking that a veteran in Missouri get the medical treatment she needs, should Change.org point out another veteran's petition, another Missouri petition, or another medical-treatment petition? By gathering internal data about Change.org user behavior, the company can improve how it solves this puzzle.[4]

---

[4] As I will discuss in chapter 3, Change.org also uses algorithms and analytics when it is deciding which petitions should be featured on the landing page of its website.

The distinction between first-, second-, and third-party data deserves further elaboration. First-party analytics are data associated with one's own content or website. Dan Siroker's optimization test for the 2008 Obama campaign (discussed in chapter 1) is a good example. The Obama campaign controlled the website. It created different variations of the website. It used digital trace data to determine which variant performed best. Second-party analytics are associated with one's own visitors, customers, members, or supporters. Amazon.com's recommendation system is a clear example of second-party analytics. Amazon's database includes a file for every registered user. Every click, every purchase, every interaction is stored in that database. Amazon can then look for patterns in the data that suggest "user A and user B have similar tastes." Hence, Amazon can better target (or "microtarget") its offerings to each individual in the database. Both first- and second-party analytics are what I would term *internal* analytics, because both monitor an organization's own interactions. Google's database includes billions of people's search histories . . . as long as they are not using Bing.

External analytics feature a third-party intermediary. If Google or Amazon sells data to the National Security Agency (or the NSA takes that data without asking), then that data becomes external analytics. Google or Amazon then becomes an intermediary party. Fourth and fifth parties can also become involved in external analytics, combining multiple databases to form master profiles. As a practical matter, the difference between internal and external analytics relates to who has the *technical capacity* to gather and assemble the underlying analytics data. A small bit of code installed on my website can provide me with data on who visits my site. If those users register as site members, then I can reliably track their activity. If I want similar data on someone *else's* website, that becomes harder to ascertain. I will be at the mercy of that website's manager and will not be able to verify what errors and limitations are hiding in the dataset.[5]

For this reason, control of and access to analytics is a form of computational power that tends to accrue to already large and powerful organizations. Google and Facebook, for instance, have a tremendous capacity to observe how citizens behave online. Since the activity is happening internally across their digital properties, they are free to test, monitor, and observe our actions. Facebook has the capacity (and the economic incentive) to fiddle with its newsfeed algorithm, changing an advocacy group's ability to reach its supporters (or charging an advocacy group for that privilege). Individuals on these sites have limited access to this behavioral data; they can access whatever data about other users

---

[5] See Hindman (2008) for a discussion of the flaws in publicly available web traffic software.

Google and Facebook choose to make available. Likewise, organizations on these sites must obey and adapt to the rules according to Google and Facebook. Academics are constrained further still. As a social scientist who studies digital phenomena, I often encounter stark reminders of how much more information practitioners have at their fingertips than my colleagues and I do. Google and Facebook analytics provide valuable insights into who is engaging in political speech, in what manner, and to what ends. But this data is not public, so academic researchers are often stuck relying on thin public data or pleading with political organizations to partner with them. How important, for instance, is Facebook in facilitating web traffic to political news sites? As we will see in chapter 4, companies like Upworthy have had a greater capacity to figure this out than journalism scholars, because Upworthy has better data than contemporary academics.

Siva Vaidhyanathan (2011), Rebecca MacKinnon (2012), Phil Howard (2012), Frank Pasquale (2015), and others have argued that Google and Facebook enjoy quasi-monopoly status and should probably face much stricter government oversight and regulation than they do.[6] Both companies have become central information intermediaries—far more central than any broadcast corporation that traffics in film, television, or radio communications. Indeed, as Micah Sifry (2014b) argues in his assessment of Facebook's voter manipulation study involving 61 million people (Bond et al. 2012), "One of the least-noticed implications of our new age of data-intensive politics is that one side has nearly all the marbles. Until the media and other observers develop the tools to independently monitor the uses of Big Data by third-party platforms (as well as campaigns), the integrity of the process will rest entirely on the honesty of the data scientists and engineers inside these organizations, for only they will know if they are playing fairly." Facebook and Google are central to the spread of online information, and their architectural design choices have a significant influence on how and when the public engages with politics. The data necessary for evaluating the influence of these two companies on politics is proprietarily held by the companies themselves, and thus the only data scientists who are capable of determining the impact of these two companies are, by definition, employed by or formally in partnership with them.

Analytics are how we keep score. But that scorekeeping is not necessarily public, which means we cannot always know who, exactly, is winning.

---

[6] In a similar vein, psychologist Richard Epstein (2015) has claimed that Google can incidentally "rig" a US election with algorithmic manipulation. As I argue in a review of Epstein's argument (Karpf 2015), this is a substantial overreach, based on faulty assumptions about how citizens use digital media in elections.

How Analytics Are Used: A Note on Strategy and Strategic Objects

The value of analytics increases as they become incorporated into organizational routines as a *strategic object*. Analytics reports can develop mass, density, and force as they become routinized and incorporated into decision procedures. In his study of the 2008 Obama for America campaign, Daniel Kreiss (2012) calls this process "computational management." The Obama campaign sought to meticulously measure all types of campaign communications, relying on the data in its efforts to determine the most strategic courses of action. By comparison, most electoral campaigns at that time isolated the digital communications team and did not incorporate any of their metrics into the broader debate over strategy and resource expenditures.[7] Both the Obama campaign and the John Edwards campaign used analytics to track web visits and fundraising. But the Obama campaign converted those metrics into a format that helped determine resource allocation decisions. Analytics and testing gain force (and thus importance) when they are incorporated into larger decision-making processes. Otherwise they offer little more than thin description. To understand the importance of analytics and digital listening, we have to place them in an organizational and strategic context.

The term "strategic" is used in many different ways to mean many different things. For many academics, "strategic" can often mean "intentional" or "goal-related" (Manheim 1991; Hallahan et al. 2007). In the game theory literature, "strategy" often denotes a course of action designed to maximize value in relation to the interests and likely actions of other actors (Dixit, Skeath, and Reiley 2014). Among advocacy professionals, "strategy" often carries an even vaguer meaning. In many circles, "That wasn't strategic" simply means "That wasn't how *I* would have done it." (This is particularly the case among certain brands of consultants whose "strategic" advice comes with a price tag attached.)

In this book, I adopt the definition of "strategy" laid out by Marshall Ganz (2009) in *Why David Sometimes Wins*. For Ganz, strategy is a verb. It is a thing that you *do*, not an attribute that you possess. If we conceptualize strategy as a verb, we can better think about how analytics fit into the act of strategizing. The context of strategic work is usually a meeting. A committee or a board meets and

[7] Jessica Baldwin-Philippi (2016, 39) notes that this venerated culture of testing has still not percolated down to most lower-level campaigns: "While the occasional well-funded congressional race, or exceptionally analytics-adept staffer can bring these skills to lower-ballot campaigns, dedication to the practices behind the highly touted 'culture of analytics' is less widespread than dedication to its rhetoric." It appears that learning in campaign organizations happens a bit like bankruptcy—slowly at first, then all at once.

discusses its goals, resources, challenges, and opportunities. It makes a plan to, in Ganz's (2009, 8) words, "turn what we have into what we need to get what we want."

The work of strategizing, when viewed through a Ganzian lens, is iterative. There are later meetings where the committee or the board checks in on its efforts, modifying its strategic approach and work plan on the basis of new information. Scholars like Kenneth Andrews (2004), Elizabeth Clemens (1997), Jane Mansbridge (1983, 1986), and Francesca Polletta (2002) have documented the crucial deliberative work that goes into a successful strategy. Analytics reports do not replace that strategic, deliberative work, nor do they result in objectively correct answers to hard strategic questions. After all, analytics are imperfect and incomplete. Some data is more traceable than other data, and reliance on analytics as a strategic object works only to the extent that the underlying data is both reliable and appropriate. For instance, as we will see in chapter 3, it is far easier to measure which petition topics attract the most new signatures than it is to measure which petition topics are most likely to win concrete victories. Likewise, it is easier to test which headlines attract the most clicks than it is to test which stories build a committed readership willing to pay a monthly fee to support a magazine. And it is easier to measure short-term fundraising goals than it is to measure long-term campaign victories. Analytics create new tools for listening and can yield valuable insights. But that listening has to be filtered through the iterative work of strategic deliberation. Lacking a clear strategic analysis, digital listening can do more harm than good. The best uses of analytics appear when these new strategic objects are also subject to continued scrutiny of "How should we best measure success?" and "How should we best interpret this data?"

And make no mistake: The act of strategizing is chaotic and messy—*particularly* for activist organizations. For-profit companies can rely on market signals to reliably conclude whether their strategies are working. The goal of a business is straightforward: Make money. The goal of an electoral campaign is also straightforward: Win a majority of votes on Election Day. But what about the goal of an activist organization? Whether the mission is ending structural racism, preventing international genocide, mitigating the catastrophic impacts of climate change, or passing sensible gun laws in the United States, no single activist organization currently has the latent power, resources, or capacity to create the change it wishes to see in the world. When businesses engage in the iterative process of strategizing, they can look at quarterly earnings reports to see if they are achieving their goals. When activist associations engage in that same iterative work, they have to rely on much fuzzier signals—petitions signed, members recruited, media events covered (I elaborate on this point in chapter 5). When these metrics are packaged into reports that activists can rely on for feedback on the relative success of their efforts, they become strategic objects.

Journalism researchers have offered compelling evidence of the impact of these changing strategic objects within newsrooms. In an ethnographic study of the *New York Times*, Caitlin Petre (forthcoming) notes, "Rather than big data *displacing* expert intuition . . . the reverse has occurred: metrics have become subordinated to editors' judgments about both the content of the publication and how the organization should be run."[8] Metrics cannot simply or smoothly be substituted for editorial judgment. Instead, they are incorporated into editorial and journalistic routines. They are fashioned into objects that in turn exert force within the newsroom.

Likewise, for analytic activist organizations, analytics do not alleviate the chaos and messiness of strategizing. But reliance on new strategic objects does have a substantial impact on how strategy is formulated. Consider, for instance, MoveOn.org's February 1, 2008, endorsement of presidential candidate Barack Obama. This endorsement occurred well before it was clear who the Democratic nominee would be, and well before most progressive political organizations made an endorsement (Karpf 2009). MoveOn's field director at the time told me in a phone interview that the endorsement decision was a "very scary moment" for the organization, adding, "No one thought Obama was going to win."[9] The timing of the endorsement was driven by MoveOn's passive member feedback systems. MoveOn conducts weekly online surveys of random samples of its membership. In 2007 and 2008, the survey included a question about whether MoveOn should make a presidential endorsement. When John Edwards dropped out after the New Hampshire primary, the MoveOn staff noticed a major shift in members' response to this question. The membership wanted to make an endorsement prior to the "Super Tuesday" wave of primaries. Since these weekly surveys are a strategic object in MoveOn's staff meetings, they immediately became an object of discussion. The staff took note of the shift in member sentiment and agreed to put the matter to a membership-wide vote. On January 30, MoveOn asked its members to vote on whether it should make an endorsement in the primary. Within 24 hours, MoveOn had its result. A supermajority of 70.4% said that the organization should endorse a candidate, and the endorsement should go to Barack Obama.

By comparison, the Sierra Club waited until mid-June 2008 to make its presidential endorsement, long after it had become clear that Barack Obama would be the nominee. I was a member of the Sierra Club's Board of Directors at that time and raised the question of endorsement at our February 20–23 board meeting,

---

[8] This finding mirrors a trend in the older literature (1970s–1990s) on "computerization" in society: The impact of new computational devices is mediated through an organizational process that is itself filled with conflict and strategic choices (see Kling 1991).

[9] Matt Ewing interview notes, March 31, 2010.

three weeks after MoveOn had acted. I was offered multiple reasons why the organization was not yet prepared to consider an endorsement. The most prominent was that *we hadn't had enough time to invite comments and feedback from our members.* The Sierra Club includes volunteer-led local groups and state chapters. Political endorsements are major strategic decisions, and the organization has developed a manual of more than 100 pages establishing the procedures for gathering and weighing input before making an endorsement. Both the Sierra Club and MoveOn value members' input when making important strategic decisions. Both organizations have established processes for gathering this input and incorporating it into the strategic debate. The two organizations have similar *values* but different *metrics*, which in turn become different strategic objects. And the difference between these strategic objects leads to substantially different decisions. MoveOn made a high-risk endorsement when it was unclear who the nominee would be. Sierra Club made a low-risk endorsement when the Democratic nominee had effectively been named. And that was because of the way the two organizations convert members' feedback into data suitable for strategic deliberation.

What Analytics Measure, Part I: Social Media Analytics as Activated Public Opinion

We have now established that we use analytics to keep score online, and we have established that this scorekeeping matters for advocacy organizations only when it is converted into formats that can influence the work of making strategic choices. Some questions remain: How should we interpret these digital traces? Are analytics reports on Twitter @mentions, Facebook likes, or petition signatures adequate approximations of public opinion? Can they substitute for surveys and polling, the traditional technologies of opinion aggregation? What can digital traces tell us that was previously hidden, and where do digital traces run the risk of skewing our perception of reality?

Answering these questions hinges on revisiting the long-standing limitations of "public opinion" as a concept. Since the inception of the field of political communication, scholars have remained decidedly unsure of what, exactly, public opinion comprises. We began with Walter Lippmann's musings on public opinion (1922) and the "phantom public" (1925). Lippmann believed that average citizens could not independently grasp all the complexities of public policy issues, so it was the job of the press and of strategic communicators to guide them. We developed a new hope for understanding and gauging public opinion in the 1930s, thanks to George Gallup's advances in scientific survey techniques (Anstead and O'Loughlin 2015). But sociologist Herbert Blumer (1948, 543) warned against equating the results of mass opinion polls with the broader concept of public opinion, forcefully arguing that we must reject "the narrow operationalist position that public opinion consists of what public opinion polls poll." In a similar vein, V. O. Key (1961, 8) memorably noted that "to speak with precision about public opinion is a task not unlike coming to grips with the Holy Ghost," and Richard Fenno (1978, xxvii) asked, "What does an elected representative see when he or she sees a constituency?" Poll data has never offered a complete picture of public opinion. We routinely equate the two, simply because polling has been the best tool available for representing some facet of public opinion.

The growth of Internet-mediated communications technologies—social media, in particular—has spurred a new wave of authoritative musings on the subject of public opinion. At the 2010 Personal Democracy Forum–Europe conference, the famed technology critic Evgeny Morozov quipped, "What is public opinion? A bunch of Facebook groups is not public opinion. Public opinion is when you show up to vote." There is some substance in Morozov's claim—spambots can populate a Facebook group or appropriate a Twitter hashtag (Brunton 2013); they cannot cast an actual ballot.[10] But the history of political communication scholarship is rife with evidence that public opinion is a moving target, given shape by a range of actors, institutions, and technologies. Social media traffic is indicative of *something*. That something is given force and form through traditional media, as journalists feature trending topics in their stories and active publics challenge, dispute, and extend political framing battles through the newest of our new media (Chadwick 2013). We should proceed with caution in equating social media data with public opinion, but, as with poll data, social media offers us a glimpse of some aspects of this complex topic.

The best route to understanding how social media analytics accord with our understanding of public opinion lies in the academic literature on critical public opinion. Blumer's (1948) caution to early pollsters and Susan Herbst's (1993, 1998) multiple rejoinders to political communication scholars have artfully demonstrated that the ghost we know as public opinion is both socially and technologically constructed. Taeku Lee (2002) has helpfully introduced the term "activated mass opinion" to describe presidential letter writing in the civil rights era. Mass opinion polls produce some measure of *broad* citizen opinion, while presidential letters, letters to the editor, and other participatory artifacts produce some measure of *deep* citizen opinion.

---

[10] Or, at least, they cannot cast actual ballots *yet*. I, for one, will welcome our robot overlords once they have learned to complete a butterfly ballot.

The difference between breadth and depth has always been a problem for the dominant measures of public opinion. As an example, when I became active with the environmental movement in the 1990s, we commonly comforted ourselves with opinion polls that demonstrated 70–80% of the public was "on our side." Clean air, clean water, and public spaces are very popular when weighed against their immediate alternatives. As we fought against Newt Gingrich and the "Republican Revolution" of 1994, my peers, mentors, and I were frankly astounded that elected officials would adopt such obviously unpopular stances. "Just you wait," we told ourselves. "The public will hold you accountable in the next election." The disappointing congressional returns of 1996 were an early and influential lesson for me: Opinion polls aren't boots on the ground, and they sure ain't votes! Opinion polls measure passive sentiment rather than active expression.

Opinions on Twitter, Facebook, and other digital media are active expressions rather than private, guarded sentiments. Traditional critiques of mass opinion polls often center on the artificiality of these nascent opinion statements (Zaller 1992). When interrupted by a pollster in the middle of dinner, citizens will generate opinion statements on a variety of public issues. Those statements do not necessarily bear any resemblance to the opinions they were spontaneously expressing at the dinner table moments before the phone rang. Upon prompting, I can generate an opinion on the state of my local school system. I don't have children, though, so left to my own devices, I am exponentially more likely to express opinions on the local sports franchise.[11]

Practically, we can imagine two different phenomena, both of which are commonly labeled as opinion. *Opinion$_1$* is voiced by an individual, when prompted, on a topic of public importance. Since the American public has never lived up to the ideal of the deliberative "good citizen" (Schudson 1998), aggregating opinion$_1$ has value as a lodestone for public officials seeking guidance regarding the direction of public policy (Jacobs and Shapiro 2000). *Opinion$_2$* is the voiced opinions that an individual shares without the urging of a pollster. The people who attend rallies, write letters to the editor, and knock on doors are expressing opinion$_2$. Opinion$_2$ is *loud*—and unrepresentative. Opinion$_1$ is representative, but flimsy.

There is a well-developed literature on the constructed nature of mass opinion responses, and it is not my intention to provide an exhaustive review.[12] My sole point here is that opinion as constructed through descriptive analytics is more akin to opinion$_2$ than opinion$_1$. It is an entirely different constructed

---

[11] They are uniquely terrible.

[12] See chapter 2 of John Zaller's (1992) *The Nature and Origin of Mass Opinion* for a classic treatment.

phenomenon than we are accustomed to in polling research, and it faces an entirely separate set of problems.

Activity on Twitter, Facebook, YouTube, and blogs is, well, active. You decide to post, retweet, view, like, share, or reblog something. This serves as a stronger indicator of what individuals are actually reading, doing, and discussing than a mass opinion survey. But those choices are also affected by social-psychological nudges. Talia Stroud and her research team (2013) have found that the "like" function on Facebook biases users toward upbeat, positive content. In experimental settings, a "respect" button leads to alternative sharing behavior, encouraging citizens to click on content that represents interesting but countervailing views. Likewise, our behavior on social media channels changes as the networks participating on those channels grow. Facebook was originally reserved for college students. The types of content that young people share on Facebook, and the ways that they construct and perform their online identity, all changed once their parents and grandparents signed up for accounts (boyd 2014).

Not only are the architectures of Facebook, Twitter, Google, and other sites nudging us toward certain types of action, they are also translating these actions through an algorithmic black box that promotes some forms of expression over others (Gillespie, Boczkowski, and Foot 2014). As Frank Pasquale (2015, 3) notes, "The term 'black box' is a useful metaphor . . . given its own dual meaning. It can refer to a recording device, like the data-monitoring systems in planes, trains, and cars. Or it can mean a system whose workings are mysterious; we can observe its inputs and outputs, but we cannot tell how one becomes the other." In the midst of the August 2014 protests in Ferguson, Missouri, Zeynep Tufekci (2014c) noted that #Ferguson was trending in Twitter but not on Facebook: "Algorithmic filtering, as a layer, controls what you see on the Internet. . . . Algorithms have consequences." We increasingly turn to Facebook, Twitter, and other social media sites to produce a record of the public's revealed thoughts and opinions. But the recording these sites produce is not the exact rendering that we might imagine. It is shaped by algorithmic decisions (which are themselves tested and refined through analytics and experimentation) that render invisible judgments about which hashtags or stories should be listed as "trending" (Gillespie 2011).

Furthermore, an undisclosed number of those choices are made not by citizens, but by automated impersonators. Members of Indiana University's "Truthy" research team have estimated that between 15 and 31% of Twitter users are actually bots (Ferrara et al. 2014). A team of computer scientists in 2006 likewise found that 10–20% of all blogs are "splogs," or spam blogs, created as phantom sites to artificially boost hyperlink levels (Kolari et al. 2006). Alexis Madrigal reported in 2013 that fully 61.5% of web traffic came from nonhuman sources. Much of this traffic came from search engines and other "good bots," but fully 21% of web traffic consisted of spammers and "other impersonators." A random-digit-dial phone survey may not tell us what people were talking about before the phone rang, but at least we can be confident that actual human beings picked up the phone (Woolley 2016).

We can generalize this phenomenon, in fact. In a previous methodological essay (Karpf 2012b), I offered the following rule: "Any metric of digital influence that becomes financially valuable, or is used to determine newsworthiness, will become increasingly unreliable over time." You can think of it as a digital version of Goodhart's Law ("Any observed statistical regularity will tend to collapse once pressure is placed upon it for control purposes"). The perverse result here is that digital listening works best *when no one is aware it is going on.* This is why companies like Google and Facebook refuse to explain in detail how their algorithms work. If Google provided step-by-step instructions for how to reach the top of its search rankings, motivated code writers would take up the challenge and find new ways to game the system. If governments chose to make public policy decisions on the basis of online sentiment analysis, organized interests would start figuring out how to game those government systems. Analytics work best when there is little incentive for falsely inflating the underlying trace data.

So the benefit of online public opinion is that it is active rather than passive. Opinion$_2$ consists of articulated statements and behaviors that have occurred without the intervention of a pollster. It represents a new window on political participation (Theocharis 2015; Halupka 2016). Except sometimes it does not. Sometimes these digital traces are faux opinions programmed into bots, and the more public value we place on a given digital metric, the muddier the metric is likely to become. This opinion data, which can be harvested through (external) analytics and introduced into newsrooms and strategy meetings as evidence of the will of the public, measures a different dimension of public opinion than we find in traditional polls. Twitter and Facebook are not representative samples. Their algorithms are black boxes, so we cannot know how they tip the scales, so to speak. But opinions are actively voiced on these sites. They provide evidence of what behavioral economists label "revealed preferences." And those revealed preferences, it turns out, are *also* an incomplete picture of public opinion.

What Analytics Measure, Part II: Revealed Preferences, Metapreferences, and the "Clickbait" Problem

In her 1998 book, *Reading Public Opinion*, Susan Herbst notes, "The meaning of public opinion is *contingent*: The social climate, technological milieu, and communication environment in any democratic state together determine the way we think about public opinion and the ways we try to measure it" (1). Public opinion is given shape by available technologies and by powerful institutions and elites who grasp at imperfect but available representations of the public will in order to guide their deliberations and shape their public appeals through "crafted talk" (Jacobs and Shapiro 2000). What Herbst and her peers were telling us, well before the rise of hashtags and trending topics, is that public opinion is, and in fact always has been, *constructed* through the technologies we had at hand. Before the advent of scientific polls, we had unreliable straw polls. Before straw polls, we had crowd-size estimates at rallies. Each construction of public opinion takes on a force that influences decision processes. We have more than 60 years of experience assessing the limitations of polls (Blumer 1948; Zaller 1992; Herbst 1993, 1998; Lee 2002). As analytics and big data provide new traces of public sentiment, they also come equipped with new limitations. We are novices, however, in assessing the use and misuse of analytics-based opinion measurement.

An analogy from the field of journalism studies proves illustrative. In his landmark 1979 text, *Deciding What's News*, ethnographer Herbert Gans noted his surprise "that [journalists] had little knowledge about the actual audience and rejected feedback from it. Although they had a vague image of the audience, they paid little attention to it; instead, they filmed and wrote for their superiors and themselves" (29). In recent years, C. W. Anderson (2011, 2013b) has described how the rise of the "quantified audience" has altered the editorial process. The introduction of web metrics (clicks and comments per story, easily measured with simple analytics tools) facilitated "management strategies that emphasized the widespread diffusion of audience metrics" (2011, 555). While observing editorial decisions at one online news site, he writes, "It is not an exaggeration to say that the website traffic often appeared to be the *primary ingredient* in news judgment" (2011, 561). Caitlin Petre (2015) highlights a similar theme in her research on Gawker.com. She quotes Gawker's founder and CEO, Nick Denton, who tells us, "Probably the biggest change in Internet media isn't the immediacy of it, or the low costs, but the measurability." In Gans's time, editorial boards had only a vague sense of audience demand, so they instead assumed that audience preferences approximated their own. In the current journalistic moment, web analytics have become a strategic object within the editorial board meeting. We now have tools for assessing granular audience preferences, and these preferences in turn exert a force on editorial judgments of newsworthiness. The result is often derided as "clickbait."

Clickbait can be most easily found on the Gawker network, Politico, BuzzFeed, or the *Huffington Post*. All of these sites A/B test their headlines, resulting in strident titles that often dredge up more controversy than the reported article can support. The *Huffington Post* has at times earned a derisive nickname, the "side-boob gazette," because of its prominent display of celebrity photos in various states of undress. This content attracts clicks, but degrades the civic reputation of journalism as the august "fourth estate." Defenders of these practices rely on a misleadingly simple retort: They are giving the audience what it wants! And they can tell this is what the audience wants because they have analytics reports indicating the most-clicked, most-liked, and most-shared stories of the day.

The problem with clickbait can be generalized as a disjuncture between two types of preference. Both Amartya Sen (1977) and A. O. Hirschman (1984) have discussed the difference between *first-order* (revealed) preferences and *second-order* (meta) preferences. First-order preferences can be viewed through our clicks, our actions, or our purchases. Hirschman (1984, 89) writes, "Economics has traditionally only dealt with (first-order) preferences, that is, those that are *revealed* by agents as they buy goods and services. But the concept of metapreference must be of concern to the economist, to the extent that he claims an interest in understanding processes of economic *change*." In terms of news production, we may simultaneously reveal a preference for cat photos and celebrity gossip through our clicks, while also holding a metapreference for a news environment that provides investigative journalism and civic journalism. Both preferences are real. The emergence of the quantified audience provides additional weight for the former, to the detriment of the latter. It is technically easy for a news organization or advocacy group to measure how many clicks a piece of content received. It is tremendously difficult for that same organization or advocacy groups to monitor whether its readers/supporters/members experienced pride, joy, guilt, or revulsion in the wake of their click.

In issue-based political campaigning, the analogue of decisions over headlines and published stories is decisions over what campaign topics to select. I talked with one leader of a foreign netroots organization who was outspokenly resistant to analytic activism. He told the story of two campaigns that the organization had recently tested against one another. One campaign was to protect charismatic wildlife species. The other was to take on a misbehaving corporation. Cute, fuzzy animals are more click-friendly than corporate malfeasance, and this became immediately evident from the testing results. But the staff of the organization agreed that the corporate campaign was more *important*, so they ignored the quantified member input and pursued the latter campaign anyway.

The problem with simply conflating analytics reports and simple experiments with public opinion is that they can mask these metapreferences. Are members clicking on a petition because it is important or because it is simple and makes them feel good? Does the email language that attracts the most donations increase or decrease the level of commitment that recipients feel toward the organization? Do stories that constantly sensationalize a conflict eventually lead readers to look for a different news source? The metrics that most easily fit within an analytics report are often ill-suited to answering these questions.

The interesting thing about metapreferences is that you can *also* design digital tools that help you gauge them. Consider, for instance, Avaaz.org's annual membership survey. Avaaz is an international MoveOn-style advocacy organization, founded in 2007 with the help of MoveOn alumni (Kavada 2012). It currently has a global membership of more than 41 million. Every year, Avaaz.org sends multiple emails to its membership base, asking members to weigh in on what the organization's priorities should be for the following year. The primary topics include "priority challenges," "making Avaaz stronger," and "top campaign ideas." After soliciting feedback on these organizational and issues topics, the survey includes an "Avaaz temperature check" (figure 2.1). This consists of two questions: "How is Avaaz doing?" and "How should we use this poll?" Ninety-six percent of the Avaaz members *who took the time to respond to the online poll* said that their votes should not be treated as a binding mandate, but instead should be regarded as a "guide" or "just as input." Notice the signal that this sends to Avaaz's core staff: Digital activity from Avaaz members is one gauge of member interest. The poll, along with various forms of passive democratic feedback (email A/B tests, petition traffic, etc.) indicates the members' revealed preferences. But the membership also favors staffers using their own judgment, even when it contradicts what other data sources appear to indicate. This is a metapreference, and it is equally relevant to Avaaz's strategic deliberations as an analytics report highlighting the most recent revealed preference of the membership.

Analytics and audience quantification do not *have* to give rise to clickbait issue campaigns. The foreign advocacy leader I spoke to could have used analytics to compare variant issue frames for the corporate campaign or to select one of two possible campaigns that his staff felt were equally important. Likewise, news sites like *The Atlantic* monitor web traffic analytics, but carefully build editorial processes that counterbalance the weight of these revealed preferences. Designing these new work routines, however, begins with the recognition that revealed preferences are not the totality of our preferences. Members might be

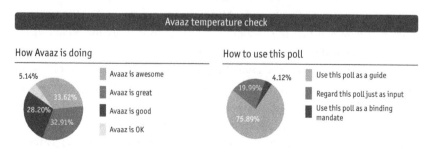

Figure 2.1 Avaaz.org temperature check.

more likely to click on the polar bear petition, while also wishing that their organization took on tougher campaign issues. Critics of "clicktivism" are often, at root, raising concerns that the ease of online action will produce social movements that prioritize actions catering to supporters' revealed preferences over their metapreferences, warping and degrading civic participation along the way (Van Laer and Van Aelst 2010; Lewis, Gray and Meierhenrich 2014). The response to this critique is not to conclude that the Internet has ruined civic organizations, but to explore how those organizations balance and mix digital inputs.

This is both the enduring strength and disheartening weakness of analytic activism. Digital sentiment tracking, like all other media, does not hold up a mirror to public preferences. It does not reflect; it refracts. That refraction reveals some images and obscures others. It produces strategic objects that can drive tactical innovation and savvy media campaigns. But it also invites tunnel vision and an obsession with the wrong metrics. Analytic activism represents an opportunity, but it also demands a recalibration of how activist leaders assess and determine the *importance* of competing issues and tactics. The danger posed by clickbait and clicktivism is an institutional danger: If activist organizations focus on the most easily tracked metrics and treat those metrics as evidence of public sentiment among their supporters, they can widen the gap between revealed preferences and metapreferences. (In chapter 5, I describe this problem as a factor in defining the "analytics frontier.")

Some of the leading netroots organizations attempt to capture both revealed preferences and metapreferences by expanding the range of their analytics signals. Thus, as we will see in chapter 3, MoveOn.org uses a combination of email response rates (revealed preferences), petition activity (revealed preferences), open-ended member surveys (metapreferences), and staff judgments (metapreferences). This range of digital trace data is an intentional effort to diversify the set of opinion signals that MoveOn incorporates into strategic deliberations. If the organization defined success solely in terms of list growth or petition signatures, it could easily optimize for campaigns that attract broad but shallow commitments.

The Ethics of A/B Testing

Thus far, this chapter has focused on what analytics *are* and how they are *used*. There is a final topic worthy of our attention, though: When and where are analytics *appropriate*? All of this discussion of digital listening, testing, and measurement and manipulation must provoke in some readers a sense of foreboding. In a book about digital listening, big data, and politics (written by an American, no less!), where is the discussion of Edward Snowden? Where is the National Security Agency? Where are the giant data vendors like Acxiom, which claims to have 6,500 data points on every individual in the United States? This book's focus on analytics *in* activism is quite far removed from the corporate and government data policies that have become the target *of* activism. In this final section of the chapter, I will attempt to explain how and why the use of algorithms and analytics in advocacy organizations presents far fewer ethical concerns than their use by governments, large corporations, and third-party data vendors.

There are indeed many causes for concern. And there are several excellent books and articles that document the myriad problems being created by unregulated data vendors and overly aggressive governmental and corporate data tracking.[13] But the meager public understanding of digital listening has produced a tendency among journalists and some social critics to lump all digital listening together. The result is a perpetual cycle of surprise and outrage whenever any form of digital listening appears in the news. Facebook, Google, Amazon, Target, the Obama campaign, and the NSA are all treated as equal examples of digital listening (or, often, "microtargeting"). But putting all of these cases in the same category serves to muddy the critical distinctions among them.

As Christian Rudder (2014), president of the popular dating website OkCupid.com and author of *Dataclysm: Who We Are (When We Think No One's Looking)*, explains in a blog post titled "We Experiment on Human Beings!":

> Guess what, everybody: if you use the Internet, you're the subject of hundreds of experiments at any given time, on every site. That's how websites work.

Rudder is right, even if he is being facile. Many uses of algorithms, analytics, and big data are commonplace, harmless business practices. Dan Siroker and Pete Koomen (2013, 38) describe many of the "surprising" findings that have come from A/B tests their company, Optimizely, has run for companies. These include insights such as "the content [Chrome Industries] put in the center block [on their homepage] seemed *always* to outperform the content they put in the left block." That's valuable information for an online retailer, and completely harmless to consumers. When you visit a website, open your email, or log in to Facebook, you are frequently placed in a treatment group without your knowledge. That's how websites and online businesses learn and improve. OkCupid's matching algorithm would not get any better unless the company routinely tweaked it through experimentation. Google's search results would be less useful

---

[13] For those interested in these topics, I particularly recommend Frank Pasquale's *The Black Box Society* and Bruce Schneier's *Data and Goliath*.

and your Facebook newsfeed would be more cluttered if those companies did not constantly pore over our data to improve their services.

The experiments that Rudder is talking about are a central source of data on what users want. Organizations that don't run tests or monitor analytics are failing to listen to their users, customers, or members. We should certainly demand that organizations listen responsibly and listen effectively. But, on balance, more listening and responsiveness is probably better than less.

Yet alongside Rudder's celebratory view of big data, we also have evidence of some far more dangerous applications. Frank Pasquale (2015, 5), for instance, asks, "Should a credit card company be entitled to raise a couple's interest rate if they seek marriage counseling? If so, should cardholders know this?" Bruce Schneier (2015) compellingly demonstrates how the NSA's bulk data collection actually undermines the NSA's goals of monitoring potential terrorist activity and keeping the country safe. Just because some forms of digital listening and experimentation are commonplace and benign does not mean there is no cause for genuine concern. So the question ought to become, "*When* should we be concerned about the use and abuse of big data?"

Even among serious scholars, the primary trend has been toward defining and critiquing algorithms as a whole rather than clarifying the situations in which their use deserves greater or lesser scrutiny. Mike Ananny (2016), for instance, asks what it would mean to treat "networked information algorithms"—algorithms that convene people, judge similarity, and suggest probable actions—in the same way we treat people and institutions that perform these functions. This leads us to think about the power, potential, and risks posed by the growing reliance on algorithmic decision making. This is a promising line of inquiry, but it runs the risk of seeing all digital listening through a singular, universalist lens. If we are going to be outraged at the NSA and credit card companies for their aggressive digital listening practices, must we apply the same critiques to political campaigns and advocacy groups? I think not. Moreover, I worry that by viewing all uses of digital trace data through the same lens, we risk losing focus on the pernicious abuses that deserve the greatest public attention and policy response.

In what follows, I map out a five-variable framework for determining the ethical risks posed by various types of digital listening. Each of these variables is related to two key distinctions:

(a)   Where does the data come from (internal vs, external analytics)?
(b)   What is the data used for (predictive vs. descriptive analytics)?

In general, descriptive, internal analytics create the least risk of public harm, while predictive, external analytics offer the greatest risk of public harm. But we can make further distinctions within the external/predictive category. They are as follows:

1. Actor Identity: Is the data being used by state or quasi-state actors? Are there natural checks on data abuse?
2. Potential Harm: What (unintended) harm might befall an individual if algorithmic modeling produces a faulty decision?
3. Approximate Transparency: To what extent can end users or other intermediaries observe and critique how the model operates?
4. Data Quality: Who controls the collection of the data inputs that are fed into these algorithms? What legal guarantees, social norms, or industrial incentives influence the quality of the underlying data?
5. Potential Redress: Since algorithms and analytics are never perfect, what avenues for redress exist for persons who feel they have been algorithmically wronged?

Let's examine each of these variables independently.

1. CONSIDER ACTOR IDENTITY: STATE/QUASI-STATE ACTION

The first variable concerns the identity of who is gathering the data. There is an important difference between governments, corporations, and advocacy groups. Governments have citizens. Companies have customers and shareholders. Advocacy groups have members or supporters. Citizenship comes with inalienable rights that must be preserved and protected. Companies operate within markets that can be well functioning or malfunctioning, depending on factors such as monopolistic behavior and regulatory oversight. Membership is a much looser, more fluid relationship. If government agencies abuse data, they can rob citizens of their rights. If companies abuse data, they can exploit potential customers while avoiding market-based punishment. If those companies are in the information industry, which exhibits a tendency toward quasi-monopolistic behavior (Wu 2010; Crawford 2013), there is an added danger that they will affect the ability of citizens to access political and civic knowledge. The stakes are much lower in the civic/advocacy/activist arenas.

Eitan Hersh (2015, 201) offers an example in the concluding chapter of his book, *Hacking the Electorate*:

> If a constituent contacts a legislator, depending on the state of residence, the [data] vendors can show the legislative office whether the voter participated in a recent Democratic or Republican primary. . . .

The use of commercial segmentation strategies in constituent communications and especially in casework may seem inappropriate. When
campaigns use databases of linked public records to target segments of
the electorate or to estimate which voters are supporters, this is a less
objectionable behavior than when similar strategies are used in official
responses to constituent requests. The latter behavior seems ripe for a
kind of abuse by which government officials treat perceived supporters differently than perceived opponents.

Voter data in the hands of electoral campaigns leads *mostly* to more efficient targeting and outreach in electoral campaigns. That same voter data in the hands
of congressional offices presents a real potential for misuse and harm. If a candidate for Congress chooses to knock only on the doors of voters who are likely
to vote for her, then she is efficiently allocating scarce campaign resources. If a
member of Congress chooses to provide services only to constituents who likely
did vote for her, then she is violating a central tenet of representative governance.
Hersh (2015, 203) notes that using voter data to provide differential constituent
services would in fact be a violation of the US House of Representatives Ethics
Manual, but also points out, "The problem is that incorporating public records,
such as registration data, into constituent services databases makes it all too easy
for legislative offices to violate this ethical standard." The problem lies not in the
existence of voter file data, but in the migration of this data from an electoral unit
to a government unit.

Data scientist Cathy O'Neil (2015) offers a second, more troubling example
in a research presentation titled "Weapons of Math Destruction." O'Neil explains
that some judges in the United States now rely on predictive models to estimate
"recidivism risk scores," which in turn factor into their sentencing decisions.
Likelihood of recidivism is indeed an important consideration, so the use of
analytics and algorithms to improve sentencing decisions may seem intuitively
appealing. But the problem is that many of these recidivism models incorporate
factors like race, employment, education level, and whether one's parents served
time in prison—factors that may indeed show a statistical correlation with historical crime data but that are also prima facie unconstitutional considerations.
O'Neil argues that by hiding these considerations within algorithmic models,
the justice system becomes systematically less just. One could argue that judicial
sentencing *already* incorporates many of these biases, but O'Neil's central point
is that cloaking them in the language of mathematics renders them less visible,
dampening our capacity to debate or challenge them. Scenarios like this one
are particularly troubling specifically because criminal sentencing is a function
reserved for the state. The state has a responsibility to provide equal justice to all
citizens. When the state fails in this task, both journalists and activists have just

cause to hold the state accountable and pursue corrective action. When agents of the state attempt to mask their decisions behind algorithms and analytics, they are rendering them less visible. Ethically, we should react with increased scrutiny of the biases and judgments that are encoded within the algorithms and underlying data.

In a similar vein, although Facebook and Google are not countries and do not have citizens, it is worth noting that they both possess quasi-monopolistic market shares in communications industries that make them virtually indispensable and unavoidable in present-day society. Rebecca MacKinnon (2012, 149) has labeled them "Facebookistan and Googledom" to denote the state-like power each company sometimes yields. Consider: Though the occasional upstart social network site may make claims that it plans to challenge Facebook's dominance, the site is an unmatched social utility. Your options as a consumer are to abide by Facebook's testing and data reuse policies or to forgo Facebook altogether. Likewise, Google's policy decision regarding what types of political advertisements to accept and reject are arguably more influential today than the decisions made by the Federal Election Commission (FEC).[14] There is no effective option for switching to a competitor, and the sheer market dominance of these two companies renders them functionally immune to competition. As a result, several observers argue that Facebook and Google should be treated like utilities—electricity, water, and phones—and regulated accordingly (Vaidhyanathan 2011; Howard 2012).

We should exercise increased caution and demand greater transparency in our roles as citizens than in our roles as consumers. Consumers should also demand increased government regulation and oversight from Internet companies that hold near-monopolistic market share, since they are not subject to the normal competitive pressures of a well-functioning market (see Hindman forthcoming). When evaluating the ethics of digital listening, it is important that we consider who is doing the listening and whether we have the capacity to avoid their prying eyes.

---

[14] This is, in no small part, due to the designed ineptitude of the FEC itself. Ann Ravel, the chair of the FEC, publicly called the commission "worse than dysfunctional" and concluded that the FEC would be incapable of enforcing election laws or preventing election abuse in the 2016 election (Lichtblau 2015). By design, the FEC has six commissioners—three Republicans and three Democrats—and those commissioners now vote in lockstep, leaving the commission incapable of enforcing election rules.

In light of the FEC's toothless behavior, both Google and Facebook have sought advice from campaign finance and political communication scholars on what their own advertising policies ought to be. Google and Facebook are now effectively left to perform the statelike work of determining what types of online advertisements will be permissible.

2. EVALUATE POTENTIAL HARMS

As Bruce Schneier (2015, 112) puts it in *Data and Goliath*, "Any time we're monitored and profiled, there's the potential for getting it wrong. You are already familiar with this; just think of all the irrelevant advertisements you've been shown on the Internet on the basis of some algorithm misinterpreting your interests." When we consider the growth of digital listening and algorithmic authority, it is helpful to ask: *What (unintended) harms might befall an individual if this algorithmic model produces a faulty decision?* I would argue that we should treat algorithms, analytics, and big data with greater caution and scrutiny as their potential for harm increases. Some algorithms are more threatening than others. To illustrate this point, consider two examples of algorithmically informed decision making: campaign microtargeting and Election Day "vote cleansing."

Campaign microtargeting has received the more thorough attention of the two. Every election cycle, journalists and public intellectuals opine on the use of big data to warp electoral communications. Zeynep Tufekci (2014a) warns in "Engineering the Public" that advances in big data, emergent computational methods, experimental and behavioral sciences, and algorithmic monitoring are ushering in a new era of hyper-targeted political propaganda, with dangerous consequences for the public sphere. She argues that "big data and associated new analytic tools foster more effective—and less transparent—'engineering of consent' (Bernays, 1947) in the public sphere."[15]

But other scholars, such as Eitan Hersh (2015) and John Sides and Lynn Vavreck (2014a), argue that most claims of "data wizardry" in present-day campaigning are overblown and not supported by the available evidence. Hersh (2015, 169), for instance, provides strong evidence that "consumer records and proprietary party records are not as predictive of voters' political attributes as public records, and that social network–based contacting strategies have not been able to reach the voters that campaigns most want to target." Simply put, first-party and second-party analytics offer far more value to electoral campaigns than the third-party consumer records that take center stage in most conversations about microtargeting. What's more, the potential harm of campaign microtargeting is relatively small. The worst-case scenario is that different voters will

---

[15] Phil Howard warned of a similar threat in his 2006 book, *New Media Campaigns and the Managed Citizen*. Howard depicted an oncoming threat of "political redlining," in which electoral campaigns aggressively segment the public into supporters, opponents, and nonvoters and then narrow their campaign efforts to engage only with supporters and likely voters. The trend in political campaigns, at least in the past decade, has been in the opposite direction, though. Campaigns are opening up more field offices and investing more heavily in mass voter contact, partially because enhanced voter files expand the universe of potential supporters that campaigns can identify (Masket, Sides, and Vavreck 2016).

receive different messages based on their predicted interests and preferences (see Hillygus and Shields 2008) and that some unlikely voters will receive no mobilization messages at all (Howard 2006). Hypertargeted political propaganda should receive some of our attention, but it probably attracts more attention than it deserves.

Compare the threat of algorithmic microtargeting with the use of algorithms in "voter roll purges." As Ari Berman (2015a, 209) documents in *Give Us the Ballot*, during the 2000 election,

> the widespread and wrongful purging of registered voters was the most consequential—and least discussed—aspect of the Florida election. A lawsuit by the NAACP after the election revealed that at least 12,000 voters had been stricken from the Florida voting rolls because a company named Database Technologies (DBT) had incorrectly labeled them as felons. That purge of (mostly African-American) Florida voters amounted to over 22 times George W. Bush's 537-vote margin of victory. [N]ames were added to the purge list if there was only a 70 percent match between a name on the voter rolls and a name in the state's felon database. This meant that voters could be tagged as felons even when middle initials, suffixes, nicknames, and even race and sex data didn't match perfectly. ()

Here we see algorithmic matching being used to aggressively reshape the contours of the US electorate. The potential harm from "vote cleansing" is much greater than the harm caused by microtargeted campaign communications. In the one case, citizens receive more narrowly tailored information before casting their vote. In the other case, citizens are denied their right to vote altogether. *Yet the vast majority of attention surrounding the Internet and campaign politics focuses on the former rather than the latter.* When campaign microtargeting goes wrong, the wrong person gets the wrong mailing. When vote cleansing goes wrong, the wrong person is turned away from the ballot box. If we incorporate the evaluation of potential harm into our judgment of analytics and algorithms, we can appropriately calibrate our attention, applying greater scrutiny to the more substantial threats.

3. DEMAND RELATIVE OR APPROXIMATE TRANSPARENCY

The analytics director of a major netroots advocacy group explained this third point as an internal rule of thumb that his organization follows: "If someone asks why an algorithm categorized them as it did, they should be able to receive a clear answer." If a company or advocacy organization is going to use predictive modeling to decide who gets which communications, it should be prepared to explain what factors went into that decision. If it would be embarrassed to identify them, it should not use predictive modeling in that case. This rule can be generalized beyond advocacy organizations to virtually any use of analytics, algorithms, and big data: If a meaningful decision process is going to be automated, the logic of the algorithm should be clear and defensible. If a citizen, customer, or journalist would have reasonable cause for alarm, that process deserves stricter scrutiny and attention.

I refer to this as *relative or approximate transparency* because there are some quite good reasons to keep the specific details of a predictive algorithm obscure. As Tarleton Gillespie (2014, 176) explains:

An information provider like Twitter cannot be more explicit or precise about its algorithms' workings. To do so would give competitors an easy means of duplicating and surpassing its service. It would also require a more technical explanation than most users are prepared for. It would hamper their ability to change their criteria as they need. But most of all, it would hand those who hope to "game the system" a road map for getting their sites to the top of the search results or their hashtags to appear on the Trends list.

If Facebook and Google were fully transparent about their algorithms, malicious actors would be much more successful in gaming their ranking systems. If the Transportation Security Administration or the National Security Agency were fully transparent about what specific flags attract heightened governmental scrutiny, actual terrorists would be better able to skirt detection. If a predictive model is being used to make valuable decisions, we should assume people will attempt to distort that model. A little bit of opaqueness can go a long way in helping the models to perform effectively over time. But if a model is completely secret, we are unable to consider its merits and its flaws.

In the area of political microtargeting, political journalists enforce a type of approximate transparency. In the 2012 election, for instance, ProPublica set up an elaborate system of dummy email accounts that monitored how both presidential campaigns were microtargeting their messages. Nick Diakopoulos (2015) describes this type of work as the "reverse engineering" of algorithms. Political journalists and academics paid close attention to online political advertisements as well. This was not *full* transparency—the Obama campaign was not going to reveal its granular strategy for determining who received which messages—but it was enough to keep the worst potential excesses in check. Any benefit the campaigns might enjoy from excessive targeting efforts is paired with the risk of a front-page story about their deceptive advertising practices.

As Jessica Baldwin-Philippi (2015, 130) writes in her ethnographic study of campaign communications practices, "While campaigns may have once gotten away with presenting slightly different views to various populations, or going to extremely partisan rallies without hopes of upsetting moderate voters, digital technologies have changed those assumptions. Currently, campaigns see the potential for radical publicity within any message they post to a website, send to an email list, or say at a small public event." Electoral campaigns are functionally constrained by attentive journalists and volunteers for the opposition candidate who carefully monitor what they say, to whom, and how.

Frank Pasquale (2015, 157) argues that a necessary component of any government/corporate intelligence apparatus must be "to make sure that independent individuals *who are not themselves part of the intelligence apparatus* have some role in processing the staggering amounts of data that even an oversight program will generate." In a sense, he is suggesting that the analytics used by governments and corporations ought to face the same monitorial constraints that we see in electoral campaigns. Note that this is still a far cry from complete data transparency, though.

There are some good reasons why we cannot expect complete data transparency, but we should demand that journalists or other neutral parties be able to observe the operating logic and operational results of any large, data-driven program. By extension, demanding relative or approximate transparency highlights the cases where companies invoke trade secret protections in order to completely avoid scrutiny of their algorithmic models (O'Neil 2015). If the underlying model is not public, and if journalists, customers, lawmakers, and citizens are prevented from evaluating the algorithm, then there is no check on this automation process to ensure that it is either morally just or mathematically sound.

4. REMAIN SKEPTICAL ABOUT DATA QUALITY

This next variable is a reformulation of an old computer science phrase: GIGO, or "garbage in, garbage out." An algorithm is only as good as the data that is fed into it. When judging the use and abuse of big data, we should also evaluate the underlying quality and reliability of the data going into these algorithmic models. Commercial data firms and consultants have strong incentives to boast about the power and quality of their data. (Academics pursuing grants and trying to make it through peer review have strong incentives as well, to be frank.) When judging the use of algorithms, we should ask not only what judgments and biases are enshrined in the code, but also what holes and limitations are present in the data.

The weaker the dataset, the more we should treat the algorithms and analytics with suspicion. The 2000 Florida voter purge again serves as a helpful example. If DBT had perfect data, its automated removal of names from the voter rolls would be a trivial matter. But DBT could make only approximate predictions of whether its list of felons' names could be correctly linked with similarly named Florida voters. Likewise, Eitan Hersh (2015, 171) notes that one major reason why electoral campaigns rely so heavily on public voter file data rather than private commercial data is that private data is "typically inaccurate" and "offer[s] very rough predictions of true attributes." Even though commercial databases continue to increase in scale, they still are riddled with outdated information and outright errors. Commercial marketers may not mind approximating on the basis of this data, since slightly better advertisement targeting can be a substantial improvement over traditional broadcast advertising efforts. But electoral campaigns lean toward overinclusion rather than overexclusion in their communications. They would rather knock on extra doors, make extra phone calls, and produce more generic messages than incorrectly remove potential voters from the target universe or accidentally send those potential voters a message that will offend them. This is the main reason why predictions of political redlining (Howard 2006; Tufekci 2014a) have not yet come to pass. Electoral campaigns treat their models with caution and err toward reaching out more broadly.

Remaining skeptical about data quality also highlights an important difference between internal and external analytics. The data gathered through first-party and second-party (internal) analytics is generally of a higher quality than the data generated through external analytics, because a company or organization has the tools and the capacity to gather exactly the data it wants or needs. At a minimum, the flaws in an internal analytics program are much more visible than the flaws in an external analytics program (we tend to *know* what we don't know when we are gathering the data ourselves). As an extension of this point, recall that academics almost universally are forced to rely on publicly available external analytics refashioned through third-party intermediaries (the exception is when academics enter into formal data-sharing partnerships with organizations like Facebook). It follows that much of "big data" research in academia is inherently more limited than research conducted by in-house data scientists for large corporations like Facebook and Google. This represents an inversion of a historic gap in expertise. It used to be that academic researchers had the time, skills, and training to conduct much richer and more nuanced studies than day-to-day corporate professionals. In the arena of big data, we academics likely still have more time, skills, and training, but the asymmetry in our access to high-quality data sharply limits our empirical reach.

5. EVALUATE POTENTIAL REDRESS

Finally, we should apply stricter scrutiny where analytics-based decision making leaves no space for corrective human intervention. This point flows naturally from the previous four. If we grant that algorithms and analytics are often flawed, it follows that there should be a clear avenue for redress when a person has been algorithmically wronged. The case of the Florida voter purge, for instance, could have been rendered effectively trivial if voters had been able to easily and effectively challenge their incorrect classification. We should be less concerned about analytics and algorithms when citizens, customers, or supporters have clear routes for effective redress; we should be more concerned when they have little or no capacity to challenge automated algorithmic judgments.

Potential redress can be particularly important in the area of digital reputation tracking (which includes credit ratings). Pasquale (2015, 32) warns:

> Runaway data can lead to *cascading disadvantages* as digital alchemy creates new analog realities. Once one piece of software has inferred that a person is a bad credit risk, a shirking worker, or a marginal consumer, that attribute may appear with decision-making clout in other systems all over the economy. There is little in current law to prevent companies from selling their profiles of you.
>
> Bad inferences are a larger problem than bad data because companies can represent them as "opinion" rather than fact.

Pasquale shares the story of a data broker (ChoicePoint) that incorrectly added a criminal charge of "intent to sell and manufacture methamphetamines" to Arkansas resident Catherine Taylor's file. After Taylor learned of this error and contacted ChoicePoint, the data broker corrected its file. But by that time the file had been sold to several other companies, effectively replicating the error. Taylor's credit was ruined and she was unable to find work as long as this error was included in her digital reputation profile. And as Pasquale (2015, 33) points out, "For every Catherine Taylor, who was actually aware of the data defaming her, there are surely thousands of us who don't know that there are scarlet letters emblazoned on our digital dossiers." Third-party data brokers like ChoicePoint have an ethical obligation to act as information fiduciaries (Balkin 2016), but that ethical obligation is not yet enshrined in case law or regulatory practices.

It bears noting that the importance of potential redress increases in direct relation to the increase in potential harm.[16] In cases like microtargeted campaign

---

[16] It also increases as data migrates from first- and second-party sources to third-, fourth-, and fifth-party data brokers, who can apply it toward unknown ends.

communications or Netflix or Amazon recommendations, citizens and consumers have relatively little opportunity to seek redress, but also face only miniscule harm. Being incorrectly classified by a political campaign means you might be exposed to the wrong political messages. Being incorrectly classified by Netflix means you might miss out on your new favorite show. When the banks misclassify you as a credit risk or search engines wrongly associate your profile with a convict, avenues for redress are more important because the stakes are much higher.

When viewed through the lens of these five variables, analytic activism appears to be categorically different than many of the more foreboding uses of analytics and algorithms. It is conducted by political associations and advocacy groups, not governments or quasi-monopolistic corporations. It is meant to guide tactical and strategic choices, so its potential for harm is low. Its algorithms can be rendered approximately transparent through the collection and analysis of publicly available data. It relies primarily on first- or second-party internal data, limiting the GIGO problem. And members of these political associations who disapprove of how they are being digitally sorted and engaged can seek redress by either raising their voice or quietly exiting the relationship.

My sanguine reaction to the use of digital trace data in activism should not be confused with complacency over the use of algorithms and analytics in all circumstances. There are plenty of cases where the use of analytics and algorithms deserves public outcry and policy response. But we ought to calibrate our sense of outrage, directing it not at every use of A/B testing or trace data, but at the actors and activities that represent the real potential threats.

Conclusion

"Analytics," "algorithms," and "big data" are popular buzzwords. They are blanket terms, used interchangeably in the discourses of international security, business and finance, health tracking, journalism, politics, and many, many more. There is no singular, overarching analytics industry or a single set of common skills or practices among analytics professionals. The terms have too many referents and can mean entirely different things. Analytics may indeed be how we keep score, but they are applied to a host of different "games," each with their own rules, norms, stakes, and boundaries.

As such, the intent of this chapter has been threefold: first, to define and clarify some of the key terms that are used in this book; second, to situate the field of analytic activism among the broader set of analytics-related fields; and third, to elaborate on how the ethical concerns in analytic activism differ from the ethical concerns in other digital listening–related fields. This is not a book about all of the ways that data affects politics. Nor is it a book about the technical application of data analysis to politics, or about digital security, or encryption, or the expansive power of digital behemoths like Google and Facebook. Each of these is a worthy topic, but each is also distinct enough to deserve its own book-length treatment.

The focus of this book is on how digital listening, based primarily on internal analytics, is changing large-scale, organized activist campaigning. We have seen in this chapter that analytics can take many different forms—internal and external, descriptive and predictive. We have seen that the importance of these new digital traces depends on how they are converted into strategic objects that can be interpreted in strategic conversations to alter an organization's course of action. The chapter has also discussed how analytics offer an alternative perspective on public opinion and member preferences. All measures of public opinion are constructed and include underlying biases. The bias of public opinion as revealed through analytics is that it more closely resembles revealed preferences than metapreferences. This in turn introduces new risks and challenges for advocacy groups that mistakenly treat opinion$_1$ as a complete reflection of complex, multidimensional public opinion.

The next two chapters offer concrete examples of analytic activism in action. Chapter 3 evaluates the digital petition industry, examining how massive open petition platforms use analytics-driven signals to promote divergent forms of political engagement. Chapter 4 explores how a commitment to analytics and the culture of testing has led to massive changes in how political information spreads online. As we will see in both chapters, analytic activism does not inexorably lead all digital organizations to embrace a single set of issues or best practices. Analytics provide a new toolset for large activist organizations to engage in power-building and contention. There is significant diversity and variation in how they make use of these digital listening tools.

3

The Organizational Logic
of Petition Platforms

A petition can be many different things. It can be a demonstration of public support for a proposed course of action—either the carrot or the stick directed at powerful decision makers (Carpenter 2003, 2015). It can be a membership sign-up form—a growth engine for political associations that have defined membership downward to include the entire reachable universe of supportive citizens. It can be a gateway—the first step in a long-term collective action campaign. It can be a media signal, a marker of newsworthiness that launches an individual story or cause into the limelight (Chadwick and Dennis 2016). Within the realm of analytic activism, a petition can also act as a governance-signaling device or a testing ground for alternative tactics and strategies.

Petitions are the most flexible and essential tool of analytic activism. While other forms of digital citizen engagement—Facebook likes and shares, Twitter retweets and trending hashtags, and views on YouTube and Vine—share the limelight in discussions of digital activism, social petitions have a few key affordances that render them particularly valuable. Most important, the act of signing a digital petition leaves an email address behind as part of its digital footprint. Retweets, views, likes, and shares do not. When Twitter users gather around a shared hashtag, they form a network of followers and the followed—what Zizi Papacharissi (2014) calls an "Affective Public." But try to reach out to this hashtag network one week, one month, or one year later and you'll find that its force has vanished in the wind. The digital traces of hashtag networks and viral videos yield tremendous data for Facebook, Twitter, and YouTube. But the authors of those tweets, posts, and videos are left with limited capacity to access that data or engage with the public that formed around them. A viral petition can give birth to a political organization. A viral video rarely gives birth to more than a meme.

Digital petitions are simultaneously celebrated as evidence of a new style of bottom-up, networked political engagement (Earl and Kimport 2011; Bennett and Segerberg 2013; Margetts et al. 2015b) and mourned as synonymous with clicktivism and the digital degradation of political activism. On the one hand, the ease of creating a digital petition and the potential for such an action to spiral into a successful political reform movement seem emblematic of the way that digital media unlocks new structures of social engagement. On the other hand, signing a digital petition is considered *too easy* by some critics (Gladwell 2010; Shulman 2010; White 2011). Clicktivism's critics argue that taking part in these simple, token efforts leaves people less likely to engage in more substantive actions, rendering the formation of large-scale social movements less likely online (Kristofferson, White, and Peloza 2014; Lewis, Gray, and Meierhenrich 2014). Clicktivism's proponents argue that we are seeing new forms of collective action that unleash the potential for revitalizing civil society in the twenty-first century.

Both the critics and celebrants of digital petitioning tend to focus entirely on the petition creators and the petition signers themselves—the members of the mass public who use online tools to fashion new forms of political speech. For analytic activism, the more important feature of digital petitioning is the opportunity it presents for novel forms of listening, list growth, and experimentation. Digital petitions are an *industry*. A viral petition can have useful hybrid-media ripple effects, while also helping political associations to build a larger supporter base and rise above the analytics floor. What the literature on "network-based" digital protest tends to miss is the crucial mediating role played by the petition platforms themselves. Sites like Change.org and MoveOn Petitions operate according to distinct organizational logics, and they combine digital listening and experimentation to help determine which petitions go viral and how those viral moments are transformed into long-term movements. What's more, treating these petition platforms as an industry reveals that *not all open petition sites are equal*. The two largest petition platforms in the United States operate under dramatically different philosophies. They highlight different issues, different personal narratives, and different calls for political engagement. The field of social petitioning is not characterized by purely spontaneous collective action or half-hearted clicktivism. It is fueled by analytic activism and provides evidence of the multiple endpoints that analytics can help political organizations to pursue.

The Media Logic of Social Petitioning

Let's consider a simple example of how digital petitions are used in present-day citizen politics. The critics of clicktivism maintain that digital petitions carry little power because, being so easy to create and so easy to sign, they offer little evidence of robust citizen opinion. But, as I suggested in chapter 1, the power of any activist tactic is amplified or muted by its alignment (or lack thereof) with the broader media system. Digital petitions, in isolation, have little impact on political elites. But the same can be said of ink-and-pulp petitions. To understand the value of online petitions, we must pause to consider them as *media objects*.

As an example, consider the experience of the Trumbull High School Thespian Society in Trumbull, Connecticut. This begins as a simple story; its contours should seem familiar to anyone who attended an American public school. For the spring 2014 semester, the Thespian Society had selected the school edition of the musical *Rent*. *Rent*, which deals with homosexuality and the AIDS crisis, was a pretty edgy musical when it was released in the mid-1990s. But it has migrated into the mainstream over the past 20 years, and today it is standard cultural fare. Trumbull High got a new principal for the 2013–2014 school year, and he decided that his students simply couldn't handle *Rent*. He informed the drama club in late November 2013 that he would be canceling the spring production. The students were outraged, and they decided to fight his decision.

If this had been the mid-1990s, they would have circulated a petition, asked their parents to contact the PTA, and perhaps held a rally. But this was 2013, so the drama club's first steps were to launch an online petition through Change. org and start a Facebook page. The students communicated directly with other students and with their parents, but their communication tools were mostly digital instead of mostly analog. More than 1,500 students and parents signed the digital petition, representing about two-thirds of the school. Alas, neither the principal nor the school board seemed to care. The direct, independent power of an online high school petition turned out to be quite small. And we should not expect otherwise: High schools are not democracies, and high school principals are not in the habit of changing their minds on the basis of students' complaints. Had the members of the Thespian Society organized an ink-and-pulp student petition, they would have fared no better with their principal or the school board. And with an ink-and-pulp petition, the conflict would have ended there.

But digital petitions can function as media beacons, drawing attention from traditional media outlets by signaling, "There's something here!" There is an appealing David and Goliath texture to this conflict, featuring young artists clashing with buttoned-down adults in authority. A writer for the *New York Times* "ArtsBeat" section was alerted to the story and felt it worthy of a column. On December 4, the *New York Times* published an online column titled "Connecticut High School Cancels Student Production of *Rent*." *Playbill* magazine, the *Philadelphia Inquirer*, the *Hartford Courant*, and the *Connecticut Post* all followed suit, publishing columns as well. Now the principal was no longer facing pressure from his students; he was facing the possibility that his school would become a national laughingstock. High school principals may not be in the habit of changing their policies because of student complaints, but they also aren't particularly used to being the subject of ridicule in the national paper of record. The principal immediately began looking for a face-saving compromise, and by mid-December he had completely relented. The students at Trumbull High got to perform their musical.

The power of the Trumbull High petition lay less in the raw number of signers than in its status as a hybrid-media object. And it wasn't pure luck that landed the Trumbull High petition on an arts reporter's desk. As one senior Change.org staffer pointed out to me in 2012, "Half of our staff are media staff."[1] Change.org looks to promote, shepherd, and support citizen petitions that can be packaged into stories in the nonpolitical media. It keeps an eye on which petitions are gaining velocity, then helps to place them on programs like *The Ellen DeGeneres Show* and *Good Morning America*. This can be a tremendously effective strategy, simultaneously putting massive pressure on target decision makers unaccustomed to the media spotlight and further improving Change.org's brand and reach among potential petition signers. The students at Trumbull High were not themselves engaging in analytic activism. But their effort benefited from the analytic activism of Change.org. And, as we will see, their petition far better matched the organizational logic of Change.org than the organizational logic of other competing petition platforms.

The Politics of Petition Platforms

Digital petitions have a specific set of affordances that make them distinct from other forms of low-cost digital participation.[2] Signing a digital petition allows for repeated interactions between the petition signer, the petition host, and (potentially) the petition creator. This is because, through the act of signing a digital petition, users leave behind an email address as a digital trace of sorts. Through an email address, petition signers can reliably be reached to engage in future

---

[1] That proportion has decreased over time and depends on how the term "media staff" is operationalized. His point remains salient, however: Change.org continues to place a strategic priority on helping online petitions attract offline media attention.

[2] This is a point of contention within the research community. Helen Margetts and colleagues (2015b, 77), for instance, argue that "petitioning epitomizes the tiny acts of political participation via social media" and fail to differentiate between the affordances of social petition sites and the affordances of Twitter or Kickstarter. There is a strong tendency among scholars of Internet politics to treat all digital media as though they share the same affordances, which are then contrasted with the affordances of older communications technologies (see Bimber 2003; Castells 2009; Bennett and Segerberg 2013; Fung and Shkabatur 2015). The evidence in this chapter strongly suggests that, by lumping all digital media together, these researchers are overlooking some critical explanatory variables in the development and success of online collective action.

actions. In a 2010 article, I noted that this potential for repeated engagement makes digital petitions particularly useful as the first step in issue campaigns that feature a "ladder of engagement" (Karpf 2010). Hahrie Han (2014) has also written extensively about the role that these first-step engagement tactics can play in larger organizing and mobilizing strategies. A petition in isolation generally will not affect policy outcomes, but petitions can form the bedrock of a larger, more aggressive political mobilization strategy.

By comparison, the act of watching a YouTube video leaves no such digital trace. This makes viral videos less practically useful to social change organizations. Consider the "Kony 2012" viral video, created by Invisible Children. "Kony 2012" rapidly became the most frequently watched video of all time. It did so because of an insightful strategy that began with the leveraging of its network of existing supporters and then grew to include celebrity supporters that massively expanded its reach through social media (Fung and Shkabatur 2015). For a brief time, the video dominated mainstream media discussion and prompted the introduction of bills in Congress that urged the US military to pursue the African warlord Joseph Kony. But while the video attracted more than 100 million views in less than a week, the act of viewing left no digital trace that Invisible Children could use to reconnect with all of these supporters. YouTube has records of which users viewed the "Kony 2012" video, but Invisible Children does not. As a result, Invisible Children had far less capacity to plan mass follow-up actions. The organization dissolved just two years after its viral success, despite Joseph Kony's remaining at large.

Crucially, the act of signing a digital petition creates a repeatable relationship between the signer and the host of the petition. It *may* create a relationship between the signer and the creator of the petition, but this depends on the petition host's terms of service. It is an internal policy decision and depends on the mission, the vision, and the business model of the petition hosting organization.

Political associations can approach digital petitioning in three ways. First, an organization can create its own petition around an existing campaign, send it to current supporters, and hope the petition spreads. Second, an organization can launch a "sponsored petition" through Change.org or Care2.org and pay those large petition sites for the email addresses it acquires. Third, an organization can host an open (or "distributed") platform on its own website and encourage existing supporters to launch new campaigns of their own. Option 1 is the cheapest and was the standard route to achieving scale for netroots organizations in the early 2000s. Option 2 has been a particularly common strategy for well-resourced legacy organizations looking to expand their digital reach without completely revamping their organizational model. Option 3 is a more recent development. There is some real brand risk associated with option 3—if anyone can start a petition on your website, then you must develop policies and procedures for weeding out offensive or ill-conceived petitions—but it also carries the greatest potential for expanding a membership base.

Digital petitioning is the central path for a political organization to expand its universe of known members/supporters and reach a scale that allows it to operate above the analytics floor.[3] In recent years, the digital petition industry has moved from relatively passive, "warehouse" sites like PetitionOnline.com (see Earl and Kimport 2011) to more active sites like Change.org and MoveOn Petitions. If we are to clearly understand the role of digital petitions in campaigns for social and political change, it is worth taking a deeper look at these petition hosts. You can start an online petition at plenty of sites, but how much support, attention, and engagement it will receive depends on how it aligns with the values and vision of the hosting site.

CHANGE.ORG

Change.org is the world's largest social petition company. Though the ".org" in its name often leads people to assume that it is a nonprofit organization, Change.org is actually structured as a for-profit "B-corp" (or "benefit corporation"). B-corps are set up to incorporate public values into their corporate charters. They are distinct from traditional nonprofits or nongovernmental organizations (NGOs) in that they seek to turn a profit and prioritize growth. But their corporate charters include provisions indicating that investors should not expect pure profit-maximizing behavior. The "B-corp" designation carries with it an underlying set of internal business logics: To succeed, Change.org must pursue ongoing growth. Some petition topics are "growthier" than others (see chapter 5 for a lengthy discussion of "growthiness").

The company's business model is, in a sense, a "reverse speakeasy" or "reverse mullet" model: There is a user-generated *party in the front* with a lead-generation *business in the back*. Most of the petitions on the site are user-generated, launched by everyday citizens fighting some (usually small) injustice. The petition creator can contact petition signers with updates through Change.org's system, but cannot export a list of supporters for future organizing through other platforms. The funding model revolves around *sponsored petitions*. Sponsored petitions are a form of advertising—a lead-generation source for nonprofits,

---

[3] Colin Holtz (2015) of Greenpeace Mobilization Lab estimates the analytics floor threshold to be somewhere between 500,000 and 1 million for organizations that want to engage in high-volume distributed email campaigning. Organizations with an email list smaller than 500,000 have trouble achieving the volume of activity necessary to glean analytics-based insights that, in turn, produce additional growth and participation. Organizations with more than 1 million members can use a host of digital tools to optimize and fine-tune their strategies.

political campaigns, and companies. Large nonprofits and political campaigns turn to Change.org to build a list of potential donors. They pay Change.org for every name that they acquire through their sponsored petitions. The company offers these sponsored petition services to all comers, regardless of ideological affiliation—Change.org runs ads for Republicans and Democrats, for unions and union busters.

Most of the company's nontechnical staffers have been hired from progressive political organizations. At the 2012 RootsCamp convention, some of the top left-wing political activists in the country made a joke video titled "Sh!t Online Organizers Say," filled with inside jokes about the most common conversations among digital campaign professionals. One of the main punchlines was "I need to hire some great campaigners . . . how about _____?" "Nope. Change. org." "What about _____?" "Nope. Change.org." While many Change.org staffers are steeped in nonprofit culture, they are clearly aware of how the organization's for-profit status alters its position in the broader social change ecosystem. In both formal interviews and informal conversations, they routinely refer to the organization as a *company*.

The decision to make the company's advertising policy neutral was both formative and contentious. In its early years, Change.org's client policy stated, "We accept sponsored campaigns from organizations fighting for the public good and the common values we hold dear—fairness, equality, and justice. We do not accept sponsored campaigns from organizations that consistently violate these values, support discriminatory policies, or seek private corporate benefit that undermines the common good" (Karpf 2012c). As the company grew, though, the client policy came under pressure for being overwhelmingly vague. What counts as "fighting for the public good"? What counts as "seek[ing] corporate benefit"? As a practical matter, just how *open* did Change.org want to be? It is easy enough to prohibit explicit hate groups from doing business with the organization, but what about Republicans, libertarians, abortion opponents, Second Amendment advocates, or other organizations whose vision of "the public good" stands starkly at odds with liberal/progressive interests? Online petitions, writ large, are not a partisan technology. But petitions that build mass support for these charged issue spaces are deeply political and firmly partisan.

In the summer of 2012, these questions were pushed to the forefront by an active online petition campaign targeting Change.org itself. At issue was a sponsored petition from the education reform organization Stand for Children. The petition was titled "Tell Chicago Board of Education and Teachers' Union: Get Back to the Table," and it was created in response to a strike authorization vote. From Stand for Children's perspective, a teachers' strike in Chicago would undermine the public good. Stand for Children has a long history of fighting with teachers' unions. From the perspective of the American Federation of

Teachers, Stand for Children was calling for union-busting activity—the polar opposite of "fairness, equality, and justice." Stand for Children and the American Federation of Teachers are engaged in a pitched political battle with one another, just as fierce as the electoral fights between local Democrats and Republicans. Did the anti-union petition violate Change.org's client policy? Union supporters launched petitions of their own, arguing that it did.

Over the course of several months, Change.org engaged in a leadership-wide discussion of the client policy. In the end, the company decided to expand the policy, replacing the ideologically progressive language of "fighting for the common good" with language that embraced an ideology of openness. The current advertising guidelines, adopted in October 2012, read, "As an open platform with tens of millions of diverse users, Change.org hosts sponsored petitions representing a wide range of viewpoints. We do not endorse nor are we affiliated with any sponsored petition or associated organizations." The new policy language carves out only one exemption, stating, "Change.org does not accept ads from hate groups, or persons/entities directly associated with them."[4]

The internal debate over these advertising guidelines was heated. Several staff members resigned in the wake of the new advertising policy, and one went so far as to leak an internal memo about the discussion to Jeff Bryant, an associate fellow at Campaign for America's Future (the leaker was quickly discovered and promptly fired). In an interview with Ryan Grim (2012), the Washington bureau chief of the *Huffington Post*, Bryant expressed disappointment, noting, "Change.org built its reputation on arming Davids to take on the Goliaths of the world. Now it seems that the company thinks David and Goliath should be on the same team." Several left-leaning nonprofits responded by ending their contracts with Change.org. If Change.org was open to accepting sponsored advertisements from coal industry "astroturf" (fake grassroots) groups, then many climate advocacy organizations would find some other venue for generating potential supporter leads.

Change.org's CEO, Ben Rattray, fiercely defends the company's neutral stance. In response to the controversy, Rattray (2012) wrote a piece for the *Huffington Post* in which he described the decision as "embracing openness": "If we weren't open to everyone, and if we limited access based on a set of political viewpoints, we would undercut the power of our petition creators and users. We would be perceived as an advocacy group ourselves, and the media and decision makers would often typecast petition creators as players in our supposed issue agenda, rather than the independent agents of change they are. The result would be to strip our petition creators of the power of telling their own

---

[4] https://www.change.org/policies/advertising (accessed August 3, 2014).

story on their own terms, making them less likely to gather broad support and less likely to win."

So Change.org definitively does not align itself with one partisan ideology over another. But this does not mean the site displays no preferences at all. Some issues have more list-growth potential than others, and the site has constructed a sophisticated system for identifying and promoting the "growthiest" issues. Rattray spoke about this system in a 2013 keynote speech at the Personal Democracy Forum conference, titled "The Next Generation of People-Powered Movements." First, he described a typical winning campaign on Change.org that was "not about policy arguments; it was about personal stories." He went on to note:

> In Turkey this week, in the wake of the violence [in Gezi Park], there are tons of citizen-petitions started, hundreds of them, but not about big national revolution. It's about daily change. About many, many small issues that can change, that aggregate into large impact things . . . around police behavior, around media censorship, around the private use of public lands.

Notice the attention shift here: In the midst of the Gezi Park protest, when the eyes of the world were focused on that small patch of green space, Change.org petitions in Turkey were not focused on the conflict in Gezi itself. Instead, they were focused on "small issues" that featured personal stories and were more winnable. In a 2011 keynote talk, Rattray likewise addressed this point under the theme of "big problems and small solutions":

> The thing about big problems is they exist for a reason. There are powerful forces resisting change. If you try to hit them head on, directly, meeting force with force, you very rarely win. So I have no doubt the Internet has huge potential to empower people to address these big problems, but not primarily in the way most people think. *I think primarily it's the Internet's ability to organize around small solutions.* Tens of thousands. (emphasis added)

According to Katie Bethell, Change.org's director of campaigns, the company seeks out these personal, narrative-based campaigns: "The campaigns that rise to the top are based in strong stories of individuals standing against injustice that anyone can understand" (Bluestein 2013). The company graphically summarizes this model as its "Victory Pipeline" (figure 3.1). Personal stories become petitions, which lead to signatures and media exposure, which in turn lead to decision-maker engagement and victories. The Trumbull High Thespian Society

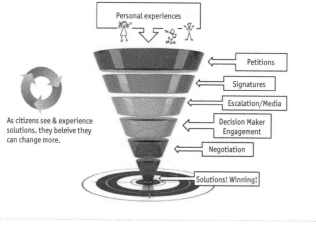

Figure 3.1 Change.org's "Victory Pipeline"

petition illustrates the process nicely. The students started a petition and gathered signatures. The petition became a media object that attracted stories from key media outlets. That media exposure created additional leverage on the principal, who then gave in to the students' demands.

Several steps in the Victory Pipeline represent unique features of Change.org's platform. In October 2013, Change.org rolled out a new "Decision Makers" feature, which seeks to engage petition targets around civic petitions. The feature allows petition targets—members of Congress, local representatives, or corporations—to write responses to the citizen petitions. The organization highlights this feature as an opportunity for more collaborative engagement between petitioners and their targets. Jake Brewer (2014), director of external affairs, described it thus: "The Internet has created the biggest citizen megaphone ever, but not the headphones to help leaders listen and engage effectively." He offers the example of a petition aimed at the Red Cross urging the organization to accept blood donations from gay men. The chief medical officer of the Red Cross responded to the petition, stating that he agreed with the petitioners, but the policy was dictated by a federal regulation that needed to be changed. This encouraged the petitioners to redirect their efforts, collecting a valuable ally along the way.

According to Brewer, "We totally expect that users won't always like the responses, because they'll be press release-y, inauthentic, or might not address the problem. But what I'm most excited about is the ability of users to respond to the response. That's a conversation" (Lapowsky 2013).

The Victory Pipeline is a clear engine for growth, brand exposure, and small victories. Anyone can start a petition at Change.org, and the company's business model relies on promoting these user-generated petitions, helping them to reach a wide audience, tell a story that attracts media attention, and engage decision makers to increase the likelihood of small victories. The company expresses a preference for petitions that tell a clear, compelling, personal story. It aims to take on small issues rather than big problems. It seeks petitions that can help to increase its user base, because that growth is central to its revenue model.

But the Victory Pipeline also rests on an untested assumption, depicted alongside the pipeline: "As citizens see & experience solutions, they believe they can change more." This is Change.org's contestable underlying premise: Political associations generally operate on the premise that, to address large problems, you need to unite people around those problems. Small solutions aren't worth much unless they help to build a public that will demand that large problems be addressed. Change.org's central assumption is that there need be no link between the small solutions and the big challenges—that citizens will be inspired by their victories ("We get to perform *Rent!*" "There are potholes on Istanbul streets.") to unite around unconnected larger problems ("National gun laws have done nothing to make the next Sandy Hook shooting less likely!" "The government is teargasing peaceful protesters!").

To its credit, Change.org's focus on compelling personal stories has led the site to play a key role in major campaigns for social justice. Consider, for instance, the case of Trayvon Martin. The death of the Florida teenager initially barely registered in the public arena. The old media slogan "If it bleeds, it leads" did not seem to apply in the case of this black teenager gunned down while walking home from a convenience store. His (white) killer, George Zimmerman, had been immediately released without charges, but this attracted scant media coverage. After nearly two weeks of mainstream media silence, Martin's parents started a petition on Change.org, titled "Prosecute the Killer of Our Son, 17-Year-Old Trayvon Martin." The Change.org petition went viral, attracting more than 2 million signatures nationwide and sparking offline actions like the "million hoodie march" in New York City. In the following six weeks, Martin's story attracted national media attention, eventually leading to the local police chief's resignation and second-degree murder charges against Zimmerman (Graeff et al. 2014).

The Trayvon Martin petition was not simply a story of individual citizens selecting a petition "warehouse" to seek justice for a slain boy. The Change.org staff played an integral part in identifying, shaping, and supporting the Trayvon Martin campaign. Trayvon's parents, Tracy Martin and Sybrina Fulton, were not, in fact, the first to launch a Change.org petition on this topic. The petition was originally created by Howard University alumnus Kevin Cunningham after he saw a Reuters story about Martin's death on a listserv. The initial signatures came through listserv-based petition sharing and were amplified by activist organizations like ColorOfChange.org and Black Youth Project. Change.org staffers were alerted to the petition by analytics reports; they evaluated the potential of this campaign and then reached out to Martin's parents and spoke with them about crafting the petition language that would eventually go viral through blast emails to Change.org's national membership. Change.org staffers refer to this technique as "Get Out the Petition," or GOTP—a reference to GOTV (Get Out the Vote) mobilization that occurs in the last few days of an electoral campaign. The Change.org staff also solicited support from a cadre of celebrities, including Talib Kweli, Wyclef Jean, Spike Lee, Mia Farrow, and Chad Ochocinco, which created a massive spike in social media traffic around the issue (for a detailed case analysis see Graeff et al. 2014).

The Trayvon Martin petition did not passively luck into a viral online attention cycle. The Change.org staff and other savvy online political organizers actively worked to create the conditions for potential virality. Zimmerman was arrested, though a jury failed to convict him. Today, the outpouring of public protest surrounding Trayvon Martin is largely considered to be the first episode in the much larger Movement for Black Lives (#BlackLivesMatter), which has drawn connections between this and other shooting deaths in Ferguson, Missouri, Cleveland, Baltimore, and elsewhere around the country. Each of these episodes of contention has included a Change.org petition. As of August 2015, 34 #BlackLivesMatter petitions have been created on Change.org, and these petitions have collectively received more than 3.7 million signatures.[5] While Change.org is not the center of the Movement for Black Lives, it has provided valuable, invisible, and free digital infrastructure for the burgeoning movement.

But Trayvon Martin's case is rare among Change.org petitions, both in terms of the results it achieved and in terms of the politically contentious nature of the issue. Not all user-generated petitions at Change.org are equally likely to succeed, and the "big problems" in politics are often rendered invisible in favor of smaller, more winnable issues. I visited the homepages of Change.org and MoveOn Petitions during the week of October 14–20, 2013, to take a look at which petitions each site was featuring as "trending right now." This was a hectic week in US politics. A fight over the pending implementation of the Affordable Care Act had resulted in a government shutdown with no end in sight. Turn on the nightly news, scan the front page of a national newspaper, or tune in to political talk radio, and the government shutdown would be an inescapable topic of discussion. During that same week, the top petitions at MoveOn.org were, unsurprisingly, focused on ending the shutdown and supporting the Affordable Care Act. The top petitions at Change.org were stories of personal tragedy—one called for

---

[5] https://www.change.org/campaigns/black-lives-matter.

an investigation into the death of a special needs child in Oklahoma; the other claimed that a suspended cheerleader at North Andover High School had been wrongly accused of drunk driving and called for her reinstatement. MoveOn. org was using its distributed petition site to help members capitalize on the issue at the top of the political agenda. Change.org was using its site to promote nonpolitical issues on the broader media agenda. Both of these Change.org petitions proved tremendously effective, if viewed through the Victory Pipeline. The Oklahoma petition eventually drew more than 500,000 signatures and resulted in an investigation. The North Andover High School petition attracted a wave of local media attention (which left an embarrassed cheerleader admitting that she had been drinking after all).

As we will see later in this chapter, the week of the government shutdown is emblematic of a broader pattern among Change.org's featured petitions. Change. org's mission, vision, and business model favor small issues, personal stories, and collaborative engagement with decision makers. Those priorities lead to growth, public attention, and (ultimately) revenue. At times, they also align with broad movements for social justice and civil rights. But, encoded within work routines, analytics, and algorithms, they can create a blind spot against pitched political fights where the battle lines are already clearly drawn.

MOVEON PETITIONS

MoveOn.org originated with an online petition. Its cofounders, Wes Boyd and Joan Blades, launched a petition in 1998 asking Congress to "Censure Bill Clinton and Move On" from the Monica Lewinsky scandal. Theirs was not the first online petition in US politics, but Blades and Boyd had a key insight: A petition signature can also function as a membership sign-up. By launching their own website to gather the petition signatures, Blades and Boyd built the foundation for repeated interactions with their fellow petitioners. When Congress ignored the 500,000 people who signed their petition, the two founders followed up, organizing a citizen lobby day in Washington, DC. Over the next decade and a half, MoveOn would build an online membership of more than 8 million and become practically synonymous with a reinvigorated netroots progressive base (Karpf 2012a).

Though MoveOn began with a petition and spearheaded the development of many petition-based online campaign techniques, its open petition platform is a relatively recent development. It began in 2011, when the organization launched SignOn.org as a Change.org-like, bottom-up offshoot. SignOn (later renamed MoveOn Petitions) allowed individual visitors to create their own petition-based campaigns. The initial goal of the SignOn tool was to enable more small-scale and locally based MoveOn campaign activities: Since anyone taking action with MoveOn was considered a member, SignOn effectively placed the tools for small-scale action in the hands of anyone who chose to show up. Members were encouraged in a monthly email to create their own campaigns.[6] If a member-led petition attracted substantial activity, the MoveOn staff would then consider "boosting" it by emailing the petition to a subset of the organization's 8 million-person member list. MoveOn crowdsourced the vetting of these petitions, beginning by sending them to existing members under the headline "Should MoveOn support this petition?" These subsets were determined through predictive analytics, based on either zip code or propensity to sign similar issue petitions.

In the aftermath of the 2012 election, MoveOn decided that SignOn should play a larger role in its work. SignOn represented the activated public opinion (or opinion$_a$) of MoveOn members, and the organization determined that this feedback should play a larger role in determining its political strategy. In a December 4, 2012, article titled "MoveOn Moving On," political reporters Amanda Terkel and Ryan Grim outlined MoveOn.org's "radical new approach" to strategic direction setting, "ced[ing] large elements of its strategic planning directly to its . . . members." Executive director Justin Ruben described the change as follows:

> "The old way of doing things, you could think of it as there are three steps in the campaign process," Ruben said. "Step one, listen hard to what members want. Step two, figure out what we can do on that. Step three, turn around and kick that back out to folks and say, 'Ok, if everybody stands on their head on Thursday, we'll get health care,' or whatever the strategy is that we've come up with. So the game here is to take that middle step, which is really the leadership step, and hand as much of it over to members as possible." (Terkel and Grim 2012)

As part of the new strategic direction, SignOn.org morphed into MoveOn Petitions, migrating from the periphery of the MoveOn model to its core. The change represents a substantial advance in "listening hard to what members want" and a dramatic shift toward monitoring diverse forms of revealed member preferences. The old and new MoveOn models are illustrated by the flowcharts in figures 3.2 and 3.3.

In the old MoveOn model, listening to the membership occurred through a mix of weekly member surveys and passive democratic feedback obtained through email A/B testing. A/B testing allowed MoveOn to compare different

---

[6] A necessary disclaimer on the site indicates that "MoveOn Civic Action does not necessarily endorse the contents of petitions posted on this site. MoveOn Petitions is an open tool that anyone can use to post a petition advocating any point of view, so long as the petition does not violate our terms of service."

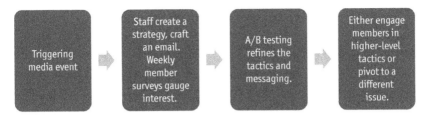

Figure 3.2 Old MoveOn.org decision process

Figure 3.3 New MoveOn.org decision process

campaign topics, campaign tactics, and issue frames on a day-to-day basis. But A/B testing produces a "local maxima problem" (Pariser 2011; Siroker and Koomen 2013): It gives MoveOn information on which of the staff-generated campaigns perform best, but provides no member input into which alternatives ought to be tested to begin with. The staff may focus on national domestic issues (filibuster reform or judicial nominations, for instance), while members may independently be interested in localized issues (natural gas fracking activities, for instance). MoveOn Petitions offers a signal of strong member commitment, which in turn can guide the priority-setting process for the national organization. By adding member-led campaigns into the mix of signals that the organization uses for making agenda-setting decisions, MoveOn creates a pressure release valve from the local maxima problem.

Allied organizations can launch petitions through MoveOn Petitions as well. Groups like Food and Water Watch, the Working Families Party, and the Center for American Progress have launched massive issue campaigns through MoveOn Petitions. As is the case at Change.org, the petition creator can repeatedly send messages to petition signers through MoveOn.org's system. Unlike the situation at Change.org, organizational petition creators can include a checkbox (autocompleted) stating that the signer would like to receive future messages from, for instance, the Working Families Party (WFP). The people who leave that checkbox checked can then be contacted by WFP at no additional cost to WFP. The net result is that WFP promotes its MoveOn-hosted petitions through its own campaign efforts, attracting new people to MoveOn, and the high-velocity campaigns reach existing MoveOn members, attracting them to WFP. It is a form of free collaboration within the progressive movement.

In practice, many of MoveOn's biggest national campaigns still draw heavily on staff judgment and creativity. But the distributed petition platform creates space for MoveOn to try out new tactics that bring members' voices to the forefront of its political actions. During the government shutdown, MoveOn deployed an array of pressure tactics aimed at shaping the public narrative. The organization wanted to make sure that this major public issue was framed as evidence that the radical Tea Party fringe had taken control of the Republican Party. MoveOn used in-person, grassroots tactics, organizing active members to visit congressional district offices and hang tea bags on doors alongside signs saying, "We've had enough tea, thanks." MoveOn commissioned public opinion polls in 65 Republican-held congressional districts and trumpeted the results to reporters.

Note that the power of both these political tactics is rooted in how they interact with the media system. The value of constituent visits and of the polls stems from how these tactics are fashioned for and taken up by media organizations. These tactics did not originate from member-led petitions, but the distributed petition platform nonetheless helped the organization target and tailor its efforts for each individual district. The organization directly emailed millions of its members, asking them to start a petition to their member of Congress. MoveOn provided framing language, but also encouraged its members to add personal stories about how the government shutdown was affecting them. A petition like this is called a "clone petition" or a "wildfire petition." MoveOn amplified the clone petitions by sending them out to all of its members, segmented by congressional district. The result was a clearer signal of revealed constituent opinion: Rather than representing 500,000 liberal activists around the nation, the district petitions represented 5,000 *constituents* who opposed the shutdown and were likely to vote in the next election. The personal stories, meanwhile, provided yet another hook for local media seeking to cover the shutdown.

Clone petitions and wildfire petitions are part of how MoveOn incorporates its open petition platform into a feedback loop that promotes grassroots activity around high-profile issues. Another example is MoveOn's "fracking fighters" program (Sheppard 2014). After noticing an increase in fracking-related petitions on the platform, MoveOn decided to further promote grassroots campaigning around the issue. Fracking is an issue that is contested primarily at the state and local levels, and MoveOn wanted to support activism that extended beyond petitioning. The fracking fighter program offered members $500 mini-grants, along with training and networking with their fellow activists. All of the fracking fighters began by creating petitions about their local campaign. Those petitions were explicitly treated as the first step in a local environmental campaign. The online petitions helped MoveOn identify potential leaders, which helped the organization direct resources to support offline action through deeper organizing work in local communities.

MoveOn is not the only progressive activist organization with a distributed petition platform. Avaaz.org's global membership list of more than 41 million has been built partially on the basis of an open petition platform that allows members to craft their own petitions in over a dozen languages. MoveOn also has a global network of peer organizations, collectively called the OPEN network (Online Progressive Engagement Network), that host similar distributed petition sites. GetUp in Australia, 38 Degrees in the United Kingdom, Campact in Germany, and Leadnow in Canada all provide space on their web platforms and in their email programs for supporting bottom-up, member-initiated campaigns. Most of these platforms have been created by software developer Nathan Woodhull and his team at ControlShift Labs. ControlShift Labs has also created distributed petition platforms for Coworker.org (discussed further in chapter 5), Greenpeace, Democracy for America, and Credo Action. MoveOn has, however, been the most aggressive organization in placing distributed petitioning at the center of its organizational model.

As with Change.org, there is an organizational logic underlying MoveOn.org's distributed petition platform. But it is a *different* logic than we see with Change.org. As a for-profit B-corp, Change.org seeks to build an international user base and become "the Google of modern politics" (Finley 2013). In so doing, it attempts above all else to *grow*. Change.org eschews direct political stances—it is anti–hate groups but otherwise wants to be the neutral home for teachers' unions and school privatization advocates alike. MoveOn.org, on the other hand, is seeking to deepen the progressive power base by expanding its reach among members. Milan de Vries, MoveOn's director of analytics, has publicly stated that the organization "does not care about list growth when choosing which petitions to promote."[7] With 8 million members, MoveOn.org is effectively *big enough*. What it needs instead is deeper member commitments and clearer signals of what supporters want to do. MoveOn Petitions is a tool for activating and engaging an explicitly partisan membership base that will then donate and volunteer for (Democratic) candidates that MoveOn.org endorses. Change.org seeks to remain nonpartisan and stay out of the day-to-day scrum of US politics.

[7] Comment by Milan De Vries during a panel titled "Moving Beyond Petitions: How Organizations Can Harness Distributed Campaigns to Build Progressive Power," *Netroots Nation*, Detroit, July 19, 2014.

THE WHITE HOUSE'S WE THE PEOPLE PETITION SITE: PETITIONING THE GOVERNMENT VIA THE GOVERNMENT

The US Constitution guarantees the right of the people "to petition the Government for a redress of grievances." After observing the success of the United Kingdom's Downing Street E-petition system (Wright 2012, 2015a), the Obama administration launched petitions.whitehouse.gov, or "We the People," in the fall of 2011. Unlike independent platforms like Change.org and MoveOn Petitions, the White House site offers a direct pipeline from citizen petitioners to government decision makers. It also promises that any petition exceeding a specified signature threshold within a single month will be guaranteed a governmental response. That threshold was initially set at 5,000 signatures, but was then extended upward, first to 25,000 and later to 100,000. The promise and potential of the White House petition site is unique: It provides a direct avenue for citizens to petition their government, a "promise" that political decision makers are, in fact, listening.

Since its launch, the site has attracted signatures from somewhere between 12 million and 19 million citizens on more than 400,000 petitions (Howard 2015).[8] More than 200 petitions have received governmental responses, and a handful of these have prompted genuine policy change. In one such case, more than 114,000 citizens signed a petition urging the government to support unlocking cell phones, fostering greater competition among cellular providers. The Obama administration agreed and directed the Federal Communications Commission to issue new regulations (Compton 2013). The best-known petition was a humorous request from Star Wars fans to "build a Death Star." The administration issued a tongue-in-cheek response, titled "This isn't the petition response you're looking for," that estimated the cost of a Death Star at 850 quadrillion dollars and asked, "Why would we spend countless taxpayer dollars on a Death Star with a fundamental flaw that could be exploited by a one-man starship?" The Death Star response received an avalanche of positive media coverage, in turn alerting the broader public to the existence of petitions.whitehouse.gov. The White House also published the recipe for the first beer brewed on-site, at the urging of more than 12,000 petitioning home brewers. And the administration used a joking 2014 petition to "deport [Canadian pop star] Justin Bieber and revoke his green card" to highlight the importance of comprehensive immigration reform legislation.

---

[8] In a July 2015 update, the White House digital team announced that it had 19.5 million "total users" and 12.3 million "verified users." The "total users" category includes an unknown number of duplicate or fake accounts.

Total April Petitions

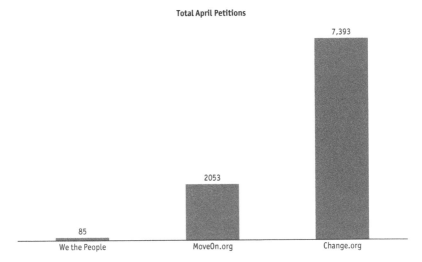

Figure 3.4 Total petitions created in April 2014

The number of accounts at We the People (more than 19 million) is compara-ble to that at MoveOn Petitions (MoveOn.org has an online list of over 8 million members) and at Change.org (Change has over 110 million users, but is global in scope). But by every other available measure of participation, the White House site dramatically lags behind these two competitors. As I described in a 2014 article for techPresident.com, We the People is akin to a "virtual ghost town," whose typical residents register a single visit but never return (Karpf 2014b). With 19,507,060 users and 27,771,912 total signatures, the average "member" of the We the People community signs only 1.42 petitions. And this average is skewed by the well-known power law distribution of online activity (Hindman 2008), with a small group of active users signing many petitions and the vast majority signing only one.

During the month of April 2014, I cataloged all of the petitions registered on We the People. Figures 3.4 and 3.5 reveal what I found. While Change.org and MoveOn Petitions received 7,393[9] and 2,053 new petitions, respectively, during the month of April, only 85 petitions were launched on We the People that month (less than three new petitions per day). Zero April petitions reached the 100,000-signature threshold necessary for a government response, and only three petitions even received more than 10,000 signatures.

Four problems plague We the People, and each has a(n organizationally) *logical* explanation. First, whereas MoveOn.org and Change.org encourage

---

[9] Noland Chambliss, email correspondence. This figure includes only US petitions on Change.org. There are Change.org petitions in nearly 200 countries, so the global total is much higher.

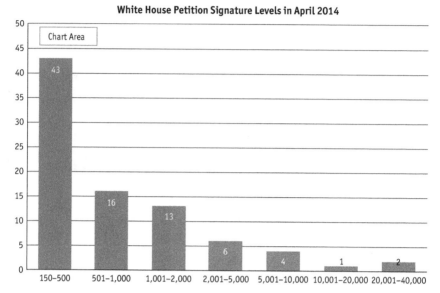

Figure 3.5 Signatures per petition at We the People

continuous user engagement through email and social channels—promoting petitions through Facebook and Twitter, and emailing supporters petitions they might like—We the People provides nothing but a static website. Less than 5 percent of MoveOn.org's and Change.org's petition signatures come from organic visits to the website; the rest come through email and social media.[10] But the static website is all that the White House has built. Second, the White House site gives petition creators no follow-up tools for movement-building. Derek Khanna, one of the creators of the successful cell phone unlocking petition, remarked to Alex Howard that, after the petition was finished, "we had no list-serve of our signatories, no organization, and no money" (Howard 2014).

The explanation for these first two problems is simple: Civil society organizations can make choices that governments can't. We the People has no "featured" petition list, no Twitter or Facebook account broadcasting "hot" petitions,[11] and no email account matching past signers with new petitions of potential interest. Change.org and MoveOn.org can play favorites. They can decide which petitions are the most promising. They can encourage follow-up actions offline. The can partner with advocacy groups to launch long-term campaigns. They can actively

---

[10] Personal correspondence with staff members at both organizations.

[11] It does, however, have a Twitter account that publicizes White House petition replies.

move their online communities in the direction of desirable forms of participation. If the executive branch of the US government played favorites in this way, it would invite righteous (and rightful) outrage. The White House is both the target of We the People petitions *and* the venue for those petitions.

The third and fourth problems with We the People are self-inflicted. The 100,000-signature threshold is arguably too high, and the White House responses are too unreliable. Without the aid of email, social media, or allied advocacy groups, citizen petitions on WhiteHouse.gov are unlikely to gain enough exposure to reach 100,000 people. Indeed, those few petitions that have surpassed this threshold have tended to gain popularity on Reddit.com or some other part of the Internet's "attention backbone" (Benkler et al. 2015). And though the White House guarantees a response to all petitions that exceed the threshold, they make no promises of a *timely* response.[12] In practice, We the People petitions are little more than fodder for the White House press shop. If replying to a petition helps advance White House priorities or create a positive news cycle, the White House issues a timely response. Most of these responses merely reaffirm previously stated White House priorities. But where petitions critical of the White House have surpassed the petition threshold—such as petitions to classify the Muslim Brotherhood as a terrorist organization, pardon Edward Snowden, or investigate the abuse of power in the Department of Justice case against the deceased technologist/activist Aaron Swartz—the petitions can languish unanswered for months or years.

The for-profit and nonprofit organizational logics of Change.org and MoveOn Petitions compel them to "pick favorites," respond to user demands, and pursue "growthiness" and victories. The administrative logic of We the People compels the White House to *avoid trouble* above all else. Both Change.org and MoveOn.org are engaged in forms of analytic activism—they use digital listening to actively promote strategic interactions between citizens and decision makers. If We the People were to highlight petitions through social media and mass email channels, it would invite media controversy and outraged citizen countermobilization. The executive branch can create a venue for citizen petitions, but it does so under the expectation that it will remain an impartial arbiter. The limitations of that hands-off approach render the site less vibrant as a result.

---

[12] In July 2015, the White House chief digital officer, Jason Goldman, announced a new internal rule that all petitions that pass the 100,000 threshold must receive a response within 60 days. It is not yet clear whether the White House will live up to this new rule. It is equally unclear how the next presidential administration will make use of We the People, or whether the site will even be maintained in 2017 and beyond.

Change.org and MoveOn Petitions, by the Numbers

Change.org and MoveOn Petitions are the two largest nongovernmental open petition platforms in the United States. In order to move beyond individual cases, I constructed a simple scheme for assessing the petitions at the two sites: daily content analysis of the top 10 "featured" petitions highlighted on each site. This is known as a "lobster trap" data collection process (Karpf 2012b). I set up a lightweight method of gathering publicly available online data that otherwise would disappear. Lobster traps like this are particularly valuable for creating datasets of shifting phenomena: Twitter follower counts, email programs, blog traffic levels, or fundraising numbers. Most public online data of these types goes uncollected and then becomes irretrievable. A lobster trap captures the data flows, then allows the researcher to examine them at a later date.

From November 2013 through May 2014, I visited Change.org and MoveOn Petitions (Petitions.MoveOn.org) every day and recorded the list of petitions featured at each site. These are not necessarily the petitions with the most signatures. They are the petitions that, through a combination of algorithmic and human monitoring, the two organizations consider to be representative of "what's trending right now." I took note of the petition topic, the petition target, the petition author, and the number of signatures on the petition. I also revisited all of these petitions one year later to see which ones had been declared victories.

I chose to focus on featured petitions for two reasons. First, the top of the homepage is valuable digital real estate. Even though the petitions are selected partially through algorithms, *algorithms can automate value judgments*. The petitions that an organization chooses to promote tell us something about the organization's priorities and identity. Second, featured petitions are rendered publicly accessible in a way that other petitions are not. We cannot peer directly within the algorithms used by these organizations, nor can we assess the full stream of petition data that they interact with on a day-to-day basis or monitor the results of the A/B tests that they choose to run. Featured petitions are imperfect and incomplete data (as virtually all data is), but they also help us see the two organizations through the frame that they themselves are creating.

There is one important limitation to viewing these sites through the featured petitions lens: Website homepages are not a major source of signature traffic for either organization. Facebook, Twitter, mass emails, and friend-to-friend emails are much larger drivers of petition traffic than organic visits to the homepage, which generate less than 5 percent of petition signatures at both sites. A great deal of engineering effort goes into refining and optimizing social sharing and email sharing of petitions. The homepages, by comparison, are a lower priority.

Senior staffers at Change.org initially expressed surprise that I was studying their organization by visiting the homepage every day. That isn't how most people access the site, nor is it how the staff visualizes its data flows. That being said, one key audience of the "featured" petition list is composed of journalists looking to write stories about the organizations. Featured petitions may be a biased representation of the full population of petitions at either site, but that very bias overemphasizes the issues that Change.org and MoveOn.org wish to display as representative. The resulting convenience sample is thus particularly well suited to facilitating an understanding of the types of petitions that these sites use in constructing their public-facing image.

My six months of daily visits to the two sites yielded 269 distinct petitions featured on MoveOn Petitions and 283 distinct petitions featured on Change. org. In the process of content-analyzing the featured petitions from these two sites, four major themes came clearly into view. First, despite both being open petition platforms where anyone can launch a petition, the two sites cater to very different types of political mobilization. MoveOn Petitions is an outlet for promoting liberal, grassroots political mobilization. Change.org is an outlet for civic mobilization that largely avoids traditional political topic areas. Second, Change.org generates substantially more petition signatures than MoveOn Petitions. If we measure open petition sites solely on the basis of their ability to reach signature milestones, Change.org is without peer. Third, there are noteworthy differences in the petition creators, the petition frames, and the petition targets that MoveOn.org and Change.org feature. MoveOn's petitions come from MoveOn volunteers and organizational allies. Change.org's petitions come from unaffiliated citizens. MoveOn's petitions tend to adopt collective action frames. Change.org's petitions tend to adopt personal action frames. MoveOn's petitions are aimed at national and state political elites. Change.org's petitions tend to be aimed at the local or corporate levels. Fourth, these differences in the types of petitions that the two sites choose to feature appear to explain the different victory rates at each site. Change.org boasts on its website (https://www.change.org/impact), "Nearly every hour, a petition on Change.org achieves victory." Part of the reason for this success rate is that Change.org encourages petitioners to focus on easier wins (or, as Rattray calls them, "small solutions") than MoveOn Petitions does.

THE DIVERGENT ISSUE AGENDAS OF CHANGE.ORG AND MOVEON PETITIONS

Petitions are created in response to a perceived problem or injustice. Sometimes we witness that problem or injustice in person: a pothole outside your house needs fixing, or a teacher at your school is fired. More often, we witness it through the existing media system: a television personality makes an offensive statement, or a governor fails to address an important policy issue. Under the "warehouse" model favored by many researchers (Earl and Kimport 2011; Margetts et al. 2015b), we should expect similar petitions to rise to the top across multiple petition sites. The reasoning here is straightforward: Even in an age of polarization and "filter bubbles," we are, for the most part, still engaging with the same stream of breaking news events (albeit through ideologically confirming news frames). When the government shuts down, the Supreme Court announces a major decision, or a state legislature considers a controversial bill, competing ideological enclaves still discuss the same topics. In the traditional language of policy agendas research, we are reacting to a single "problem stream" (Kingdon 1984). Given two open/distributed platforms, each with millions of users, we ought to observe a fair degree of topical overlap in the petition-based responses to the problem stream.

If petitions are being started at both sites in response to the same political and media events, there is no evidence of it among the featured petitions at the two largest US sites. Over the course of the study, *only six petition topics* were simultaneously featured at the two sites. That is less than 2.5% of the total featured petition population, or roughly one petition per month.

Of the six overlapping petition issues, only two were focused on mainstream political institutions. One pair of overlapping petitions called on Shell Oil and the Russian government to release the "Arctic 30," a team of Greenpeace activists who had been jailed by the Russian government. The other pair of overlapping petitions called on Arizona governor Jan Brewer to veto SB 1062, a controversial piece of anti-gay legislation. Another two pairs of petitions concerned racism in our political culture—one asking Shawn "Jay-Z" Carter to end his partnership with Barneys New York in response to a news story about routine harassment of African American shoppers by store security, the other calling for the cancelation of a celebrity boxing match between rapper DMX and George Zimmerman (whose celebrity status stems solely from having shot and killed Trayvon Martin). The fifth pair of overlapping petitions focused on a local gay rights issue in Seattle. The vice principal of a Catholic high school was fired for being gay, and petitions calling for his reinstatement were featured at both sites. The final overlapping-petition topic actually featured two petitions on opposite sides of the same issue. When Phil Robertson, star of the A&E television program *Duck Dynasty* was suspended by the network for making inflammatory statements about homosexuality and race relations, a fan of the show launched a Change.org petition asking A&E to lift his suspension. A MoveOn.org petition was launched in response the following day, asking that Robertson remain suspended.

Figure 3.6 reveals the breakdown of primary topics that Change.org and MoveOn Petitions featured over the six months of the study. The most popular

Issue Breakdown

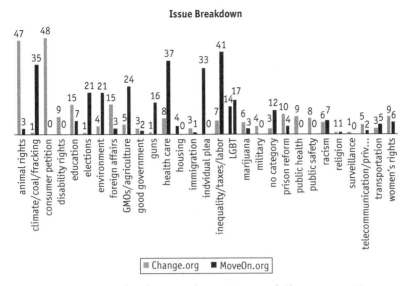

Figure 3.6 Primary issue classifications of MoveOn.org and Change.org petitions

issue areas on Change.org were (1) consumer/fan petitions, (2) animal rights petitions, (3) individual pleas,[13] (4) education petitions, and (5) foreign affairs petitions. The most popular issue areas at MoveOn.org were (1) income inequality/taxes/labor petitions, (2) health care petitions, (3) climate/coal/fracking petitions, (4) GMO/agriculture petitions, and (5) electoral reform petitions. There is no overlap in these top-five lists. Though both sites featured a medium amount of LGBT, women's rights, and racism-related petitions, the gaps in the issue landscape featured by the two sites paints a clear picture of their divergent social visions.

Many of the featured MoveOn.org petitions focused on the dominant political news stories of the day. MoveOn's electoral reform petitions were created after the Supreme Court struck down key sections of the Voting Rights Act. Its health care petitions were focused on the expansion of Medicaid. These are expressly political issues. They are both timely and important. They are also consistent with the political news agenda that we would see constructed on *All In with Chris Hayes* or *The Rachel Maddow Show* on MSNBC. And they are completely absent from the featured petition section of Change.org.

Instead, Change.org brings personal injustices and cultural communities to the forefront. Many petitions took the form of personal pleas or fan requests. The

---

[13] Many of these individual pleas related to health care. A common plea was "My relative needs a rare drug. Please, health company, make an exception and give it to him/her." There is no collective action frame in these requests—they do not question the status of American health care; they ask solely for a favor from the powerful.

North Andover High School petition referenced previously is a good example of an individual plea: A high school student was suspended for alcohol use, even though she claimed she was acting as the designated driver for her friends. This is a personal tragedy for the young woman but has no broader ramification for society as a whole. Though it occurs within the context of our education system, it is not a petition about education reform. The approximately 20,000 people who signed the petition were not taking the first step in forging a collective identity as part of a shared movement. They were just registering agreement that "this is a shame and ought to be addressed." Petitions of this sort were very popular on Change.org (33 petitions), and they often introduce media-friendly personal narratives with the potential to go viral on social media. (In this particular case, the digital petition leveraged the young girl's story into the local media, which investigated it further and eventually exposed it as a lie.)

An example of a fan petition is "Seth Macfarlane, and Fox Broadcasting Company: Bring Brian Griffin Back to Family Guy" (128,318 signatures). This was a petition launched after the dog character on the cartoon program *Family Guy* was killed in an episode. The petition asks that the dog be brought back. Macfarlane did bring the dog back two episodes later (the script had already been written), but in the meantime fans used Change.org to demonstrate his popularity. The *Family Guy* petition spent ten days on the featured list, including five days at number one or number two. It is listed by Change.org as a "confirmed victory." Cultural and consumer petitions like these are sources of substantial list growth for Change.org. While anyone is free to launch petitions like these through MoveOn Petitions,[14] they are unlikely to reach the featured list. On the same day the *Family Guy* petition appeared as number one at Change.org, the top two petitions at MoveOn.org were "Whole Foods CEO: Stop Spreading Lies About Obamacare" and "Bring Secret Corporate Spending Out of the Shadows!" Neither petition resulted in a confirmed victory. But I would venture that both issues are more important to the future of civil society than any cartoon dog.

The different issue areas featured by the two sites provide telling evidence of the niches that Change.org and MoveOn Petitions seek to fill. Change.org features petitions that frame their call to action in very personalized terms, a hallmark of what Bennett and Segerberg (2013) have labeled "crowd-enabled connective action." MoveOn.org uses petitions to put more agenda-setting power in the hands of its politically engaged membership. It features petitions with more traditionally collective frames and is more in line with what Bennett

---

[14] Including a 2014 fan petition to fire the coach of the Washington Wizards basketball franchise. I must admit that I signed this petition and, at the time, felt it was among the most important issues facing the public.

and Segerberg would call the "organizationally brokered" or "organizationally enabled" model of digital activism. Change.org is a great place to gather mass support for your personal plight. But if you are trying to protect social security or preserve the Voting Rights Act, MoveOn Petitions is a better place to start.

A noteworthy exception to the divergent issue agendas of the two sites is civil rights and LGBTQ rights. As I previously noted, Change.org has been a valuable and frequently used tool for activists mobilizing around the #BlackLivesMatter movement. The site has also featured several high-profile gay rights petitions, including a successful campaign by Scouts for Equality that resulted in major policy changes by the Boy Scouts of America (Gast et al. 2013). During the six months I was gathering data, there were not many national-profile controversies in either of these areas. But since the data collection phase has ended, both issues have regularly been in the news. These issues are part of both the national political agenda and the broader cultural conversation. They are discussed by both political elites and cultural elites, on political news programs and morning talk shows. It is in these cultural crossover areas of racial and sexual inequality that Change.org and MoveOn Petitions experience the greatest overlap.

SIGNATURE TRAFFIC AT THE TWO SITES

The simplest and most public metric for judging the relative success of distributed petition sites is the total signature count of featured petitions. Petitions aren't *necessarily* more likely to win because they boast large signature counts, but more signatures are clearly preferable to fewer signatures. And it is in this area that Change.org earns its accolades as the world's largest petition site. Across the five cases where both sites featured petitions advocating the same position on the same topic, Change.org petitions received an average of 6.2 times more signatures than their MoveOn.org equivalents.[15] Figure 3.7 provides a box-and-whiskers chart of the final signature levels for featured petitions. I provide similar data on growth rate per petition in table 3.1.

In terms of signature volume, Change.org is simply unmatched. The average (mean) featured petition at Change.org boasted 67,701 signatures. At MoveOn, it was 12,973. The median Change.org petition had 26,695 signatures, while MoveOn's median petition attracted only 3,310. In terms of daily growth rate, Change.org had a mean growth rate of 4,464.5 and a median of 2,053.7, while

---

[15] Jay-Z petition: Change.org, 44,346; MoveOn.org, 8,379.
Celebrity boxing petition: Change.org, 104,790; MoveOn.org, 2,335.
Greenpeace 30 petition: Change.org, 88,728; MoveOn.org, 29,404.
Arizona governor petition: Change.org, 71,724; MoveOn.org, 7,114.
Seattle Catholic School petition: Change.org, 29,697; MoveOn.org, 7,655.

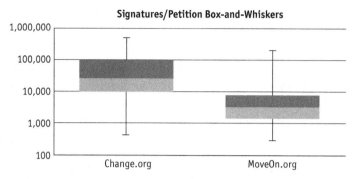

Figure 3.7 Change.org and MoveOn Petitions totals (log scale)

Table 3.1 **Petition Growth Rate at Change.org and MoveOn. org (signatures per day)**

Growth Rate	Change.org	MoveOn.org
Mean	4,464.5	763.6
Min	30.4	2
q_1	733	70
Median	2,053.7	159
q_3	6516	408
Max	42,717	19,946.3

MoveOn had a mean growth rate of 763.6 and a median of 159. With the exception of a few high-performing petitions, MoveOn's featured petitions experienced daily growth in the hundreds, while Change.org's featured petitions experienced daily growth in the thousands.

It is worth noting three additional points about the difference in signature counts. The first point is that, since most petition signatures come via email and social sharing, not via organic web visits, MoveOn's petition *growth* looks smaller because many petitions appeared on the featured list *after* they had been emailed to the membership. As one example, MoveOn member Neil Heslin's petition, "Remember Jesse & Honor Newtown Families: Divest from Guns," appeared on the featured list on December 15, 2013, one day after the anniversary of the Sandy Hook elementary school shooting. The petition already had 58,713 signatures and gained an additional 12,998 signatures during its thirteen days on the featured list. So what looks to this study like a 1,000 signature per day growth rate excludes the initial email-driven two-day spike of roughly 29,000 signatures per day.

The second point is that, as I document later, MoveOn Petitions features many more state and local petitions than Change.org. MoveOn.org's algorithms pick petitions that are doing particularly well *relative to their denominator population*. So a petition with 380 signatures in Nebraska will appear more popular than a petition with 15,000 signatures nationally. Nonetheless, it is unlikely that any MoveOn petitions with more than 10,000 signatures would fail to appear in the recommended list. Change.org petitions receive more signatures than their MoveOn counterparts, full stop.

But this brings us to the third point, the subject matter of the petitions themselves. The single most popular petition at Change.org (so popular that I excluded it from the box-and-whiskers chart) was titled "Open Investigation into Judging Decisions of Women's Figure Skating and Demand Rejudgement at the Sochi Olympics," with more than 2 million signatures. The premise of this petition is easy to understand: Millions of figure skating fans felt that the wrong skater had won the gold at Sochi. They were outraged and took to the Internet to express that outrage. Change.org was a natural place for them to lodge their complaints. At MoveOn Petitions, the most popular petition was "We Denounce the Koch Brothers," by former secretary of labor Robert Reich, with 213,705 signatures.

It isn't hard to understand why Sochi Olympic controversies or Seth Macfarlane cartoons receive larger signature counts than petitions about money in politics or gun control: Entertainment has always been more entertaining than politics. Change.org has succeeded in building the largest petition engine in the world, but it has done so largely by eschewing petitions aimed at traditional political institutions.

PETITION CREATORS

Petitions can be used for a wide variety of purposes. They can be a one-shot action or the first step in an ongoing campaign for political change. They can be used to build a larger organization, to engage media entities, to develop a more stable base of support, or to demonstrate the viability of a proposal. An important determinant of the role a petition will play is the originator of the petition. This is the person who will have the ability to send follow-up messages to petition signers. The petition creator and the petition-hosting site are the only two actors with follow-up access to petition signers. If a digital petition is going to spiral into a social movement, it will need leadership (or at least acquiescence) from the person who got the ball rolling.

MoveOn's featured petitions tend to favor allied organizations, while Change's petitions tend to favor unaffiliated individuals. In the six cases where both sites featured petitions addressing the same controversy, five of the six MoveOn

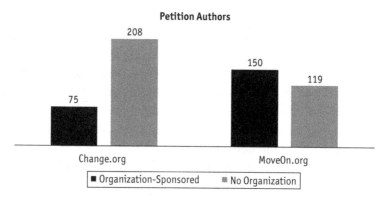

Figure 3.8 Petition authors

petitions were associated with an established progressive advocacy group (Greenpeace, Color of Change, GetEQUAL, and Faithful America); none of the Change.org petitions were associated with any existing organization. Figure 3.8 reports the larger breakdown of independent and organizationally affiliated petition creators at each site.

Roughly one-quarter (26.5%) of Change.org's petitions included an organizational sponsor. Meanwhile, 58% of MoveOn's petitions were sponsored by an organization. And many of the unaffiliated MoveOn petitions were elements of a coordinated MoveOn-organized grassroots campaign. On January 25, 2014, for instance, 5 of the top 10 featured petitions were titled "Divest from the Gun Industry!" These were state-level "clone" petitions, each one authored by a MoveOn volunteer who had decided to take a leadership role on the issue. While my coding scheme records these petitions as "unaffiliated," it is more accurate to state that they are affiliated with MoveOn itself, in which volunteers across the country adopt the same petition language, customized to local targets, and assume a leadership role for follow-up campaign actions. The discrepancy in the amount of organizationally affiliated content points to a key difference in the role that these two petition engines play in the broader ecology of online organizing.

PETITION TARGETS

Two petitions in the same issue area can take very different forms depending on the targets they choose. Some climate petitions are aimed at the Russian government, others at Shell Oil or the local legislature. Some animal rights petitions are aimed at the local dogcatcher, others to Walmart. As Walker, Martin, and McCarthy (2008, 36) have noted, "The target that a movement selects—whether it be a domestic state, a private corporation, or an educational

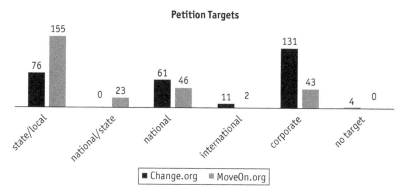

Petition Targets

155

76

0   23

61   46

11   2

131

43

4   0

state/local   national/state   national   international   corporate   no target

■ Change.org   ■ MoveOn.org

Figure 3.9 Change.org and MoveOn Petitions targets

institution—shapes the character and range of tactics that movement will employ." Figure 3.9 reveals the breakdown of petition targets at the two sites.

Two clear differences are readily apparent. First is the abundance of state and local petitions on MoveOn's distributed system. MoveOn featured more than twice as many state-targeted and locally targeted petitions as Change.org. Many of these were state-level petitions calling for gun control legislation, restoration of the Voting Rights Act, or adoption of Obamacare. Others were local attempts to influence transportation or zoning policy, or to pressure the governor on taxes or education funding. Second is the abundance of corporate petitions at Change. org. Change.org featured more than three times as many corporate petitions as MoveOn Petitions. Some of these were attempts to pressure or shame a corporation, but far more were individual pleas that the corporation grant an exemption or respond to fan/consumer support.

The 23 national-state petitions at MoveOn are a good example of how algorithms can shape petition-based campaigns. An example of a national-state petition is "Oregon: Tell the EPA to Ban Bee-Killing Pesticides" (433 signatures) by Peter Stocker of Friends of the Earth. Stocker created identical petitions for Colorado, Washington, and California, all of which appeared on the top 10 featured list. When a petition is created at MoveOn, it moves through a distributed filtering system called "PileOn." PileOn automatically emails the petition to 1,000 MoveOn members, with the subject line "Should MoveOn Support This Petition?" Members are asked to indicate yes by signing the petition, or "no," with the option of leaving a comment explaining why they think the petition is a bad fit for MoveOn. If the petition receives enough signatures within 72 hours, it is sent to a larger testing pool and the process is repeated. MoveOn staffers use a dashboard tool to monitor this process, and petitions that pass through PileOn are then turned into mass emails. Petitions that are geographically limited to a single state are sent to members who live in that state. By creating multiple state-level versions of the same national petitions, some organizations hope to increase their chances of bypassing the PileOn filters and gaining mass distribution. And by featuring state-level petitions on the top 10 list, MoveOn Petitions shines a spotlight on local political fights with smaller total signature counts.

DECLARING VICTORY

It is clear from this data analysis that Change.org favors cultural petitions with personal action frames, while MoveOn favors political petitions with collective action frames. It is also clear that Change.org succeeds in attracting more petition signatures, but MoveOn features petitioners backed by stable organizations, which are better situated to engage their petition signers in follow-up actions. Judging which of these models is more successful is a thorny proposition, since the two organizations are deploying their open petition platforms in pursuit of different ends (for alternative perspectives on success see Wright 2015b; Margetts et al. 2015a, 2015b). But one useful indicator is apparent from the featured petitions that are eventually declared a "victory."

Change's featured petitions boast a better success rate than MoveOn's. Of the 269 MoveOn petitions, 24 had been declared victories more than a year later (9%). Of the 283 Change.org petitions, 60 had been declared victories more than a year later (21%). The most frequent successes at Change.org were found in the categories of animal rights (13 winning petitions out of 47 featured petitions), individual pleas (9 winning petitions out of 33 featured petitions), and consumer/fan petitions (8 winning petitions out of 48 featured petitions). The most frequent successes at MoveOn were in the categories of climate/ environment/agriculture (12 winning petitions out of 80 featured petitions), inequality/taxes/labor (4 winning petitions out of 41 featured petitions), LGBT rights (3 winning petitions out of 17 featured petitions), and gun reform (2 winning petitions out of 17 featured petitions).

Nearly half of the victorious Change.org petitions were focused on corporate targets (28 of 60). These included several large-scale animal rights petitions launched by Mercy for Animals—petition-based campaigns that pressured grocery stores and food producers to alter their production and sales practices. A petition-based campaign also convinced musician Tricia Yearwood to cancel her performance at SeaWorld, part of a broader (and ultimately successful) effort to pressure the company over its mistreatment of animals. But the Change.org corporate victories also included many fan petitions whose independent effect is more debatable. Seth Macfarlane did not bring back the *Family Guy* dog in response to fan outrage. The script had already been produced. A&E didn't bring back Phil Robertson because of a fan petition. It brought him back because *Duck Dynasty* is the network's most popular program. By comparison, only four of the winning MoveOn petitions were corporate-focused, but all four concerned contentious issues where citizen campaigning was likely a necessary condition for the corporation's eventual course of action.

National-scale victories were less prevalent at both sites. Unsurprisingly, it appears that democratizing the basic tools for citizen engagement has been no match for the historic partisan gridlock of the US Congress. Change.org featured 12 victories that were targeted at the national level, but half of these were individual pleas aimed at the US government rather than at corporate targets. MoveOn Petitions featured only three national-level victories, but all three concerned major contentious issues at the center of the nation's political agenda.

The bulk of MoveOn's victorious petitions occurred at the state level (17 state/local victories out of 24 total). These included victories around local environmental protection issues, state-level LGBT legislation, marijuana reform, and gun reform. At the state level, Change.org once again had more successes than MoveOn (18 state/local victories out of 60 total), but many of these were, once again, individual pleas or calls on the state government to launch an investigation or drop (potential) charges.

What becomes clear from this analysis is that the types of petitions that each site is most likely to promote also prove to be the petition types most likely to achieve victory through that site. Change.org features personal battles with compelling narratives around nontraditional political issues. The site attracts signatures in the tens or hundreds of thousands and helps these animal rights petitions, fan petitions, and individual pleas to succeed. MoveOn features collective battles around traditional politics at the state and national levels. Its victories appear mostly at the state and local levels, while its failed petition campaigns help to broaden and deepen the mass supporter base for the organization and its allies.

Conclusion

Any individual can create a petition at Change.org, MoveOn Petitions, or We the People. From the individual's perspective, all three sites indeed appear to be little more than digital warehouses, practically interchangeable depositories of civic appeals. Scholars, journalists, and public intellectuals who have focused on the individual's perspective have both celebrated these sites as examples of network-based/organization-less organizing (Trayvon Martin's parents can launch a petition, see it go viral, and ignite a movement! High school students can gain power, voice, and agency in their everyday fights with the principal!) and derided them as purveyors of clicktivism or slacktivism (The digital mob rushing to support the North Andover High cheerleader doesn't actually know whether she was drinking at that party or not! Digital petitions about the Sochi Olympic judges or cartoon dogs leave people with a false sense of efficacy! What happens when it fades over time?).

But this surface similarity masks deep divisions in how the sites guide and promote some petitions over others. Change.org is in the business of being the world's petition platform. The logic of the company's for-profit endeavor leads it to select petitions that feature personal stories and small potential victories. Along the way, it attempts to rebuild civic capacity and empower the agents of cultural change. MoveOn.org uses petitions as a gateway for larger progressive campaigns. Both individual members and allied organizations launch petitions through MoveOn in order to invite participation from their politically attentive peers. We the People attempts to provide an impartial platform for citizens to petition their government. But the tension created by simultaneously being the venue and the target of these petitions paralyzes the White House platform, leaving it with minimal activity and unfulfilled promise.

Both MoveOn.org and Change.org are engaging in forms of analytic activism. Both routinely run tests to optimize their existing tactics and tinker with new ones. Both treat petition activity as a signal of member interest. So why are the two sites so different? The reason, quite plainly, is that the two organizations are trying to achieve different ends. Change.org wants to be a neutral platform that fosters civic engagement across the ideological spectrum, turning a profit along the way. MoveOn.org wants to win victories for progressive issues and candidates at the local, state, and national levels. The culture of testing does not move all analytic activist organizations toward a single, uniform style. Analytic activism and computational management produce new signals of activated public opinion and new measures of tactical effectiveness. Those signals can point different organizations, operating under divergent organizational logics, in very different directions.

Next, in chapter 4, we'll turn to a very different set of analytics-driven organizational logics. Companies like Upworthy.com specialize in curating the social web, using analytics to identify, target, and frame progressive messages so they can reach dramatically larger audiences. These organizations signal the emergence of relatively new forms of digital persuasion techniques, collectively termed "big listening." Where Change.org and MoveOn Petitions specialize in simple acts of online mobilization, Upworthy.com and its ilk operate one step earlier in the process, harnessing and redirecting online attention.

4

Analytic Audiences

Zach Wahls, age 19, stood before an Iowa State Senate hearing in January 2011 and delivered the speech of his life. The State Senate was considering a constitutional amendment that would ban gay marriage. Wahls, the son of two lesbian parents, rose in defense of his family: "I scored in the 99th percentile on the ACT; I'm actually an Eagle Scout; I own and operate my own small business. If I were your son, Mr. Chairman, I believe I'd make you very proud. I'm not really so different from any of your children. My family really isn't so different from yours. . . . Will this vote affect my family? Will it affect yours? Over the next two hours, I'm sure we're going to hear plenty of testimony about how damaging having gay parents is on kids. But in my 19 years, not once have I ever been confronted by an individual who realized independently that I was raised by a gay couple. And you know why? Because the sexual orientation of my parents has had zero effect on the content of my character."

Wahls's moving testimony failed to convince the State Senate committee, which voted in favor of the constitutional amendment. Had his speech been delivered in 1991 or 2001, his moment would have ended there. State Senate committee hearings don't tend to be festivals of media attention. At best, the local papers and television station might have covered the hearing, and Wahls's eloquence might have landed him a mention on page A17 of the paper or a sound bite on the C-block of the evening news. But this being 2011, his three-minute testimony was captured on handheld video and uploaded to YouTube with the headline "Zach Wahls Speaks About Family." The progressive blogosphere, including cultural kingmaker BoingBoing.net, linked generously to the video. Karine Nahon and Jeff Hemsley (2013) argue that elite blogs like BoingBoing function as "network gatekeepers" that help drive attention and influence in the digital era. Indeed, within a few weeks, the video had been viewed more than a million times. *The Economist* wrote a brief article about the testimony, describing it as "This is what it looks like to win an argument." Wahls was invited to appear on *The Ellen DeGeneres Show*, where Ellen asked him, "What do you feel when people say that you're a hero? Because I actually would say that right now to you, that you're a hero. To me, you're a hero for what you did." Wahls's brief offline moment created online echoes, expanding the reach of his message and extending his time in the spotlight.

But the downside of our current hybrid media system is that moments like this one tend to fly by. BoingBoing publishes dozens of blog posts every day. YouTube's algorithms are programmed to briefly highlight and promote Wahls's video, then move on to the next new thing. Twitter, Facebook, and Google are all designed to reward recency. Wahls's moment of fame was supposed to fade from memory. He was supposed to go back to his engineering classes at the University of Iowa. His friends, family, and fellow activists would remember the video, but everyone else's attention would surely move to the next exciting thing. In the constant churn of present-day social media, public attention almost never rests in a single place for long.

But almost a year later, the video of Wahls's speech resurfaced online. And this time, its reach increased 16-fold.

Eli Pariser, former executive director of MoveOn.org and *New York Times* bestselling author of *The Filter Bubble*, was leading a team that was experimenting with MoveOn.org's homepage. MoveOn has always interacted with its membership primarily through email. The homepage displayed stale and rarely updated content. The team's project, called ShareMachine, was an attempt to see whether new headlines could inject fresh life into old content. Through the ShareMachine program, MoveOn volunteers searched the Internet for shareable progressive content; then the MoveOn staff tested the content to see which images and headlines had the most potential to spur viral sharing. ShareMachine was also an attempt to turn the MoveOn homepage into a clearinghouse for resonant political messages.

The original Wahls video combined a powerful speech with a terrible headline. As Pariser later explained during a public interview with journalist David Carr (SXSW 2014), "When we found it, it was 'Zach Wahls speaks about family.' And we figured, 'Nobody knows who Zach Wahls is,' and 'speaking about family' isn't a big category of interest. So we put another headline on it, which was 'Two Lesbians Raised a Baby and This Is What They Got." (Carr replied with "Not bad. Not bad. Mic drop.")

MoveOn promoted the video through its usual social media channels— sharing it on the Facebook page, the Twitter account, and emails to segments of the membership. The headline attracted clicks. The powerful speech led viewers to share the video further. The video spread through the Facebook social graph, attracting an additional 16 million viewers. In the aftermath of the runaway viral phenomenon, if you Googled the phrase "two lesbians" with Safe Search off, the Wahls video was the number one result.

The underlying theory of ShareMachine is very simple: If digital media has dethroned the industrial broadcast media system, it has also created new opportunities for exposing people to matters of public importance. Pariser and his collaborators believe that high-quality content about important topics can be just as viral as celebrity gossip and cat videos. But to reach beyond the activist choir, these issues of public importance have to be framed in ways that engage curiosity. People encounter unexpected information through social channels like Facebook and Twitter. When they like what they encounter, they share that content, spreading it further. You need compelling content if you want people to share progressive messages, and you need engaging headlines if you want people to click on those messages in the first place.

The second life of Wahls's video boosted the young man's profile. As Sara Critchfield (2015) puts it, "A funny kind of meta thing happens when media goes viral: the media starts doing media stories about the media that went viral." Wahls would go on to give a speech at the 2012 Democratic National Convention. He wrote a book and became executive director of Scouts for Equality. ShareMachine's success also led Pariser and his collaborator, Peter Koechley—a former managing editor of the famed satire site *The Onion*—to launch a new company called Upworthy.com. Within a year of its founding in 2012, Upworthy would be heralded as the fastest-growing media company of all time and crowned the new "king of content" (Sobel Fitts 2014). In November 2014, the site's traffic peaked at more than 80 million unique visitors, giving it a larger reach than CNN, the *New York Times*, or virtually any other major media property. Its success proved so great that Koechley would eventually announce at the 2015 Changing Media Summit, "Sorry, we kind of broke the Internet last year." Along the way, Upworthy has unsettled much of what we thought we knew about how political news travels online. It has changed the rules for how activist organizations seek to deliver messages to broad public audiences. And it has done all of this through an intentional, laserlike focus on analytics.

This chapter discusses Upworthy.com as a window into how analytics and the culture of testing interact with the new dynamics of public attention online. According to the media theory of movement power, the success of any social movement tactic is steeped in the ways that the tactic interacts with the dominant media system of the day. Our understanding of analytic activism will thus be necessarily incomplete unless we also cultivate a keen understanding of the media system and the types of activity it affords and encourages. Upworthy is not an activist organization. But Upworthy is emblematic of a changing social media environment that supports and rewards new types of activist interventions in the public discourse. Digital activism in 2016 is different from digital activism in 2010 or 2004 because the hybrid media environment continues to evolve. The academic literature has stayed surprisingly silent about Upworthy-style social sharing. This chapter addresses that gap.

The Previous Future of Digital News

When Zach Wahls testified at that Iowa State Senate hearing, a company called Demand Media was widely thought of as the future of the news business. That future was dark. It was grim. In a 2009 feature story for *Wired* magazine, "The Answer Factory," journalist Daniel Roth described Demand Media as "fast, disposable, and profitable as hell." And, worst of all, that future seemed inevitable.

At least, that is, until it wasn't.

Demand Media was the largest "content farm" on the web. As the owner of Cracked.com and eHow.com, the Demand Media empire cranked out roughly 4,000 new videos and articles per day. It was the single biggest producer of YouTube videos and enjoyed a relatively symbiotic relationship with YouTube's content partnerships team. "I know we do deals with the ESPNs and ABCs of the world, but Demand is incredibly important to us," YouTube executive Jordan Hoffner told Roth. "They fill up a lot of content across the site" (Roth 2009). The company was ubiquitous, dominating search traffic and reaping hefty profits from online advertising.

It appeared as though the site had cracked the digital advertising economy, using predictive algorithms to identify gaps in the supply and demand of Google search traffic. Demand Media's algorithms spit out writing and video assignments that were picked up by an army of freelancers who were paid a meager $15–$20 per piece. Their production model relied on a three-part formula that tracks (1) search term volume, (2) the market value of potential ads associated with those search terms, and (3) what competitors were already providing in response to those search terms. From these three inputs, Demand Media's algorithms calculated the potential "lifetime value" from a piece of content. It then engaged tens of thousands of freelancers to select titles ($0.08 per headline), write articles ($15 per story), film videos ($20 per video), copyedit ($2.50 per article), fact-check ($1 per article), check quality ($.025–$0.50/video), and transcribe content ($1–$2 per video). This was the pinnacle of the search engine optimization (SEO) era. The goal of Demand Media articles and videos was to claim the top spot in the search rankings for obscure, high-ad-value topics. The company had no loftier goal than that. Byron Reese, Demand Media's chief innovation officer, told Daniel Roth that the ideal Demand Media story was "Where Can I Donate a Car in Dallas?" Online car ads provide high margins, Dallas is a huge, sprawling metropolis, and few competitors already provide answers to that question. And Demand didn't need to provide *good* answers to these queries.

It just had to provide *relevant* answers that would match Google's search algorithms and generate ad revenue.

The data told Demand Media what people were interested in. The data told Demand Media what advertisers would pay. The data told Demand Media what topics were under-covered. The data told Demand Media how much journalism, video production, fact checking, and quality control were worth. And the data didn't lie.

The ubiquity of Demand Media videos prompted some blood-curdling reactions from journalists and media critics. The immediate problem was that Demand Media's algorithms left no room for the type of editorial judgment that has historically supported journalism's public value. Demand's Lifetime Value Model prioritized "evergreen" content over breaking news, local news, and investigative journalism. But, as media critic Jay Rosen put it in an interview with Demand CEO Richard Rosenblatt, "What happens when editorial quality requires costs greater than what's available in search revenue? And who's watching out for that point?" Rosenblatt's response was revealing: "We only make content that we think can be done responsibly and within our cost structure" (Rosen 2009).

The ascendancy of Demand Media fed into a long-brewing narrative about the journalism crisis in America (Shirky 2008b; Starr 2009; Schudson and Downie 2009; McChesney and Pickard 2011; Anderson, Bell, and Shirky 2014. The types of journalism with the highest public value—those that provide in-depth investigative reporting, foreign news, and local coverage—don't tend to be big profit centers. They have typically been subsidized by other elements of the news business: sports reporting, lifestyle content, classified ads, and so on. With content farms like Demand Media soaking up the revenue from click-friendly evergreen content, how are real news operations supposed to pay for public-interest reporting? As Daniel Roth memorably put it, "Imagine a classroom where one kid raised his hand after every question and screams out the answer. He may not be smart or even right, but he makes it difficult to hear anybody else." For this reason, media critic Jay Rosen routinely referred to Demand Media as "(the demonic) Demand Media."

And Demand Media's quality-control process generally established the bottom threshold for "good enough" in online media. Media critic David Carr (2010) pointed to the company's article "How to Throw a Super Bowl Party": "Buy several six-packs of beer. Keep the beer in a cooler close by so you don't have to run to the fridge when it's third and inches. Restock the cooler at halftime." Relevant? Yes. Ad-friendly? Sure. But is this really the quality advice that digital searchers were seeking?

When Demand Media went public in January 2011, its initial stock price rose 37% on its first day, establishing a valuation of $1.5 billion. Lauren Kirchner of

Columbia Journalism Review noted with alarm that this placed the company's net worth higher than that of the *New York Times*. The market seemed to have spoken. The future of journalism was going to be one that "works every day to lower the standards of online content, that devalues the skills of reporting and writing, and that removes any incentive for original thought in exchange for quantity and speed" (Kirchner 2011).

But the dystopic future where Demand Media took all of the ad revenue and further impoverished the news business along the way never came to pass. Demand's brilliant algorithms stopped working so well. Its stock price soon tumbled and has been in a steady decline ever since (see figure 4.1). By the summer of 2015, the original members of Demand Media's executive team had all departed for greener pastures. The company quietly laid off employees, closed offices, and looked into selling eHow and Cracked (Kelly 2015; Rosales 2015). Today, Demand Media more closely resembles an old digital prospecting town than a bustling city of the future. What happened?

Demand Media was undone by two problems—one fast, one slow. The fast problem arrived within weeks of the initial public offering. Google implemented a change in its search algorithm that was designed to punish content farms.

Figure 4.1 Screenshot of Demand Media stock performance (September 9, 2015)

Months of criticism from technology journalists, media commentators, and Google customers (who began blocking Demand sites using a Chrome browser extension, signaling to Google HQ and its engineers their dislike of the company) had apparently soured the symbiotic relationship between Google and Demand Media. Demand was filling up "a lot of [YouTube's] content," as Jordan Hoffner previously noted, but to Google's engineering team the large quantity and low quality of the content eventually looked like a bug instead of a feature. Google engineer Matt Cutts (2011) took a jab at content farms while explaining the reweighted algorithm: "We hear the feedback from the web loud and clear: people are asking for even stronger action on content farms and sites that consist primarily of spammy or low-quality content."

There is a clear logic to Google's decision making here. Demand's algorithmic editorial process was creating a race to the bottom in content quality. Rewarding low-quality content with high-value advertising creates a perverse incentive that does not benefit Google's user base. Demand Media's algorithms failed to measure how visitors felt about Demand Media itself.

Google's algorithmic manipulation further points to a distinction I introduced in chapter 2: the difference between internal and external analytics. The problem with basing your business model on predictive analytics from an external site is that it leaves you vulnerable to the shifting whims of the people who run that external site. And the more you succeed, the greater the likelihood that a change will eventually come. In retrospect, this may seem obvious: *Of course* Google would eventually punish the content farms. The content farms were too successful and too unpopular to keep working in perpetuity. Compare this with, for instance, the Obama campaign's reliance on internal analytics to increase online fundraising totals. All of that clickstream data and experimentation was based on internal engagement measures. Obama for America could monitor anything it wanted and did not have to rely on the goodwill of larger platforms to continue succeeding. Demand Media's algorithms were bigger business, but they were also less reliable over time.

Aside from Google's algorithmic modification, Demand Media also faced a slower-moving trend in user behavior, from search engine optimization (SEO) to social sharing optimization. The American public is increasingly turning to Twitter and Facebook for news. The Pew Research Center found that, by 2013, 52% of individuals with a Twitter account were turning to it for news, as were 47% of users with a Facebook account (which includes far more people in total, since Facebook's user base dwarfs Twitter's). Those numbers increased to 63% for both sites in 2015 (Barthel, Shearer, Gottfried, and Mitchell 2015). The Reuters Institute for the Study of Journalism likewise identified a dramatic increase in social media–based news discovery across multiple countries, noting, "We seek news on Twitter but bump into it on Facebook" (Newman 2015).

Google rewards search term relevance. Facebook and Twitter reward social sharing behavior. People might click on the eHow video explanation of how to host a Super Bowl party. But if the video offers boring, generic advice, they aren't likely to share it.

Demand Media's algorithms were optimized to win the SEO wars. The company was built for an Internet that rewarded keyword relevance with advertising dollars (or, more often, advertising pennies, nickels, and dimes). And if the Internet had remained static, with Google taking no corrective action to dampen Demand Media's search dominance, it likely would be flourishing today. But Google adapted, and the Internet continued to evolve. Demand Media faded as a result.

When Demand Media was the future, the future was fast, high-volume, and disposable. As Demand Media started to fade, Upworthy became the future. And, as we will see, the future of journalism as it looked through the lens of Upworthy prioritized *different* analytics, *different* algorithms, and *different* user behavior. Most important, Upworthy prioritized content quality and shareability over content volume and search rankings. Both companies used algorithms and analytics to guide their decision making and editorial choices. But, as we saw with Change.org and MoveOn Petitions in chapter 3, those analytics led them in very different directions.

The difference, once again, can be viewed through the combination of mission, vision, and business model. As we will see, Pariser and Koechley's vision for Upworthy is built around social sharing and escaping "filter bubbles," so Upworthy optimizes for shares rather than clicks. Since Upworthy's mission is centered on promoting "stuff that matters" instead of simply maximizing profit, the company developed novel metrics that helped it track attention while ignoring the shifting calculus of digital advertising markets. And, as an important bottom line, Upworthy's business model isn't based on ad revenue. Optimizing for online ads means optimizing for clicks— hence the incessant slideshows at online news sites (20 slides = 20 clicks!). Upworthy decided instead to optimize for attention and constructed a revenue model that treats attention as a valuable commodity.

Building Upworthy: Pariser and Koechley's Improbable Bet

The original underlying model for Upworthy was simple enough. Step 1: Scan the Internet for high-quality content—videos, infographics, and (to a lesser extent) stories—that hadn't found their potential audience. Step 2: Fiddle with the headlines and images associated with the content, repackaging it to optimize for social sharing. Step 3: Spread that content through Facebook, Twitter, and email channels, engaging a massive community of supporters along the way. It had certainly succeeded with the Zach Wahls video, and that proof-of-concept was enough for Pariser and Koechley to attract venture funding for their new start-up.

Most observers assumed that Upworthy would cater to a niche audience at best. The common wisdom circa 2012 was that the audience for left-leaning political content simply was not that big. Substantial news content was (and still is) routinely compared to urging the public to "eat their vegetables." The Internet, filled as it is with a never-ending panoply of jokes, memes, celebrity gossip, and pet photos offers an unlimited sugar rush. Analytics from news sites seemed to confirm our worst suspicions about human behavior. Salacious gossip draws clicks. In-depth reporting from Afghanistan draws the chirping of crickets.

Indeed, the literature on the Internet and political knowledge is filled with warnings about just how difficult it should be to attract mass audiences to online political stories. Cass Sunstein laid the foundation for this trend in the research community with two books, *Republic.com* (2001) and *Republic.com 2.0* (2006). His books warned that personalized digital news could lead to the creation of online echo chambers or "information cocoons." Liberals and conservatives would be served different news stories from different sources, and different subjects with different political slants. Under the guise of satisfying reader demand, society ran the risk of continuously reinforcing existing biases. To Sunstein, the potential of news personalization signaled a risk of "cyber-balkanization." His first book was published prior to the rise of the political blogosphere, so the second book highlighted the ways that political blogs function much like the information cocoons he had warned about. Recent research has extended this line of thinking. Magdalena Wojcieszak and a team of researchers (2015) have found through survey experiments that exposure to "pro-attitudinal" partisan news (partisan news that aligns with your ideology) increases citizens' will to participate in politics. Partisan news exposure doesn't just confirm our biases; it also motivates highly partisan minorities to get more involved.

Markus Prior expanded on these issues with hard empirical data in his 2007 book, *Post-Broadcast Democracy*. Prior highlighted the impact of "Relative Entertainment Preferences" on political knowledge and political participation. Prior's work deals primarily with the shift from broadcast television to cable news, but it holds clear implications for the Internet as well. Prior argues that the limited media choices of the industrial broadcast era resulted in a leveling effect of sorts. In the broadcast era, everyone was essentially limited to the same half-hour of serious six o'clock news. You couldn't get much more political news than that on television, and you couldn't avoid exposure to that news by changing the channel. The adoption of the cable spectrum expanded the choice environment, letting viewers act on their entertainment preferences. Political "news junkies" could watch constant political news, while sports fans could avoid politics altogether by tuning in to ESPN. The result, according to Prior's argument, is a political "knowledge gap" between those who can indulge their thirst for political news and those who are now less likely to be incidentally exposed to public affairs news. Providing a wider range of media choices quickly demonstrated how limited the demand for public affairs turns out to be. And with the Internet expanding the range of media choices even further, it stands to reason that this political knowledge gap may only get worse.

Prior's knowledge gap and Sunstein's information cocoons are distinct phenomena, but they reinforce one another. The danger of information cocoons is that political partisans will be able to avoid news that challenges their beliefs, thus creating a feedback loop that heightens political polarization between the Left and Right. The danger of the knowledge gap is that everyday citizens will manage to avoid politics altogether. Polarization also results from Prior's knowledge gap, but it is a polarization driven by the absence of the great mass of disinterested, generally moderate citizens. In the final chapter of *The MoveOn Effect*, I discussed some of the practical implications of this set of findings: "The subset of the American populace that actively participates in political activities beyond voting has simply never been all that large" (Karpf 2012a, 161). Elsewhere, I have frequently written about the "Field of Dreams Fallacy" that tends to plague civic technology projects (Karpf 2012d, 2013a). A great many online initiatives have presumed a pent-up demand for civic information and civic participation. All of these initiatives have resulted in "virtual ghost towns," as they offered a product that most Americans showed little interest in.

Eli Pariser understood these challenges better than almost any political practitioner or media entrepreneur. His 2011 book, *The Filter Bubble*, has itself made a major contribution to literature on digital participation, digital news, and the challenges of digital politics. Pariser added an important new wrinkle to Sunstein's and Prior's line of research, updating it to account for the rise of Google, Facebook, and the social web. News personalization and search results are *engineered* phenomena. The entire Internet is an engineered phenomenon, and the Internet that we have today is, in important respects, different from the Internet we had in 2001 or 2007.[1] Companies like Twitter and Facebook now

---

[1] This is the case primarily at the content layer of the Internet—the sites we access and the media we use. It is not as true at the protocol layer or infrastructure layer. The actual software code that allows machines to talk to each other evolves slowly, through a negotiation process that Laura DeNardis (2009) calls "protocol politics." Meanwhile, the infrastructure of the Internet—the actual pipes, cable, and fiber that facilitate our connections—changes slowly and is dominated by quasi-monopolistic industrial providers (Crawford 2013).

play a central mediating role as information conduits. Their programmers and software engineers face the hard problem of crafting search results and prioritizing newsfeeds to help their users encounter stories, news, and content that are most relevant or interesting. In the process, Google and Facebook can make the problems of information cocoons and knowledge gaps better or worse, depending on what kinds of behavior their programmers choose to engineer.[2]

Facebook's priorities circa 2010–2011 certainly did not seem promising. CEO and founder Mark Zuckerberg, in response to a question about Facebook's role in the news system, notably replied, "A squirrel dying in front of your house may be more relevant to your interests right now than people dying in Africa" (Pariser 2011, 1). News, in the eyes of Facebook's engineers, is not civic or public affairs. News is whatever seems most likely to generate clicks, likes, and shares from the individual user.

In *The Filter Bubble*, Pariser shares two stories about why this digital transition is so troubling. First, he highlights the disappearance of conservative peers from his newsfeed. Pariser himself had made attempts to diversify his Facebook news stream, making friends with conservatives in the hope of escaping the liberal information cocoon. But Facebook's algorithm detected that he rarely clicked on the links that his conservative friends posted. The algorithm adjusted his newsfeed, serving him more liberal content and less conservative content. Facebook's algorithm was treating political diversity as an engineering problem with an engineering solution. As an individual citizen, Pariser could not escape this "filter bubble" even when he tried!

In his second story, Pariser discusses the engineered filtering of Google's personalized search algorithm. Google employs 57 signals to personalize search results *even for users who aren't logged in to Google.* This means that two individuals searching the same term will encounter different results—with occasionally dramatic repercussions. To illustrate this, Pariser asked several friends to Google "Egypt" in the midst of the Arab Spring. Some friends received news stories about the protests in Tahrir Square, but others received travel and vacation information. Egypt was either in the midst of revolutionary turmoil or a sunny getaway, depending on how the search algorithm classified you.

The standing wisdom at the time of Upworthy's founding was that "serious" content was vegetables, and the entire digital click economy was directed toward providing a constant sugar high. Demand Media dominated search results for evergreen content. Meanwhile, if you wanted to go viral online, the best content

---

[2] Claes de Vreese and his colleagues (Zuiderveen Borgesuis et al. 2016) describe this as the difference between "self-selected" content personalization and "pre-selected" personalization. Sunstein's warning was geared toward self-selection, while Pariser introduced the threat of pre-selection through algorithmic filtering.

was wedding dances, stupid human tricks, and cute kids. War footage, cancer documentaries, and police harassment videos are buzzkills and wither from lack of attention. Pariser knew all of this. *The Filter Bubble* was written as a call to action of sorts, urging technologists to prioritize aspirational signals (metapreferences) alongside behavioral signals (revealed preferences). In his 2013 TED talk, which introduces and promotes the book, Pariser clearly articulates the nature of the problem:

> We may have the story of the Internet wrong. The founding mythology of the Internet is that, in a broadcast society, we had these gatekeepers, the editors. And they controlled the flows of information. And along came the Internet, and it swept them out of the way and it allowed all of us to connect together and it was awesome. But that's not actually what's happening right now. What we're seeing is more of a passing of the torch from human gatekeepers to algorithmic ones. And the thing is that the algorithms don't yet have the kind of embedded ethics that the editors did. So if algorithms are going to curate the world for us, if they're going to decide what we get to see and what we don't get to see, then we need to make sure that they're not just keyed to relevance. We need to make sure that they also show us things that are uncomfortable or important.

Upworthy, at its core, is an attempt to create the algorithms that Pariser talks about in his book. Pariser believed that the American public had an untapped thirst for political substance along with its appetite for light, fun digital entertainment. "Upworthy," Pariser would later state during a keynote speech, "is basically media for people who haven't totally given up on the world" (DLD 2014). In his early days at Upworthy, he and Peter Koechley produced an infographic (pictured in figure 4.2) that summarized "What Makes Up the Internet" ("Weird old tips about belly fat," 27%; "200-word articles turned into 15-part slideshows," 19%; "Social media about social media," 7%; "Stuff that actually matters," 0.1%). The analytics and algorithms used by news sites, search engines, and social sites (the very same data and algorithms that Demand Media had been exploiting up until early 2011) were part of the problem. With different analytics and different algorithms, could more important, substantive content find a much larger audience? As Pariser and Koechley set out to launch Upworthy, they were making the seemingly improbable bet that it could.

Upworthy launched on March 26, 2012, with the help of seed funding from Facebook cofounder Chris Hughes. In the first two months, it had attracted 35,000 Facebook fans and 7,300 Twitter followers—solid numbers, but entirely in line with the niche-audience expectations of most skeptics. Then

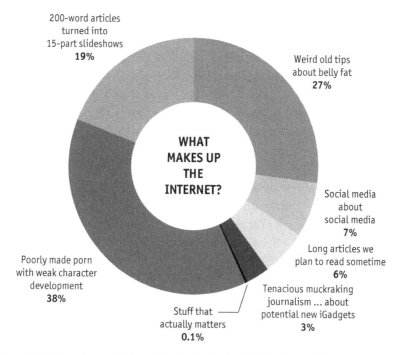

Figure 4.2 Upworthy.com infographic, "What Makes Up the Internet"

the site took off. By December 2012, the site's following ballooned to 791,000 Facebook fans, 10,000 Tumblr followers, and 43,000 Twitter followers. Less than a year into the experiment, Upworthy had been dubbed the "fastest grow-ing media company in the world" (Shontell 2012). Viewers kept pouring in over the following year, their numbers peaking in November 2013 with 80 mil-lion unique visitors, giving Upworthy a larger audience than FoxNews.com, CNN.com, or the NYTimes.com. The success drew an avalanche of media com-mentary and a rash of copycat sites like ViralNova.com and PolicyMic.com. Upworthy had become the new "future of the news business." Though changes to the Facebook algorithm have tamped down Upworthy's reach, today the site has approximately 20 million visitors per month. And it accomplishes this with a small staff team and no fluffy content.

How Upworthy Works

In its early years, Upworthy developed and refined its business model for help-ing "stuff that matters" reach a mass audience. The most important elements of that model include (1) curation, (2) headline testing, and (3) new types of analytics data. Upworthy's digital curators (not journalists and not content creators) gather "seeds"—videos, infographics, and other distinct pieces of online content—scattered across the web. Once they settle on something worthwhile, they move on to creating a frame for the content, turning those seeds into "nuggets." Upworthy's frame-development process centers on a combination of human-driven and analytics-driven decision making. Curators brainstorm potential headlines, then rigorously test those headlines in a proprietary analytics engine nicknamed the "magical unicorn box." The magical unicorn box (basically a sophisticated A/B testing platform) determines which headline is most likely to attract social media clicks and shares. Then the site promotes the content through Facebook, email, Twitter, Tumblr, and the Upworthy website, relying on unique analytics metrics that prioritize viewer engagement and sharing over pageviews and unique visitors. All three of these elements offer distinct lessons about analytics and digital media, so they are worth expanding upon at length.

CURATION—UPWORTHY IS PEOPLE

Much like ShareMachine with the Zach Wahls video, Upworthy begins by searching the web for existing high-quality content. During its initial three years, Upworthy did not employ a single journalist or content creator. Instead, it relied on the judgment of its team of curators to determine what sorts of stories fit the mission and vision of the organization. The original Upworthy team included a heavy dose of former MoveOn staffers. It has appeared at times that Upworthy is, in effect, the company that former MoveOn-ers retire to. Several other early Upworthy staffers, including Jennifer 8 Lee and Adam Mordecai, also hailed from the progressive netroots. As the organization grew, Pariser and Koechley placed a premium on hiring curators with "lived experience": "We believe that lived experience + intellectual experience = better curation. We hire people who have a strong grasp of the big-picture systemic issues facing our world, not just in their heads but also in their lives" (Upworthy 2014d).

Upworthy's hiring choices are important, because this initial stage is the one part of the process that is guided by ideology, not math. Upworthy imitators have made this point abundantly clear as they have attempted to replicate its success on social media. A/B testing and digital optimization are not inherently progressive or political in nature. Brainstorming headlines, framing content, and focusing on social media channels for distribution can be equally effective for conservative news stories, low-content cat photos, and general internet "junk food." Independent Journal Review (IJR) was founded in late 2012 as a conservative Upworthy clone. ViralNova was founded in 2013, applying Upworthy-style headlines and social media optimization strategies to the same sorts of low-content stories Pariser had criticized in *The Filter Bubble*. At the time of this writing, IJR has approximately 20 million visitors per month, and ViralNova has recently been sold for $100 million. Upworthy is a progressive organization by virtue of the people it hires and the tastes and preferences they bring to their work.

Each of Upworthy's curators identifies only five to seven stories, articles, and videos per week. Curators find these stories through their own web searching and from tips and suggestions sent to them through email and social media channels. They also make use of CrowdTangle, a Facebook analytics add-on service that surfaces popular content on the global social network (Sobel Fitts 2015). They then devote the bulk of their attention to crafting the headlines and frames that help their pieces average more than 43,000 likes on Facebook. Ezra Klein (2013) has noted that this is a major difference between Upworthy and other social media giants: "Prior to Upworthy the model for success online was to use fewer people than traditional news outlets do to create and curate much more content. Upworthy is using very few people to create no content and to curate very little. . . . The lesson of the social web is that in terms of traffic—and traffic is not the only metric publishers should worry about, but it's important—one piece of content that goes viral is worth hundreds of pieces of content that don't." Klein, of course, is referring to the previously dominant Demand Media model. Where Demand Media was aiming for cheap and plentiful, Upworthy aims for high-quality and potentially viral.

The company's editorial choices draw from a mix of human and algorithmic judgment—a theme that Upworthy (2014d) has cleverly labeled the "Iron Man Principle":

> The idea is to balance creativity and editorial judgment with technology and data that test assumptions and guide decision-making—one part human, one part machine. (Dig it?) When you layer in data on how audiences are actually responding, it can help you answer a different set of questions. Does the presentation of the content break through and grab attention? Does the content appeal to a broad audience or just the people who've pretended to read Foucault? . . . It's one thing to presume you know what will make people engage with a story you really care about and quite another to see it tested against your next-best guesses. . . . The key to the Iron Man Principle is to create a culture that uses data in a balanced, heuristic way—not to override human intuition (as data often does), but to guide and challenge it.

The editorial direction of the company is also shaped by social science research on the nature of viral news. In particular, Jonah Berger and Katherine Milkman conducted a 2012 study of online *New York Times* articles. Through a large-scale content analysis of sharing behavior around nearly 7,000 articles, they observed that viral social sharing behavior is psychologically rooted in a condition of physiological arousal. "Content that evokes high-arousal positive (awe) or negative (anger or anxiety) emotions is more viral. Content that evokes low-arousal, or deactivating, emotions (e.g., sadness) is less viral" (Berger and Milkman 2012). Relatedly, Upworthy's editorial director Sara Critchfield (2013) has urged her team, "Don't forget to use your emotions as data!" Alongside the analytics reports on which headlines and seeds are performing best, Upworthy staff are encouraged to engage and draw on their emotional reactions to the underlying content.

The "greatest hits" at the site include a documentary about a teenager with pancreatic cancer, a 13-minute documentary about stop-and-frisk police tactics in New York City, a video of a Senate banking hearing, a tutorial on how to use Photoshop to airbrush images, and an audio clip of an Irish radio host telling a story about confronting a Tea Party member. All of these videos have attracted more than 1 million viewers. The company produced a report on the 100 most popular pieces of 2013, cataloged at Most.Upworthy.com (Upworthy 2014a). These topics include a wide range of progressive social issues, many of which routinely receive limited coverage in mainstream media and repeatedly suffer from being trapped within partisan echo chambers.

One month after Upworthy released this report, the company sent out a survey to its entire email list, asking which issue areas Upworthy supporters felt were the most important. The three most popular responses were (1) climate change and clean energy, (2) income inequality and poverty, and (3) human rights. It bears noting that, as we see in figure 4.3, these topics were far from the most popular in 2013. Four of the top 100 posts in 2013 were devoted to environmental issues, six were devoted to poverty and income inequality, and three were devoted to human trafficking and prostitution (the closest analogue to human rights on the 2013 list). Here, once again, we can see the gap between revealed preferences and metapreferences (or, as Pariser puts it, the gap between our aspirational selves and our behavioral selves). Upworthy (2014c) responded to this survey data by hiring additional curators focused specifically on climate, income inequality, and human rights. By mixing the types of data it gathers from supporters (click data plus survey data), Upworthy develops a clearer impression of what its curators should focus on.

"YOU'VE GOT TO FRAME YOUR CONTENT; OTHERWISE THE TERRORISTS WIN"

A critical element of Upworthy's editorial process is borrowed directly from *The Onion*, where cofounder Peter Koechley formerly acted as managing editor.

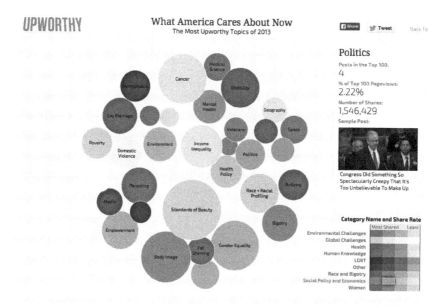

Figure 4.3 Screenshot of Most.Upworthy.com (September 22, 2015)

In *The Onion*'s writers' room, it was common to write 25 headlines for every story. Some of these headlines would be terrible. Some would be brilliant. But the act of brainstorming so many headlines forced the writers to expand their creative horizons. And only after the writers' room had settled on the best headlines would *Onion* writers be free to write their satirical articles. Upworthy has adopted a similar rule. Curators are required to write 25 potential headlines introducing a piece of seed content. They then pare down this list to a handful of headlines that can be A/B-tested against each other to determine which has the most potential. They also decide which "share image" should be linked to the seed. (Share images are the graphics that appear when a video is shared on Facebook.)

Time and again, Upworthy has demonstrated that the right headline can unlock the viral potential of a video. In one case, two Upworthy editors found the same video and uploaded it with different headlines and share images. The video records a TED talk by biologist Frans de Waal, originally titled "Moral Behavior in Animals," in which he discusses experimental findings about how primates react when they receive different rewards for the same task. Upworthy editor at large Adam Mordecai uploaded the video under the headline "Remember Planet of the Apes? It's Closer to Reality Than It Seems." Upworthy editorial director Sara Critchfield uploaded the video under the title "2 Monkeys Were Paid Unequally; See What Happens Next." Mordecai's post attracted 10,000 pageviews. Critchfield's attracted 2.5 million.

Choosing potential headlines is an analytics-driven process. As Adam Mordecai (who, despite the Planet of the Apes example, is Upworthy's most successful curator) explains it, "[In 2013] I predicted 100 of my posts would break a million pageviews, and seven did. . . . Without the data and math and tools, I'm 93% an idiot".[3] Upworthy shares this perspective with a lot of prominent analytics-driven organizations. Alumni from the 2012 Obama for America campaign have reported that email staffers had an ongoing betting pool to see who could predict which email headlines would be most successful. No single staffer was better than average. One remarked during a retrospective panel, "We basically found our guts were worthless" (Sides and Vavreck 2014b, 24). The very best email headline writers in the world had little idea which headline would win at any given time. Likewise, Mordecai and Upworthy's top writers boast that they are wrong much more often than they are right. It is their approach to and reliance on analytics that lets the company tap into the unconscious psyche of the Facebook-dwelling American public.

This emphasis on framing content points to an interesting change in how framing processes occur in a digital media environment. For political communication scholars, *framing* generally refers to the textual and rhetorical choices made by journalists, public officials, and political advocates when engaging in acts of political communication (for the classic discussion of this topic see Entman 1993). Journalists can frame waterboarding as torture or as "enhanced interrogation" (Bennett, Livingston, and Lawrence 2008). Elected officials work with pollsters and focus groups to frame their legislation with language that appeals to key constituencies—warning of mythical "death panels" in the Affordable Care Act, for instance (Hopkins 2013). Climate change activists can frame their appeals in terms of environmental preservation or potential public health impacts (Leiserowitz et al. 2013). Behavioral psychologists Daniel Kahneman and Amos Tversky have likewise demonstrated that framing the same issue in risk-averse or risk-acceptant terms can have a significant impact on public perceptions of the issue (Tversky and Kahneman 1981). Framing, in other words, has generally been studied through the analysis of texts. For Upworthy, the "frame" of a piece of content is the packaging that surrounds the text. The frame is the headline and image that will appear on Facebook, on Twitter, and in people's inboxes. A good frame will generate clicks, while good content will hold attention, generate shares, and prompt additional forms of engagement.

Headlines and share images are hardly the only items that Upworthy optimizes. Much like Dan Siroker when he left Google in 2008 to join the Obama campaign, Upworthy is invested in testing all sorts of granular design choices

<hr>

[3] Comment during a keynote presentation on "Media and Social Network Innovations," at the 2013 Progress Alliance of Washington conference.

and letting the data shape its sensibilities (Siroker and Koomen 2013). Siroker's guiding case example was running A/B tests to help the Obama campaign identify the size, shape, color, and text that would boost response rates to its "join now" button as much as possible. Likewise, Upworthy tests everything from the size and shape of share buttons on the site to the timing and delivery of email sign-up appeals and mobile web-viewing formats (Forrest and Montanez 2012). Upworthy's leadership is actively invested in the culture of testing that has been observed in political organizations like the Obama campaign (Kreiss 2012) and MoveOn.org.

One of Upworthy's most heralded and duplicated findings concerns the "curiosity gap" in headline writing. The curiosity gap is the sweet spot where you give readers enough information to spark their curiosity, but not so much information that they feel no need to click and learn more. One curiosity gap headline read, "This Amazing Kid Got to Enjoy 19 Awesome Years on This Planet. What He Left Behind Is Wondtacular." The headline takes viewers to a 22-minute documentary about a teenage musician, Zach Sobiech, who died of a rare form of cancer. Seventeen million people watched the documentary through Upworthy, and millions then downloaded Sobiech's song "Clouds" on iTunes, helping it to reach no. 1 on the iTunes music charts and raising $750,000 for rare-cancer research. This sharing would not have occurred if SoulPancake.com had not produced a high-quality documentary about the young man. But it also would not have occurred if Upworthy had introduced the video as "Here's a Great Cancer Documentary" or some other merely descriptive headline.[4]

Pariser likes to animate the value of the curiosity gap with a set of headlines from traditional media outlets: "Statistics on Women: Some Good and Some Bad," "Ukraine Protests Once More Turn Violent; At Least Five Reported Killed," "EU Treaty Hampered by Broad Array of Ratification Systems," and "Global Warming Leads to Darker Arctic, Making Earth Absorb More Solar Energy: Study" (SXSW 2014, 32:22). All of these headlines accurately introduce good reporting on important topics. One (statistics on women) is too vague to be interesting, while the others (Ukraine, EU, and Global Warming) are so specific that they leave readers with no need to click and learn more.

For a while in 2012 and 2013, Upworthy's curiosity gap headlines had become so widespread on Facebook that they spurred a backlash of parody sites. The Twitter handle @upworthit offered fake Upworthy-style headlines. The comedy website FunnyorDie.com engineered 21 classic movie posters with Upworthy-style headlines—"Luke Skywalker Doesn't Know the Identity

---

[4] Notice, once again, how Upworthy's optimization goals differ from Demand Media's. Demand Media's algorithms focus on search terms and online ad markets. Upworthy's algorithms focus on social media clicks and shares.

of His Father. His Reaction When He Finds Out the Truth Is Priceless" (*Star Wars: The Empire Strikes Back*) and "I Couldn't Be More Impressed by a Group of Students Cutting Class" (*Dead Poets Society*). *The Onion* eventually launched its own Upworthy clone, Clickhole.com. The site has become a cultural touchstone, attracting both scorn and praise.

The backlash against Upworthy-style headlines extended into a wider backlash against Upworthy itself. As we saw with Demand Media, it seems that by inheriting the mantle of "future of digital news," a company becomes a focal point for news criticism. In Upworthy's case, the backlash consisted primarily of clicktivism-style worries that the ease and scale of social sharing would somehow degrade the meaningfulness of serious news exposure. Tom Scocca (2013) published a lengthy screed published by Gawker.com titled "On Smarm," in which he equated Upworthy with smarm: "a kind of performance—an assumption of the forms of seriousness, of virtue, of constructiveness, without the substance." Gawker's founder and managing editor labeled Upworthy "even smarmier than Buzzfeed" in a memo to employees cautioning that his digital gossip site was losing market share (Romanesko 2013). Al Jazeera America columnist Jordan Fraade (2014) likewise calls Upworthy cynical: "Upworthy liberalism is liberal politics stripped of any awareness of systemic barriers or perverted incentive structures. It's what happens when liberalism is treated as merely a set of lifestyle preferences. . . . What's cynical is the strategy of finding 'meaningful' content about social or political issues, and adding an emotionally manipulative headline, monetizing the results, all the while claiming that your goal is to make the world a better place."

Pariser initially responded to these accusations of smarm and cynicism dismissively, saying, "I'm not going to pay too much attention to some snarky New Yorkers who see [our headlines] too many times" (Abebe 2014). But the company also slowly adjusted its headline-writing practices as well. A year later, Koechley would publicly state, "What started out as a kind of fun, off-the-wall experiment to reinvent headlines (to bring attention to important stories) mushroomed and multiplied and sort of broke the internet. When they started to flood the internet, nobody liked what happened next, including us. And we're sorry" (Upworthy 2015).

But it is worth noting that all of the public attention to the curiosity gap has led to a substantial overestimation of its role in Upworthy's business model and editorial strategy. Curiosity gap headlines became an early Upworthy staple specifically because Upworthy's analytics showed them receiving the most clicks. It was an analytics-driven outcome. But as the Upworthy imitators started adopting the same style and as Facebook viewers grew fatigued and frustrated by their vagueness, curiosity gap headlines stopped outperforming the more straightforward options. Beginning in 2013, Upworthy curators began to notice curiosity gap fatigue among their readers. Headlines of the "You Won't Believe What Happened Next" variety stopped winning their A/B testing matchups, so Upworthy's editorial team quietly shifted away from them. While Upworthy imitators and legacy news organizations have parroted the organization's headline-writing style (CNN once ended a tweet about a child-murder story with an ill-conceived "the reason why will shock you"), the real source of Upworthy's framing success stems from the site's attention to data.

It bears repeating that the curiosity gap is a reaction to changes in the way people access information online. In the early 2000s, Google Search was the primary route to new readers, and this gave rise to the search engine optimization wars and the brief period of Demand Media dominance. The core practices related to SEO involved making headlines tremendously clear and specific, so that searches for that topic would rank your story as the most relevant and reward you with a share of the advertising dollars/cents. But Upworthy was built while news-related traffic online was shifting toward the social web—Facebook and (to a lesser extent) Twitter. And Facebook's algorithms do not prioritize clear headlines. They prioritize likes, shares, and comments. So the headlines that win the social media matchups are usually not the headlines that would win the search engine optimization matchups.

The curiosity gap is the most obvious example of how the changing Internet has altered the incentives and opportunities for engaging citizens with substantive issues. Many of the same media critics who decried Demand Media's SEO-driven search dominance have also inveighed against Upworthy for "tricking" readers into viewing its "stuff that matters" with heartwarming headlines (Fraade 2014; Waldman 2014). They label Upworthy's content "clickbait" and argue that the site is "warp[ing] the meaning of political engagement" (Waldman 2014). The concern, much like the standard critique of clicktivism, is that Upworthy headlines will foster even greater cynicism over time. What these critics mostly miss (again, much like the clicktivism critics) is the organizational context that this viewing and sharing behavior fits into. Upworthy is not a journalistic organization, but Upworthy *is* a force multiplier for high-quality journalism. Upworthy is not an activist organization, but it helps people to break out of activist echo chambers and reach beyond the standard audience of political messages.

YOU ARE WHAT YOU MEASURE: ATTENTION MINUTES AND UPWORTHY'S BUSINESS MODEL

One critical feature of Upworthy's role in the news system is its business model, particularly its decision to avoid clickstream advertising. Recall that Demand Media was built to harvest advertising revenue through maximized clicks. As a result, Demand was set on a collision course with traditional journalistic outlets: To the extent that Demand succeeded in cornering the market on Google ads, it also undercut the revenue streams that support actual online journalism. Upworthy chose to bypass this inevitable competition and conflict by avoiding on-site advertising entirely. Upworthy pages carry no sidebar advertising. They don't fight for top billing on the search engines or try to earn money from valuable AdWords. The clickstream revenue from Upworthy's curated content flows to the original content creators instead of to Upworthy itself.

When Upworthy's curators took a documentary video produced by *The Nation* about stop-and-frisk police tactics and promoted it with the headline "Meet the 17-Year-Old Who Blew the Lid Off Racial Profiling with His iPod," the company brought in an additional 800,000 viewers and pushed the video into "viral" territory. For *The Nation* magazine, this was an unmitigated success. Its reporting gained massive attention, its organization received appropriate credit for that reporting, and all advertising revenue associated with the increased YouTube viewership flowed into *The Nation*'s coffers.

But if Upworthy doesn't make money by competing for digital advertising, how does the company expect to turn a profit? The answer, launched in 2014, is Upworthy Collaborations. According to a blog post announcing the program, "Upworthy Collaborations is about finding a shared mission with brands and organizations—working together to connect the best of what they stand for with what our community cares about. Brands get an opportunity to participate in the Upworthy community, we get to go deeper on important content areas, and together we push the mission forward" (Koechley and Pariser 2014). More specifically, Upworthy Collaborations includes *sponsored content*, where a foundation, nonprofit, or company underwrites Upworthy's curation in a specific content area, and *promoted content*, where Upworthy helps to optimize and frame advertising from one of its partners.

As an example of sponsored content, the Bill & Melinda Gates Foundation helped fund Upworthy's "All 7 Billion" vertical, which featured curated stories about global health and poverty issues. These are stories that fit Upworthy's mission and vision (they are "stuff that matters" / "news vegetables") and also align with the Gates Foundation's commitment to raising public awareness of global health and global poverty. The Gates Foundation receives prominent billing on these pages, which simultaneously raises the foundation's profile and signals to readers that they are engaging with sponsored content. Figure 4.4 provides a screenshot of a sponsored post.

An example of promoted content is CoverGirl's "Girls Can't" advertisement. CoverGirl produced this one-minute advertisement with female celebrities, including Queen Latifah, Ellen DeGeneres, and Katy Perry. The advertisement offers an uplifting message about female empowerment. It ends with DeGeneres delivering CoverGirl's "easy, breezy, beautiful" slogan, but the video is focused on

What It Really Means To Be An Earthling
JULY 29, 2014
SPONSORED POST

It seems like we're constantly bombarded by sad stuff in the news. A tragedy here, violence there, people being mean to each other everywhere – it can be a real downer. So let's focus on the good for a change, on people who are trying to be their very best, and think about what their actions mean for the world. If you want to help spread those good vibes, it'd be cool if you heard what these people have to say and think about how you contribute to the question below.

Curator: Morgan Shoaff   **f Share**   **Tweet**

Made possible by the Bill & Melinda Gates Foundation.

BILL & MELINDA GATES *foundation*   *A special Upworthy series about global health and poverty, made possible by the Bill & Melinda Gates Foundation. Read more, then check out more in All 7 Billion.*

Everyone poops, but 2.6 billion people do it in a really crappy way.

Figure 4.4 A sponsored post at Upworthy

challenging negative female stereotypes rather than selling makeup. Companies like CoverGirl, Dove, and Unilever are increasingly producing this type of advertising in order to improve their brand in the eyes of consumers who consider corporate responsibility and corporate ethics when making decisions about what products to buy. Upworthy (2014f) featured the video with a prominent disclaimer: "We were paid to promote this ad, but we only do that for things we think are actually Upworthy. Read more." After subjecting the advertisement to Upworthy's headline-development process, they settled on the title "Ellen, Katy Perry, And A Hockey Player Walk Into An Ad and Shatter A Ridiculous Argument." Figure 4.5 provides a screenshot of this promoted post.

Promoted content and sponsored content are forms of native advertising, itself a topic of substantial debate among journalism scholars (Carlson 2015). Native advertising in traditional journalism can include innocuous partnerships, like Starbucks sponsoring the television program *Morning Joe* on MSNBC (the hosts prominently display their Starbucks coffee cups throughout the program). It can also take more pernicious forms, such as magazine advertisements that look like news articles and hide their sourcing or news segments about the 2010 Gulf oil spill produced in-house by BP and then aired on television stations with minimal disclaimer (yes, this actually happened). In the news industry, native advertising raises concerns that the

Figure 4.5 An Upworthy promoted post

"church and state" division between the news and advertising is disappearing. It also raises concerns about whether reporters will be able to maintain the ideals of objective reporting when they are prominently grappling with corporate sponsorship. Online news sites like BuzzFeed have pioneered the use of native advertising online, relying on a heavy dose of sponsored posts, listicles, and quizzes that, in turn, pay the salaries of a high-quality team of reporters. Since Upworthy itself lacks a news division, at least some of the harshest critiques of native advertising do not seem to apply.

Optimizing for content partnerships instead of mouse clicks has led Upworthy to develop new metrics to track its effectiveness. Chief among these is *attention minutes*, an estimate of the amount of time each visitor devotes to each piece of content. In a February 2014 blog post announcing the switch to attention minutes, the Upworthy team introduced the new metric:

> We're big believers that you are what you measure. Our mission here at Upworthy is to draw massive amounts of attention to the most important topics. So, how do you measure that?
>
> We dabbled with pageviews, but that's a flimsy metric, as anyone who's suffered through an online slideshow knows (20 pageviews! Zero user satisfaction!). Pageviews are only a great metric if you're being paid

for each pageview; we don't run banner ads, so they've never meant as much to us.

Unique visitors are fine but reward breadth over depth of user experience. Shares per piece of content are quite a valuable signal, but they don't get you all the way there. And time on site, as Google measures it, works great for e-commerce but is often confusingly broken for media companies. Google Analytics at one point had us at 21 minutes on site per visit on average; we're good, but we know we're not that good.

So we decided we needed a new approach. If we're trying to maximize attention for meaningful content, let's actually solve for that.

Introducing **attention minutes**, Upworthy's new primary metric, which we're planning to track in two forms:

- **Total Attention on Site** (per hour, day, week, month, whatever)— that tells us (like total uniques or total pageviews) how good of a job Upworthy is doing overall at drawing attention to important topics.
- And **Total Attention per Piece**, which is a combination of how many people watch something on Upworthy and how much of it they actually watch. Pieces with higher Total Attention should be promoted more.

Notice the reference to pageviews in this post: "Pageviews are only a great metric if you're being paid for each pageview; we don't run banner ads, so they've never meant as much to us." Demand Media tracked pageviews to help estimate the expected lifetime value of its content products. Pageviews were the bottom line for Demand Media's business model, just as email lead generation is the bottom line for Change.org and member donations are the bottom line for MoveOn.org (chapter 3). With collaborations as the bottom line for Upworthy, the company needed a better measure of how well its content was engaging audiences. Attention minutes becomes a *strategic object* (chapter 2), useful in pitching to collaborators the reasons they should invest in Upworthy.

It is debatable whether attention minutes are a measure of "true" online impact. Upworthy's public switch to attention mentions attracted commentary from various corners of the web, including the *Columbia Journalism Review*, *NiemanLab*, *Adweek*, and *Time* magazine (Lowenstein 2014; O'Donovan 2014; Shields 2014; Haile 2014). Max Read, the editor in chief of the digital gossip site Gawker.com, offered a counterargument to attention minutes: "If time spent becomes important to advertisers—or to a publishing company's goals as a business—writers and editors will be pressured to try to get readers to spend more time on the page, in ways that are exciting and valuable to readers and ways that are cheap and frustrating" (Tanzer 2014).

Attention minutes is not a perfect metric. There is no such thing as a perfect metric. As Donald Campbell (1976, 85) pointed out with his Campbell's Law, "The more any quantitative social indicator (or even some qualitative indicator) is used for social decision-making, the more subject it will be to corruption pressures and the more apt it will be to distort or corrupt the social processes it is intended to monitor." Charles Goodhart (1981, 116) is credited with having come up with the same insight in "Goodhart's Law": "Any observed statistical regularity will tend to collapse once pressure is placed upon it for control purposes." But what is abundantly clear is that attention minutes give Upworthy a tool to measure user engagement, which in turn lets the company make more effective pitches to its potential content partners. A business (like Demand Media) built on impression-based ad revenue will optimize for pageviews. A business (like Upworthy) built on attention minutes will optimize for user engagement. Just as we saw in chapter 3 with Change.org and MoveOn Petitions, the use of analytics in digital media operations can have divergent impacts, depending on the missions, visions, and business models of the organizations that are deploying them.

The Social Web Adjusts to Upworthy

Upworthy's highest-traffic month was November 2013, when the site attracted more than 80 million unique visitors. That was a particularly auspicious month for the site, with multiple videos that gained particularly strong traction through social media sites. But it also marked the start of a stiffening relationship with Facebook. Facebook's engineers began tinkering with the site's algorithms after that month, ostensibly in response to Upworthy's runaway popularity. Upworthy, it seems, had proved *too* successful at enticing readers to navigate away from Facebook's walled garden. John Herrman (2015) has argued that Facebook's algorithmic adjustments set the stage for Facebook-native video, which premiered in August 2014 and helped fuel the rampant success of the Ice Bucket Challenge: "Upworthy was succeeding according to metrics favored by Facebook, but not necessarily by doing the things Facebook believed those metrics would cultivate. . . . Why not just host the video directly *on* Facebook?"

The promotion of Facebook-native video has not undercut Upworthy to the same extent that Google's algorithmic adjustments undermined Demand Media. Upworthy has stabilized to a reader base of roughly 20 million visitors per month, and the site continues to perform quite well according to its attention minutes metric. But while copycat sites have crowded the field and Facebook has adjusted its algorithms, Upworthy has also collected a massive amount of data about the types of story elements that keep readers and viewers engaged with substantive content. In June 2015, the company hired Amy O'Leary, the former

deputy editor of the *New York Times* international desk, as its new editorial director. O'Leary's hiring signaled the company's intention to expand beyond content curation to include original storytelling and content creation. At the time
this book is going to press, the curators have been renamed "editors," and the site
has begun publishing its own 5,000-word articles about the fast-food industry
(March 2015). Upworthy has maintained its analytics-driven focus. The mission, vision, and business model of the site remain essentially unchanged. But
the habits and routines that Upworthy popularized in its first few years are still
changing and adapting to what those analytics inputs tell the company.

Upworthy's Role in Activism as a Resource for Activist Organizations

> We just became Upworthy. And the overwhelming support is giving
> us more momentum than we could have dreamed.
>
> Please don't stop supporting us—we're still going to be outspent
> like crazy. Every extra dollar means more voters registered, campaign
> materials, resources for our volunteers and contacts with Boulder
> voters to educate them about what's at stake in this election.
>
> Give what you can and continue to share our story!
> —Facebook post, New Era Colorado, September 3, 2013

Upworthy is not an activist organization. Though it was founded by MoveOn
alumni and features a large number of staffers with experience in progressive
politics, Upworthy's goal is to reach a massive audience with substantive content
about socially important issues. The company is not trying to pass legislation,
elect public officials, or hold corporations accountable. Its success is measured
in attention minutes, not political victories. We can best understand Upworthy's
role in political advocacy as "activism-adjacent." Upworthy is a megaphone and
a force multiplier. It changes the landscape for political associations, increasing
the value of a particular set of political tactics. Specifically, the rise of Upworthy
has *finally* created a good reason for activist groups to invest in high-quality
video production.

The case of New Era Colorado provides a telling example (one that has been
retold at many national activist conferences). New Era Colorado was founded in
2006 as a multi-issue progressive advocacy organization committed to engaging
young people in politics. It is an affiliate of the Bus Federation, a network of eight
statewide groups with similar mission statements. In 2013, New Era Colorado
was opposing Xcel Energy on a Boulder, Colorado, ballot initiative. Xcel was
spending more than $1 million on advertisements aimed at stopping the city

from setting up a municipal energy utility. New Era Colorado decided to launch a crowdfunding campaign to help it fight back against Xcel Energy. The goal was to raise a modest $40,000—not nearly enough to match Xcel dollar for dollar, but enough to hire some field organizers and help with get-out-the-vote efforts. As part of the crowdfunding campaign, New Era Colorado created a six-minute video that introduced the issue, documented what was at stake, and called on viewers nationwide to donate to the cause.

The problem with investing in six-minute videos about local power initiatives is that it is never clear who is going to *watch* something like that. New Era posted the video to YouTube with the headline "Campaign for Local Power" and featured the video on its Indiegogo fundraising page. New Era promoted it through its network of strong supporters and peer organizations and sent it around to local media. The organization also sent it to Denver resident Adam Mordecai, Upworthy's editor at large. Mordecai thought the video had all the elements he looked for in a piece of seed content. It was a compelling story about an important issue. It had solid production values and a clear, positive message. He fiddled with the framing and eventually settled on the title "A Bunch of Young Geniuses Just Made a Corrupt Corporation Freak Out Big Time. Time for Round Two." New Era Colorado had just "become Upworthy." (What happened next probably won't surprise you, though.)

Within two weeks, over a million people had viewed New Era Colorado's video. More than 5,000 of those viewers were moved to donate to the crowdfunding campaign. New Era Colorado blew past its initial goal of $40,000, eventually raising $193,018 from 5,702 supporters. Xcel Energy's ballot measure was defeated two months later by a better than two-to-one margin (Meltzer 2013). And at the New Organizing Institute's 2013 RootsCamp convention, New Era Colorado received the "Most Valuable Campaign" award (as a reference point, the 2012 award had gone to the Obama for America reelection campaign). Upworthy did not call any voters, knock on any doors, or post any lawn signs. New Era Colorado and its coalition partners were responsible for this victory, not Upworthy. But without Upworthy, New Era Colorado would not have attracted national attention, nor would it have raised nearly as much money. The six-minute video became a smart tactic specifically because of Upworthy's role in the evolving hybrid media system. Without Upworthy, the money and time put into that video would have been a far worse investment.

Here, Upworthy is indicative of a broader trend in the hybrid media system. When traffic on the Internet is driven by Google searches, the audience that can be reached by a piece of political content is constrained to the people who are motivated to search for it. Bruce Bimber and Richard Davis ably demonstrate this point in their 2003 book, *Campaigning Online*, which highlighted that political campaign websites (circa 2000) are ill-suited tools for persuasive campaigning because the only citizens who, in practice, bother to seek out candidate websites are the strong supporters and opponents who have already made up their minds about the election. This indeed is the very problem that Sunstein warned about in his discussion of information cocoons and cyber-balkanization and that Markus Prior highlighted in his discussion of information gaps and relative entertainment preferences. But the shift toward social media–based sharing creates a new opportunity for incidental exposure to political information (Bode 2012; Messing and Westwood 2014). Armed with the right (read: click-worthy) framing, worthwhile political stories can spread through the "curated flows" of the Facebook newsfeed and Twitter timeline (Thorson and Wells 2015). Long-form, high-quality persuasive messaging is no longer confined to "preaching to the choir," because the dominant tools of social news discovery encourage sharing and spreading behavior (also see Jenkins, Ford, and Green 2013; Nahon and Hemsley 2013).

Upworthy represents a change in the media system. As I have previously suggested with the Media Theory of Movement Power, this change in the media system affords new tactical and strategic opportunities for social movement organizations. Matthew Powers, for instance, has shown that international human rights nonprofits invest heavily in investigative reporting capacities, producing their own reports and filling in some of the gaps left by cuts at traditional news organizations (Powers 2014, 2015). These NGOs remain focused mainly on garnering mainstream news coverage—they measure success through *New York Times* coverage, not shares and retweets. Nonetheless, Human Rights Watch chose to invest in the Upworthy Partnerships program, most likely because they recognized that *spikes in coverage through Upworthy can generate additional exposure in mainstream media*. Social sharing is not an alternative to traditional media. It is an access point into the hybrid media system—one that can create valuable leverage for activist organizations over their targets.

The new capacity for shareable, actionable political content has opened up opportunities for traditional media and political actors to marshal new techniques for building and engaging with an audience. Comedian John Oliver, for instance, has pioneered a new style of long-form, activist storytelling on his HBO program, *Last Week Tonight with John Oliver*. His weekly 30-minute program usually includes a 10- to 15-minute segment about some major social problem. Interspersing humor with dramatic, fact-based storytelling, Oliver tends to conclude with a clear call to action for his viewers. His June 1, 2014, program on net neutrality ended with a call for his viewers to log on to the Federal Communications Commission (FCC) website to register comments in favor of a strong net neutrality policy. His viewers responded in droves, registering an estimated 45,000 comments and briefly crashing the FCC website (McDonald 2014). And there is good evidence that these long segments rely on the social sharing behavior of Oliver's viewers. According to Nielsen ratings, Oliver's program (on premium cable, no less) attracts roughly 1.1 million viewers. But his long-form, activist storytelling segments are routinely featured on Upworthy, BuzzFeed, and their various copycat sites. Oliver's FCC rant has been viewed on YouTube more than 10 million times. Without the social web, his calls to action would not spread so widely. With the social web and the social optimization practices it has afforded, Oliver has been able to carve out an innovative new space in the political comedy landscape.

Upworthy is a media company, not an activist organization. It measures success in attention minutes and social sharing, not legislative votes and citizen participation. But there is a good reason why Upworthy staffers have repeatedly given presentations at major progressive activist conferences like the Netroots Nation convention and the New Organizing Institute's annual RootsCamp. Upworthy wants to encourage activist organizations to invest in high-quality media production. Sharing Upworthy's "secrets" with activist organizations signals that persuasive media appeals have more potential value than they did just a few years ago. And when activist organizations invest in high-quality persuasive media appeals, that gives Upworthy's curators more good content to work with.

Eli Pariser (2013) has a rule for his company: "No great speeches to empty rooms. . . . It doesn't matter if you do the perfect thing and no one pays attention to it. You have to make people care." The best arguments are useless if no one hears them. They are of limited use if they are designed to persuade but never reach beyond an audience that is already nodding in solemn agreement. In the digital media environment of the past decade, most "great speeches" had no chance of reaching beyond their echo chamber. Upworthy's culture of analytics and testing massively expands the reach and scope of persuasive political content, which in turn increases the value of persuasive storytelling within activists' tactical repertoires.

5

Boundary Conditions

The Analytics Floor and the Analytics Frontier

> You are what you measure.
> —Dan Ariely
>
> The centrality of metrics to Gawker's organizational culture meant that
> behaviors that were hard to quantify were also hard to incentivize.
> —Caitlin Petre, *The Traffic Factories*

The application of analytics to politics has been driven mostly by electoral campaigns. The widely celebrated success of the Obama campaign in 2008 in particular has created ripple effects that have helped to forge a burgeoning industry
of analytics services and consultancies. Several firms specializing in political analytics were founded in the aftermath of the two Obama campaigns (Optimizely,
Civis, and Blue Labs, for example). Multiple academic and journalistic accounts
have documented the role that data, testing, and analytics now play in modern electoral campaigns (Kreiss 2012; Issenberg 2012; Rogers and Nickerson
2014; Baldwin-Philippi 2015; Hersh 2015). Scholars have begun to speculate
about what the "big data campaign" means for democratic representation writ
large: Will all this information in the hands of parties and campaigns be a net
positive or net negative force for civic voice and participation (Tufekci and
Wilson 2012; Katz et al. 2013; Tufekci 2014; O'Neil 2015)?

There are some crucial differences between electoral campaign analytics and analytic activism. These differences can all be traced back to a single
theme: Electoral campaigning is, conceptually, very simple. Activist and advocacy campaigning is tremendously complex.

These differences take form as *boundary conditions* that define the current
scope and limitations of analytic activism. There are two central boundary conditions, which I term the *analytics frontier* and the *analytics floor*. Both the analytics frontier and the analytics floor are purely theoretical constructs, not precise

empirical claims. Much of the most interesting innovation and experimentation among civic technologists and digital activists is focused on adapting to the limitations of analytic activism—pushing against the analytics floor to increase the relevance of digital tools to small organizations and niche issues, and pushing past the analytics frontier with new platforms and metrics that help large organizations trace and incentivize the types of behavior that align with their theories of change.

This chapter documents efforts to lower the analytics floor and chart the analytics frontier. It highlights early pilot projects, technology partnerships, and novel metrics that have drawn attention from the activist community but have not yet developed into robust programs or models. I can thus clearly state at the outset one lesson to be gleaned from this chapter: *The field of analytic activism is still being defined.* Today's vexing challenges might become tomorrow's object lessons or cautionary tales. The analytics floor and frontier do not define what this mode of activism *cannot* do. They determine what this mode of activism *will not* do, until and unless activist leaders craft solutions to the hard problems these concepts highlight.

Why Electoral Campaigns Are Simple

Consider what winning looks like in a US Senate race. A Senate race is a two-stage game. First, your candidate must win a primary election against competitors from the same party. Then, your candidate must win a general election against the nominee from the competing party. (Depending on incumbency and the partisan makeup of the state, victory is sometimes virtually ensured in one of these two stages—your candidate might face no primary challenger, or the opposing party might not bother to nominate a candidate.) The dates of the primary and general election are well known in advance. The victory condition is also clearly established. Whoever receives a plurality of votes is the winner. This can be 50.1% of the voting electorate in a two-way race, or even less if there are minor-party candidates on the ballot.[1]

Reaching this victory condition traditionally occurs through a three-stage campaign of (1) voter identification/registration, (2) voter persuasion, and (3) voter turnout (get out the vote, or GOTV). Those are the basic stages of an electoral campaign. And this is a completely noncontroversial claim; it is common knowledge for all campaign professionals in the United States. These

---

[1] Since there are often more than two candidates in competitive primary elections, some states employ "top two" runoff elections if no candidate receives more than 50% of the primary vote. So the specific electoral rules can vary from state to state, but only at the margins.

established steps impart a rhythm to the campaign, with campaigners, pollsters, candidates, and reporters focusing attention on quarterly fundraising deadlines, campaign advertisements, and tracking polls in order to keep approximate track of the "horse race" along the way to the fixed conclusion on Election Day. While there are competing theories about how one can best persuade and mobilize voters, and long-standing academic debates about the importance of campaigns versus "fundamentals" (Holbrook 1996; Erikson and Wlezien 2012; Sides and Vavreck 2014b), there is no disagreement over what victory itself looks like. Electoral campaigns have the *luxury* of a fixed endpoint and a clear victory condition.

Knowing what victory looks like is a boon to electoral campaigns, because that victory condition clarifies the *outcome variables* that electoral campaigns can focus their analytics on. Electoral campaigns need volunteers, (preferably positive) media coverage, and money. They convert that money into paid commercials, canvassers, and phone bankers, along with salaries for (presumably competent) advisers, consultants, and staff members. That is what electoral campaigns *do*. As a result of this clarity of purpose, electoral campaigns can gather data on all these necessary campaign elements and run experiments to try to optimize money raised, or calls placed, or viewers reached, or reporters cajoled.

In the parlance I have developed in the past few chapters, the mission, vision, and business model of electoral campaigns are clearly established. The mission is to elect a candidate. The vision is to give representation to the set of interests and constituencies that stand with that candidate. The business model is to raise funds from supporters (a mix of small donors and large donors) and use those funds to support a massive campaign "assemblage" (Nielsen 2012). While we can identify meaningful differences in how campaigns use information technology to achieve these goals (Issenberg 2012; Kreiss 2012; Stromer-Galley 2014; Baldwin-Phillipi 2015; Hersh 2015), in how they engage supporters (Alexander 2010), in where their funding comes from (La Raja 2013), and in what policies they pursue, the fixed endpoints and rhythms of the electoral campaign environment enforce a good deal of similarity among all campaigns. Campaigns knock on doors and purchase media advertisements. They do not hold sit-ins or compose poetry. We know when an electoral campaign has ended, and we can evaluate how it did according to well-established metrics. This is all a blessing for electoral analytics and testing, because campaigners know which variables to track, when.

Activism, by comparison, is hobbled by the undefined qualities of its mission. How do we know when activism has succeeded? How does an advocacy campaign know that it has reached its end goal?[2] Consider, for instance, Occupy

---

[2] For the classic discussion of this topic, see Gamson (1975).

Wall Street (OWS). Was OWS *successful*? Was it *powerful*? *What does winning look like for OWS*? Is it the complete overthrow of the global finance system (White 2011)? Is it the prefigurative political goal of exposing a wider public to alternative perspectives on wealth and inequality (Gitlin 2012; Gottlieb 2015)? Is it a set of policy outcomes that fall short of complete revolution but nonetheless curtail the unfettered power of financial elites (Bennett and Segerberg 2013)? Or is it the empowering and life-changing experience of OWS participants themselves (Gould-Wartofsky 2015)? Different scholars and activists cluster around each of these definitions. Some view OWS as a dramatic success that signals a shift in twenty-first-century politics (Castells 2012). Others view it as a flash point that eventually sputtered and failed. How we define success will determine how we ultimately view the work of OWS activists. But there is no common definition, nor will there be. The debate over the impact of social movements rests on an unstable foundation, since the very nature of "impact" is subject to debate.

As another example, consider the work of global climate activists. What constitutes winning for climate activism? Is it getting an international climate treaty passed? National climate legislation? A campus or town ordinance that promotes clean energy? Shutting down a local coal-fired power plant? Undoing the worst excesses of global capitalism by replacing the current energy extraction industry with one that promotes green jobs and climate justice? Some of the toughest strategic debates within the climate movement revolve around these very questions (Hadden 2015; Hall 2016). There is no fixed endpoint at which the climate movement has either won or lost. There is no simple victory condition like 50.1% of the electorate. Even for high-profile legislation and climate treaties, climate activists internally debate whether the politically feasible proposals supported by major climate organizations are strong enough to achieve the carbon reductions that climate scientists tell us are ultimately necessary (Skocpol 2013). In the multi-year activist campaign to defeat the Keystone XL pipeline, there was even a long-running strategic argument over whether the pipeline was the right target for climate activism (Roberts 2015).

Without a clear endpoint and a clear victory condition, the analytics that have been developed for electoral campaigns are of limited utility to social movements and activist organizations. An activist organization can use analytics to measure fundraising, or membership growth, or calls to Congress, or media coverage. But none of these metrics are clearly linked to winning or success, because the very definition of victory is itself subject to intense contestation.

Here, once again, let me return to the Media Theory of Movement Power introduced in chapter 1. Movements do not win on Election Day. Movements demonstrate their power by convincing their targets to take some action that they would not otherwise take (Dahl 1957). In the process, all social movements rely on media technologies and media organizations to amplify and refract their message. Strategic innovation for activist organizations often involves developing new media interventions that increase their leverage within the prevailing media system. But the activist and advocacy organizations that are best at generating phone calls to Congress, turning out citizens to a hearing, or raising money to fund issue advertisements are not necessarily achieving their goals. And that raises a specific danger: that an overreliance on analytics and algorithms will lead to a style of bloodless activism that generates large but hollow numbers. By focusing on the types of analytics that have been developed for electoral campaigns, activist organizations run the risk of prioritizing the outcomes that are easily measured over the outcomes that align with their strategic mission. The pioneers of analytic activism have crafted their analytics to match their mission, vision, and business model. But the danger posed by the analytics frontier is that, over time, mission and vision could instead be shaped by the availability of digital trace data, warping the organization's work along the way. I elaborate on how activist organizations are confronting the analytics frontier challenge in the second half of this chapter.

The analytics floor is a separate concern. Even within the space of electoral campaign politics, researchers and journalists alike tend to focus on the most well-resourced and visible national campaigns. There are tens of thousands of elections every year in the United States, but our national attention tends to boil down to the presidential race and a handful of competitive House and Senate seats. One result of all this attention on national elections has been a faulty impression that the practices and processes developed at the presidential level can seamlessly scale down to the local level—if Obama for America is using fancy analytics to track its supporters, then surely it is only a matter of time until the winning city council candidates are doing the same. And if electoral campaigns are using analytics to raise money and target communications today, surely advocacy campaigns cannot be too far behind.

This assumption is routinely made by theorists and journalists alike, and it highlights the lower boundary condition for analytic activism, the analytics floor. Analytics and algorithms become increasingly valuable on a large scale. For small-scale campaigns and organizations, the strategic objects that are produced by analytic activism can often be impractical or impossible to create. This leads to a tendency toward "growthiness" (defined as a focus on tactics that help to expand the organization's list size), which can exert pressure that diverts activist organizations from their mission. It also sets up a series of challenges and workarounds that I explore later: (1) efforts to build larger lists in order to rise above the analytics floor, (2) efforts to draw on external analytics to identify political opportunities and leverage points from the mass of public social media data, and (3) efforts by small campaigns and organizations to combine or collaborate in order to increase the power of their experimental findings. The next section of the chapter elaborates on the analytics floor and on the challenges posed by the impulse toward growthiness and further discusses the problems that occur at the borders of the analytics frontier. The chapter then concludes with six case examples of how analytic activist organizations are responding to the challenges posed by the analytics frontier and the analytics floor.

The Analytics Floor Defined

Conceptually, the analytics floor is intended as a reaction to the abundant hype surrounding the transformative power of "big data." Authors like former *Wired* magazine editor Chris Anderson, as well as Viktor Mayer-Schoenberger and Kenneth Cukier, have argued that the rise of big data will completely transform society, leading to "the end of theory" (Anderson 2008) and a reliance on correlational data that "help us capture the present and predict the future" (Mayer-Schoenberger and Cukier 2013, 53).

In its simplest form, the analytics floor is a limitation on the use of *internal analytics* as a routinized strategic object. Let's refer back to the uses of analytics discussed in chapter 1 (see figure 1.1): (1) small-scale tactical optimization— running quick tests or experiments to determine which variant on a campaign tactic will perform better, (2) large-scale computational management—using digital metrics to guide larger resource allocation decisions, and (3) passive democratic feedback—running tests or monitoring analytics reports to gain insights into members' public opinion.

The value of analytics increases as the size of the organization's supporter base increases. Larger email lists (or number of website visitors, Facebook fans, etc.) yield larger testing groups. Larger testing groups increase the precision of the results, allowing organizations to identify a smaller *minimum detectable effect* at a statistically significant level.[3] Larger email lists also increase the *return on investment* in testing regimes. Ideally, a small minority of the email list ought to be exposed to test messages. That way, the findings from the test can be fruitfully applied to the rest of the list.[4]

As Kevin Collins, research director of the Analyst Institute, explains it, "For optimization to be actionable, you not only have to have results with sufficiently small standard errors, you have to have a large population into which you're

---

[3] https://analystinstitute.org/power-calculator/ (accessed June 27, 2016).

[4] As a corollary, I do not mean to suggest that small-scale organizations cannot run experiments at all. Rather, small-scale organizations gain *less value* from testing than their larger peers do, so the investment in email lists, data analysts, and analytics consultants is less worthwhile.

drawing a sample. If my 10,000 voter contacts represent the most responsive half of my district, they will be less effective on average than if they represent the most responsive 10% of my district. This is true for both experimental analytics and targeting with observational models, and is probably the harder constraint on the analytics floor."[5] His key point here is that there is a *cost* to building organizational routines around data, algorithms, and analytics. The larger the organization and the more plentiful the (internal) data, the greater the return on investment will be.

Matt Hindman (forthcoming) shows that these benefits of scale are particularly applicable to online news and entertainment businesses. Companies like Netflix, Google, and Amazon are able to incorporate testing and optimization into all of their work routines, garnering insights that their smaller, upstart competitors simply cannot match. Google's advantage in search is not just its brand name and popularity. Google's advantage is that it can run tests on petabytes of data to improve search results and web page speed. Likewise, the recommendation systems at Netflix and Amazon rest on unmatched data pools that yield them an ongoing competitive advantage. Testing and optimization become more valuable as the size of the company increases. This can lead to quasi-monopolistic outcomes, where the built-in advantages for the largest web services make them virtually immune to competition.

So, as a general principle, the power of analytic activism increases with the size and scale of the activist organization that uses it. But we can derive a few internal limitations from this principle. In particular, the impulse to increase list size can skew an organization's priorities and degrade the strategic and governance signals that an analytic activist organization can obtain. All else being equal, bigger is better. But the process of building a large list carries its own risks and challenges.

The Growthiness Imperative

To rise above the analytics floor, organizations need to expand their membership rolls (in other words, they need to acquire a lot of email addresses). This simple fact has led to an interesting term of art among netroots advocacy professionals: "growthiness." A "growthy" tactic is anything (email action alert, petition, etc.) that tends to attract new email addresses (or, technically, Facebook likes or Twitter followers—but discussions of growthiness really seem to always revolve around email list growth). Growthiness is a quality that some issues, actions,

---

[5] Personal communication, April 2014.

and messages have and others do not. Emails about local zoning regulations are (probably) not very growthy. Emails about puppies in danger are (probably) much more growthy. Growthiness is a measurable quality of campaign communications. It indicates the number of people who have taken part in your action *and are not already part of your list*. It is a mobilization metric that can be tracked through analytics, favored through algorithms, and featured in reports.

Growthy petitions tend to resonate with the current news cycle. In the aftermath of a mass shooting or an incident of police brutality, condemnations of these acts tend to perform better than they would otherwise. In the midst of viral online moments like the Ice Bucket Challenge, advocacy organizations will commonly try to link their communications to that viral moment in order to increase their potential growthiness. But it is also the case that, as we saw with Upworthy in chapter 4, some topics and frames simply tend to have more growth potential than others. Campaign finance reform tends not to be a big growth engine, nor do other stories of corporate malfeasance. Charismatic megafauna (big, cool animals like polar bears and wolves) tend to perform well, while agriculture policy does not.

Growthiness can be a deceptive metric, though. The problem is that not all potential members have equal value. If your organization works on tax policy but you run a petition about the new *Star Wars* movie trailer, then the new members who join through that petition are likely to delete, spam-filter, or unsubscribe from your detailed reports about the estate tax. If your organization is looking for members who will walk door-to-door in Minnesota in January, then signing up new members with an offer of free bumper stickers and visors will be a weak starting point.

Different advocacy organizations subscribe to different membership philosophies. Some activist groups focus primarily on aggressive, staff-driven campaigning by means of creative media and elite pressure tactics. These groups look largely to their membership for donations. Others mainly mobilize a large number of supporters to take part in low-bar actions. Still others try to develop volunteer leadership capacity and seek to build power through distributed, volunteer-led activities. Advocacy organizations do not simply want massive lists of onetime supporters who never take another action. They want to develop larger membership *programs*. And this in turn means that growthiness alone, while useful for producing the scale necessary to rise above the analytics floor, can create problems for the organization's overall mission. A growthy tactic that produces email addresses of thousands of people who will never respond to another communication results in a bigger member list, but that list size is considered a "vanity metric" (Ries 2011; Holtz 2015). It may make the organization look good on paper, but it is not an accurate indicator of strength or success.

In the dataset of Change.org/MoveOn.org featured petitions that I discussed in chapter 3, the growthiest petition appeared on Change.org with the title "International Skating Union (ISU): Open Investigation into Judging Decisions of Women's Figure Skating and Demand Rejudgement at the Sochi Olympics."[6] This was a fan petition, launched by an outraged women's figure skating enthusiast in response to a controversial decision by the Olympic judges. The petition received a total of 2,041,662 signatures (apparently it was a *really* bad decision by the judges!). Since Change.org is a nonpartisan venue for citizen-generated social petitions, it is entirely possible that those new Sochi signers went on to find other Change.org petitions that fit their interests. In fact, the company has invested heavily in machine-learning algorithms that help it estimate which petitions should be presented to which new visitors, specifically in the hope of optimizing the experience of visitors who stumble onto the site.

But imagine if the Sochi petition had instead been launched through MoveOn.org's open platform. Those 2 million new members (presuming for the moment that the overlap between US political progressives and women's figure skating devotees is slim and that the bulk of these new signers are thus not already in MoveOn's member database) would represent a 25% increase in the organization's membership rolls. Would this be a good thing or a bad thing for MoveOn? On the one hand, the organization would be able to boast to reporters and politicians that it had 10 million members rather than 8 million members. That certainly sounds like a nice benchmark. But what could MoveOn reasonably expect these new digital members to do *next*? Donate to Elizabeth Warren? Host a viewing party featuring the latest Michael Moore documentary? Call Congress to urge passage of campaign finance reform? Attend a rally or sign a petition about diplomatic relations in the Middle East? This all seems unlikely. There are many paths to civic activism, but anger at a sports judging decision on television is an exceedingly odd one.

At best, the bulk of the Sochi signers would be deadweight on MoveOn's email list. As I previously noted in *The MoveOn Effect* (Karpf 2012a), on the one hand, this deadweight is less costly in the digital era than it was in the direct mail era. The marginal cost of communicating with each additional email recipient

---

[6] Incidentally, I cannot say with certainty that the Sochi petition was, in fact, the growthiest petition in my dataset. This is because growthiness is tracked through internal analytics. Only Change.org knows how many of the Sochi petition signers were new to its system. It is theoretically possible (but extremely unlikely) that all 2 million signatures came from people who already had Change.org profiles. In that case, the petition would be responsible for zero growth. Since it was the only featured petition on either site to receive more than 1 million signatures, I think it is safe to assume that many of these signatures came from new visitors. This seems particularly likely because the petition is linked to such a major media event (Dayan and Katz 1992). But readers should keep in mind that total signatures is not equivalent to list growth.

approaches zero, while each member communication through direct mail or telephone carries a noticeable marginal cost. On the other hand, a mass of unresponsive list members like this can create major deliverability problems for the organization as a whole. As Laura Packard of PowerThru Consulting puts it, "Sending to a dead email address hurts you whether you realize it or not" (Karpf 2014a). Internet service providers (ISPs) are constantly monitoring mass email traffickers, looking to identify spam algorithmically (Brunton 2013). The cost of an email's being algorithmically labeled "spam" can range from its being diverted to the spam folder in Gmail to its being automatically rejected and left undelivered. If emails are auto-filtered into the spam folder, that is a moderate problem for digital advocacy groups. But if they are undelivered, that is an unmitigated disaster. And one of the main flags for deliverability trackers is the aggregate open rate of a mass emailer's messages. Adding 2 million new addressees who are unlikely to open your message substantially increases the risk that ISPs will block *all communications* from your organization. So while the marginal cost of each unresponsive email address approaches zero, the aggregate cost of bulk unresponsive emails can create major problems for the organization as a whole.

Yet another problem could crop up if the hypothetical new Sochi signers in fact chose to start *responding* to MoveOn emails. Since MoveOn, like many other netroots organizations, makes use of A/B testing for passive democratic feedback, acquiring a mass of new members through an issue unrelated to progressive politics could easily skew the other analytics reports that the organization relies on. Netroots practitioners employ an intriguing metaphor to refer to this problem: "the shrimp that we eat." The phrase derives from the fact that pink flamingos are not born with their colorful plumage; their feathers take on their distinctive color as a result of their food supply—the shrimp that they eat. For digital advocacy organizations, "the shrimp that we eat" is a reference to the issue topics that helped build their membership rolls. If a group initially built its list around a forestry campaign, it can expect forest-related actions to generate a particularly large response from those on the list, and (for instance) civil rights–related actions to inspire a weaker response. Organizations that use passive democratic feedback to set their issue agenda often monitor responsiveness among the existing membership to determine their course of action. In so doing, they are accepting a form of path dependence that quietly guides their work. A huge influx of members who do not share the interests and values of the organization and its existing membership can exert a subtle force, pushing the group away from its mission and core member base.

So, on the one hand, growth is imperative for organizations that wish to take advantage of analytic activist techniques. On the other hand, growth for the sake of growth can lead an activist organization away from its core mission and produce an unresponsive list that further weakens digital activist campaign techniques. The problem posed by the analytics floor cannot be solved simply by mass email acquisition. And organizations that manage to build their way above the analytics floor still confront the second boundary condition: the analytics frontier.

Defining the Analytics Frontier

There is a negative corollary to the popular slogan "You are what you measure." It goes something like this: Since some things are harder to measure than others, *you probably aren't what you don't measure.* This can be a problem for organizations that engage in analytic activism, because some of the most important features of their work are difficult to directly measure or track.

Activist organizations need more than tweets, favorites, signatures, email addresses, and donations. They need more than phone calls to legislators and bodies in the streets. They need leadership, creativity, commitment, and shared identity. As Marshall Ganz (2009, 8) puts it, effective social movement organizations need to cultivate "strategic capacity" that can help them convert "what [they] have into what [they] need to get what [they] want." Ganz himself is not a critic of digital activism per se, but he has long been a vocal proponent of building power through relationships and public narratives, neither of which are simply correlated with the easiest digital metrics.

Joy Cushman (2011), the former organizing director of the New Organizing Institute, likewise adds that social movements need "courage and commitment":

> We teach and train people to do lots of things: build strong online programs; measure the reach and effectiveness of every email and every tweet; set goals and metrics, then strategize with all the data those metrics create. All of these parts and more are critical to running ambitious, effective campaigns that engage others to win. But at the end of the day they're just the engine. . . . The fuel it takes to drive the engine, the two factors most critical to great campaigns, are things we absolutely cannot teach: Courage and Commitment. No fuel, no forward progress. And no amount of planning, data analysis or training is a substitute.

Activist organizations need numbers, but they also need *vision.* But how do you quantify, isolate, and measure vision? And if it cannot be directly measured, how do you make sure it does not disappear from your work? This question represents the theoretical puzzle at the heart of the analytics frontier. The presence of analytics-based strategic objects invites organizations to focus on what they can easily measure. That easy measurement can, in turn, exert a subtle pressure on those organizations, leading them to optimize the wrong things. As Caitlin Petre (2015) finds in her study of analytics in the digital newsroom, "The centrality of metrics to Gawker's organizational culture meant that behaviors that were hard to quantify were also hard to incentivize." The analytics frontier refers to the types of movement activity and strategic goals that are either too complex or too ephemeral to be measured by the most commonly used digital metrics and indicators. It is complicated even further by the various types of activism that advocacy groups, political associations, and social movement organizations can seek to engage in. As we will see, some types of activist engagement are much harder to measure than others.

Three Modes of Activism: Mobilizing, Organizing, and Campaigning

We've seen in the preceding two chapters that the types of analytics that activist organizations make use of vary depending on their mission, vision, and funding model. Algorithms automate and extend our value choices. Change. org optimizes for growth, uplifting personal narratives, and small, winnable fights. MoveOn.org optimizes for campaigns that appeal to its existing member base and for timely actions that productively channel progressive energy around existing political issues. Those distinct visions lead them to highlight and promote very different issues and campaigns. Alongside the trio of mission, vision, and funding model, there is another critical distinction that influences the type of analytics an organization will develop and incorporate into its work: *What role does the organization envision for its members?* There are (at least) three distinct modes of activist engagement: mobilizing, campaigning, and organizing.

In her 2014 book, *How Organizations Develop Activists*, Hahrie Han makes a crucial distinction between two modes of membership engagement. Political organizations can seek to *mobilize* supporters, or they can seek to *organize* supporters. Mobilizing, Han writes, is transactional, while organizing is transformational. "When mobilizing, civic associations do not try to cultivate the civic skills, motivations, or capacities of the people they are mobilizing. Instead they focus on maximizing numbers by activating people who already have some latent interest. Organizers, in contrast, try to transform the capacity of their members to be activists and leaders" (Han 2014, 8). Mobilizing, in other words, is about breadth of engagement. Organizing is about depth of engagement. Han finds that the strongest political associations tend to combine mobilizing with organizing, allowing them to extend the reach and commitment level of their campaign efforts.

Alongside the two categories of activity Han identifies, we can add a third: *campaigning*. Both mobilizing and organizing often occur within the context of a campaign. But the metrics we use to evaluate the success of campaigns are distinct from the metrics we use to evaluate mobilizing and organizing objectives. Mobilizing is measured by the number of people who have taken action. Organizing is measured by the strength of their engagement. Campaigning is measured by the impact on an external target. Recall Taren Stinebrickner-Kauffman's (2013) statement quoted in chapter 1: "If [your campaign strategy] happens to involve empowering people along the way, then that's great. But if you can make that change by having drinks with the nephew of a Senator, so be it." Campaigners, in a sense, are *indifferent* to member engagement. Engaging members, broadly or deeply, can at times be a valuable tactic for campaigners. But the focus of a campaigner is on winning his or her specific campaign victory. If the best route to victory is a quiet lobby visit or a noisy media stunt, a talented campaigner might find him- or herself ignoring both mobilization and organizing goals.

These modes roughly map onto what Bruce Bimber, Andrew Flanagin, and Cynthia Stohl (2012, 150) have labeled the three most-populated quadrants of "collective action space": Campaigning engages "individualist" supporters in creative actions, mobilizing engages "minimalist" supporters in mass, organization-directed moments of solidarity, and organizing engages "enthusiast" supporters who develop leadership qualities and deep organizational identity.[7] The divergent modes also relate to what Chris Wells (2015) and others have termed differences in "citizenship styles," in which younger Americans subscribe to an "actualizing" vision of citizenship that is focused on civic voluntarism and coproduction, while older Americans subscribe to a "dutiful" vision of citizenship that highlights traditional acts like voting and contacting elected officials.

As one might imagine, these three modes of activism frequently overlap. Campaigners often mobilize. Mobilizers sometimes organize. Organizers tend to base their organizing around a campaign. And the strongest organizations include a mix of these three modalities. But, critically, the three modes require different skill sets and are measured according to different outcomes. A campaigner is focused on creating leverage over the campaign target. A mobilizer is focused on demonstrating wide support and engaging a large number of people.

[7] Bimber, Flanagin, and Stohl (2012) theoretically identify a fourth quadrant, termed the "traditionalist" member, but also empirically demonstrate that this quadrant is effectively an empty set. Traditionalists exhibit a high degree of personal interaction with their fellow members, but little organizational commitment or identity. Bimber et al. (2012, 154) describe this membership style as "an interesting and odd style" and demonstrate that it appears among very few members of a diverse range of advocacy groups.

An organizer is focused on fostering civic skills and building shared identity and commitment.

I'll note here that these three modes are not an exhaustive list of activist styles. As I discussed in chapter 1, there are several types of "horizontalist" radical activism and online "hacktivism" that do not map neatly onto these three modes, or indeed within the scope of this study. Activism that directly exploits vulnerabilities in software and hardware, or activism that expands our social imagination through new forms of radical expression, tends to disagree with the reformist activist tradition on the importance of engaging the mass public and/ or traditional elite institutions. It thus requires different concepts and terminology than do mobilizing, campaigning, and organizing.

We use entirely different metrics to measure these three modes of activism. Mobilizing is measured by raw numbers. How many signatures were gathered, dollars were raised, doors were knocked on, or phone calls were made? Campaigning is measured by secondary indicators of influence. How many times has the organization appeared in mainstream media? How did the targets or opponents of the campaign action react (since, as Saul Alinsky memorably put it, "The action is in the reaction")? The executive director of one aggressive netroots campaign organization once mentioned to me that his long-term measure of success was the number of members of Congress who, if he called them, would immediately take his call. His organization is capable of mobilizing hundreds of thousands of online supporters, but he measures success in a campaigner's terms, not a mobilizer's.

You might notice that the measures of effective campaigning are not as firm and precise as the measures of effective mobilizing. We can directly measure whether our actions created a lot of noise, generated a lot of signatures, or raised a lot of money. But we cannot directly observe what a targeted decision maker would do in the absence of an activist campaign (or, more important, in reaction to a *different* series of strategic interventions from an activist campaign). So campaigners are forced to rely on secondary indicators of campaign influence.

Measuring organizing is even more complicated. How large and committed is the core leadership team? How well have they learned critical organizational skills? Are people becoming more deeply committed to the organization, and are they drawing on their creative and organizational resources to participate in strategic deliberations? Organizing is a craft; it is more art than science. As a result, the measures of successful organizing are more elusive than the measures of successful campaigning or successful mobilizing. As organizations commit themselves to "listening to the data," they face the inevitably hard problem that there is far more plentiful data related to mobilizing than to campaigning or organizing.

Perhaps the most important distinction between mobilizing and organizing is what Micah Sifry (2014a, 23) terms "atomization." In his book *The Big Disconnect*, Sifry defines atomization as "a combination of 'Let's watch it by ourselves' and 'Let's respond to it by ourselves.'" The bulk of digital activism does not rely on repeated interaction or collaboration within a community of interest. It instead consists of watching a tragedy unfold on our screens and receiving a missive from an activist organization inviting us to take action through our screens. This is commonplace within both the mobilizing and campaigning modes of action. They generate political activity, but little political *interactivity*, which in turn limits the community-building and deep, identity-based ties that social movements generally rely on.

Sifry is not rehashing the same old clicktivism tirade that routinely appears in print. He is not arguing that the Internet is only good for lightweight action or that digital campaigning and mobilizing lack meaning or value. He is instead offering a commentary on the current landscape of digital political activism. We have developed some tremendous tools for mobilizing mass publics to take part in simple acts of raising a political voice. From fundraising to petitioning to spreading political messages through likes, shares, and retweets, netroots political associations have developed a robust set of tools. But Sifry voices concern that the current landscape of digital politics features few tools for large-scale deliberation and participation. Upworthy.com's viewers, and Change.org's and (to a lesser extent) MoveOn.org's members, are atomized in this sense. Millions watch and share Upworthy content, but they do so on their own. Millions sign digital petitions, change profile photos, and post status updates, all on their own. Even when these organizations look for member input—be it through passive democratic feedback or active member surveys—that input occurs in an atomized context.[8] A mass email list is great for raising money or generating phone calls to Congress. But it is a terrible format for many-to-many conversation. Digital politics, Sifry warns, has developed its *mobilization* muscles while letting its *organizing* muscles atrophy.

And therein lies the normative challenge posed by the analytics frontier: The analytics frontier is the theoretical boundary between those activities that align with an organization's mission, vision, and business model and are easy to measure and those activities that are harder to measure. Mobilization goals are easier to measure, and they tend to overlap with the metrics developed in electoral campaigns. So there is a path-dependent bias in analytic activism that

---

[8] In a similar vein, Nick Couldry and Jose van Dijck (2015) have cautioned the research community to think hard about what it means when social media "plausibly stand in for social life itself through installing mechanisms for counting and valuing action in the very domain of everyday interaction the myth (of sociality) naturalizes."

favors mobilization over organizing metrics. As we will see, this is a permeable boundary. People are still developing and co-creating how we make use of digital technologies. Leading practitioners are aware of the analytics frontier and are working to develop alternative metrics and incentive systems.

The next section details six case examples that extend beyond the current analytics floor and analytics frontier. These case examples both flesh out the challenges posed by the two boundary conditions and highlight the agency and capacity that digital activism professionals have to affect and modify the limitations of analytic activism. The section begins with three responses to the analytics floor and then turns to three advances into the analytics frontier.

Targeting Strategic Growthiness: Coworker.org and Workplace Organizing

Coworker.org is a petition-based campaign platform. To the naked eye, the website looks similar to that of Change.org or MoveOn Petitions. In fact, the site even runs on the same software code as the open petition platforms found at Great Britain's 38 Degrees, Australia's GetUp, and America's Credo Action and Democracy for America. But there is a crucial difference between Coworker and these other digital activist organizations. Coworker is built on a distinct membership premise derived from the US labor movement. As a result, growthiness is both more constrained and more strategically valuable to the organization.

Coworker was founded in 2013 by Jess Kutch and Michelle Miller, two experienced campaigners with a background in the labor movement and in digital activism. In one sense, Coworker.org is just another open petition site. Anyone can go to the website (see figure 5.1), click "start a campaign" (figure 5.2), and develop a petition in four easy steps. What makes Coworker different is the focused niche that it is trying to fill. Coworker is devoted to supporting workplace activism among America's increasingly nonunionized workforce.

The US labor movement has faced a multi-decade decline in membership. In 1954, fully 34.8% of US workers were represented by a union. That was the peak of union membership in the United States. By 1983, that percentage had receded to 20%, and today it has further declined to 11% (DeSilver 2014). During the intervening decades, unions have become a major target of conservative legislators at the state and national levels who have introduced a range of policy initiatives that make it more difficult for unions to operate (Yeselson 2013). For years, the labor movement has attempted to halt this decline, both through aggressive political mobilization that challenges anti-labor policies and through union recruitment drives. Coworker is designed to be a new pathway for workers to engage in organizing conversations in the increasingly nonunionized portion

Figure 5.1 Coworker.org (accessed November 1, 2015)

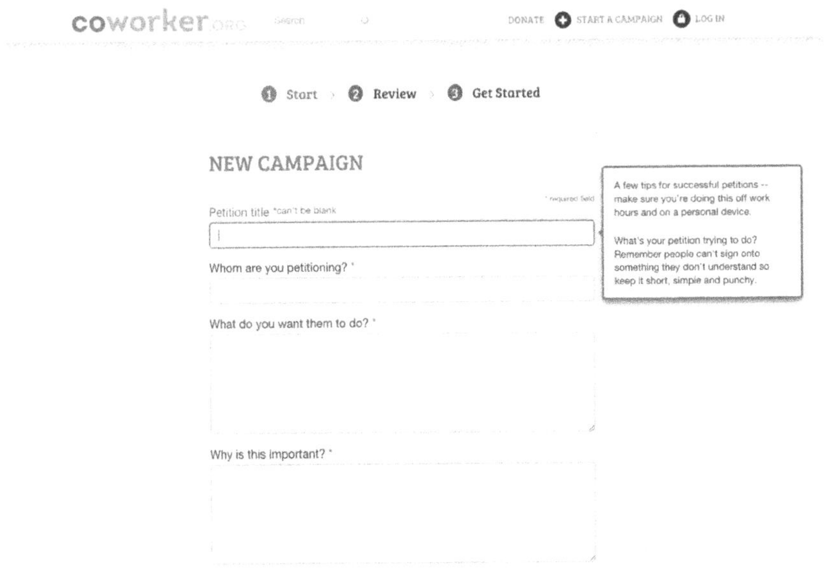

Figure 5.2 Coworker.org's petition creation page (accessed November 1, 2015)

of the US workforce. For this reason, the Obama White House partnered with Coworker for a one-day White House Summit on Worker Voice (Holst 2015).

Kutch tells the story of one particularly successful petition in a keynote speech at the 2015 Personal Democracy Forum conference, titled "Labor Codes: The Power of Employee-Led Online Organizing." In the summer of 2014, an Atlanta-area Starbucks employee, Kristie Williams, launched a Coworker petition asking her company to change its tattoo policy. Starbucks had a dress code that forbade employees to display tattoos. When the air conditioning at Williams's workplace broke down that summer, she and her fellow tattooed employees were required to wear long sleeves in the brutal Atlanta heat. Williams complained to her manager, who told her that the prohibition on visible tattoos was a national policy and the local franchise could not change it. So Williams decided to launch a petition. She reached out to her fellow Starbucks employees via Facebook groups, Twitter hashtags, and Instagram, encouraging them to sign the petition and to post photos of the tasteful tattoos that Starbucks was forcing them to cover up. The petition eventually garnered more than 25,000 signatures and convinced the company to revise its dress code (Bradford 2014).

Williams could have launched her petition at Change.org or MoveOn Petitions. These two sites have higher traffic than Coworker.org, and they likely could have helped her reach 25,000 supporters more quickly. But the key difference is that those two mammoth sites would have generated signatures from *supporters* rather than from *fellow employees.* Coworker generates fewer total signatures because it focuses on workplace organizing. This creates a different theory of membership. MoveOn uses social petitions to recruit and mobilize political progressives. Change.org uses social petitions to recruit and mobilize virtually anyone. Coworker uses petitions to encourage workers to discuss and push for better working conditions.

On its own this single victory surely felt significant to Williams and her fellow Starbucks employees, but on a grander scale it was a minor issue. The employees identified an unreasonable corporate policy. They pushed back against it. They faced resistance. They kept on pushing. The company relented. This is the (relatively) easy stuff of workplace organizing. It does not relate to wages, benefits, or the company's bottom line. But it is in the aftermath of the tattoo campaign that much more has become possible. More than 7 percent of the Starbucks workforce (more than 20,000 workers) has joined Coworker as a result of the tattoo campaign, and roughly a dozen follow-up campaigns have been launched by Williams's fellow employees. Some of these campaigns have taken on tougher issues, like wages and benefits. The victory and the media coverage it generated have also inspired dress-code campaigns at other workplaces in the service sector, including Jimmy John's, Publix, and Walmart. Every campaign launched through Coworker generates growth *within specific sectors of the US (and global) economy.* As Kutch (2015) explains, that within-sector growth "opens up a range of possibilities of what we can do together. So, we've started launching experiments around curated social content, qualitative and quantitative surveys to see what kind of tech interventions can be staged to spread workplace activism and maximize an individual worker's impact."

The important lesson we can take from Coworker is that *growthiness can be made to serve your strategic vision.* Kutch and Miller developed a vision for supporting workplace organizing in sectors of the economy that are no longer unionized. Coworker is more interested in facilitating conversations and engagement between its community members than a group like MoveOn or Change.org is. Coworker's strategic goal is to build membership within targeted sectors of the economy, listen to that membership to identify workplace organizing opportunities, and then spur workplace activism among those members. In this way, Coworker creates some of the necessary conditions for future unionization efforts. It mobilizes workers, gets them talking about workplace conditions, and demonstrates to them that they have collective power. As a result, Coworker focuses on a modified type of growthiness to help it rise above the analytics floor across a range of workplace sectors.

Upwell.us: "Your Campaign Budget Is the Internet"

> Your campaign budget is not a number in a spreadsheet. Your campaign budget is the Internet
> —Rachel Weidinger, "When Sharks Attack, Jump Into the Water"

Upwell.us was launched in 2011 as a "digital PR agency for the ocean." Even within the environmental movement, ocean concerns are mostly a niche interest. Upwell set out to raise the profile and visibility of ocean-related social issues. It was launched and incubated by the Ocean Conservancy, though Upwell explicitly set out to explore the potential for unbranded communications on social media (the goal was to increase the ocean conversation, not the Ocean Conservancy conversation). Its founder, Rachel Weidinger, was a veteran online marketer from the technology field. With Upwell, she and her team attempted to build a radically new type of digital PR operation.

Upwell had no member list. The type of internal analytics pioneered by MoveOn and the Obama campaign simply could not apply to the project. So Upwell instead decided to harvest data from social media—particularly Twitter. It purchased access to the Twitter Firehose (the full dataset of tweets over time) and it purchased Radian6, a program that helps parse, analyze, and visualize data from a variety of online media (including Twitter, Facebook, and many traditional media sources). Upwell identified a set of keyword clusters related to eight ocean issues—overfishing, sustainable seafood, marine protected areas, oceans, cetaceans (whales and dolphins), sharks, tuna, Gulf of Mexico, and ocean acidification—then used Radian6 to estimate baseline conversation levels and conversation "spikes" from the previous year (defined as one standard deviation increase in the conversation level around any given keyword cluster for a given day of the week). This data also revealed the specific actors on social media who were talking about ocean issues, and what frames and hashtags they were using in their discussion.

After spending months analyzing the state of the online ocean conversation using Radian6 and developing a transparent methodology for defining their terms and measuring their dataset, the Upwell team went to work trying to increase the baseline conversation in each of these areas, along with increasing the size and frequency of the conversational spikes (Weidinger et al. 2013). They did so through a series of "minimum viable campaigns" (MVCs), a concept that they repurposed from the Silicon Valley "lean startup" community (Ries 2011). The Upwell Campaign Lab director, Rachel Dearborn (2013), describes MVCs as campaigns that "operate on short time-frames and focus on rapid delivery of content, continuous learning and iteration." They are a bit like "throwing spaghetti against the wall," with dozens of small-scale campaigns launched in a let's-just-try-it-and-see manner. But they also tend to produce immediate feedback and can generate knowledge about how to leverage and enhance online conversation about ocean issues.

Upwell focused on "network capacity-building," specializing in developing unbranded social media content that allied individuals and organizations could use to promote ocean issues. Over its three years of operation, Upwell built a strong reputation for (1) developing and promoting visual memes and infographics, (2) engaging within existing conversations by retweeting and replying to ocean advocates, (3) organizing nimble social media campaigns that made use of a "build-measure-learn" cycle that generated immediate results, and (4) sharing their findings widely though online webinars. According to Matt Fitzgerald, Upwell's Attention Lab director, "content became a gateway to connection."[9] By creating unbranded content, carefully measuring results, and freely sharing its findings, Upwell was able to notably strengthen community and coordination and collaboration within the ocean advocacy community.

When Weidinger says "your campaign budget is the Internet," what she means is that advertising and public relations can be leveraged and spread

---

[9] Interview notes, Matt Fitzgerald, February 26, 2016.

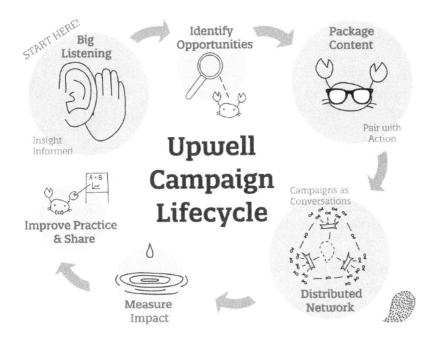

Figure 5.3 The Upwell.us campaign cycle

through networked advocates, reaching far more people than they could when confined to paid commercials. Figure 5.3, from Upwell's 2013 pilot report, makes this point graphically with its depiction of the organization's campaign cycle. The most critical elements of this campaign cycle are the "Big Listening" and "Distributed Network" stages, which are designed as a departure from more traditional PR campaigning.

Much of the value of big listening comes from identifying opportunities for engagement that traditional advocacy nonprofits might be unaware of. In Upwell's case, this lesson became particularly clear when it observed how the online conversation about sharks dramatically changed during the Discovery Channel's annual Shark Week. "The biggest takeaway was that Shark Week is responsible for the single largest spike in the online shark conversation for the entire year, and that spike eclipsed every other spike in every ocean topic we monitor. Put simply: Shark Week is the Super Bowl of the online ocean conversation" (Weidinger et al. 2013, 71). The marine conservation community has largely avoided Shark Week online, viewing it as sensationalized and negative. Upwell conducted a content analysis of Shark Week–related tweets and found it was mostly an enthusiastic fan conversation. Upwell shared these findings with ocean advocacy professionals in a "Sharkinar" online workshop. And, as we will see, these "big listening" and network capacity-building

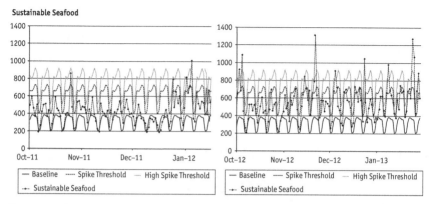

Figure 5.4 Twitter conversation about sustainable seafood keyword group in Winter 2011 and Winter 2012 (reported in Upwell pilot report)

practices resulted in a substantial increase in the online conversation about ocean issues.

Upwell is instructive in two ways. First, it demonstrates the potential value of external analytics to small organizations with limited budgets. As Fitzgerald told me, even if an organization is below the analytics floor, "you can still use listening. You can still be data-informed, and data-driven."[10] As reported in the organization's first-year pilot report, Upwell was very successful in increasing online conversation about all of its topics (see figure 5.4). These may not be tangible campaign victories, with legislators or corporations adopting ocean-friendly positions, but they are a necessary first step in that direction. As we saw with Upworthy in chapter 4, increasing engagement with political topics is a useful element of political persuasion efforts, and social media creates new opportunities for promoting these conversations.

But there is a second, less positive lesson we can take from Upwell. Despite its early success, the organization announced in January 2015, "After two years of exploring a variety of funding options and models, we've been unable to secure dedicated ocean funding that is sufficient to maintain our core ocean programming" (Dearborn 2015). Upwell's findings had been heavily distributed, its work had been frequently celebrated, and it was widely treated as a successful and promising experiment. But the organization lacked a clear funding model and had no membership base to sustain it. After the original pilot funding from the Ocean Conservancy ran out, Upwell became yet another piece of well-loved infrastructure that died for lack of funding.

The eventual fate of Upwell is particularly instructive when we compare it with a similar organization, CrowdTangle.com, which created a big listening type of

[10] Interview notes, Matt Fitzgerald, February 26, 2016.

product oriented toward Facebook. Brandon Silverman, the former communications director of the Center for Progressive Leadership, launched CrowdTangle in 2011 to help activist organizations make sense of the online Facebook conversation. He initially intended it to be an activist toolset, but later came to recognize its potential niche within more traditional media and marketing industries. In 2015, a journalist at *Fast Company* magazine dubbed CrowdTangle "the secret tool that Upworthy, Buzzfeed, and everyone else is using to win Facebook" (Kessler 2015). The logic of CrowdTangle's model is relatively simple (even if the underlying math and software code get complicated). CrowdTangle tracks clusters of Facebook pages and specific keywords. It gathers historical data on how stories, posts, and images tend to perform on these sites and then highlights the stories, posts, and images that are doing best against their own expected baseline performance rate. Silverman's company then packages this information in a daily email, alerting his clients to the content that is likely to perform best on a day-to-day basis.

In a case like this, return on investment is of paramount importance. Recall that internal analytics yield an increasing return as the scale of the organization increases. External analytics of the sort that Upwell and CrowdTangle were conducting can also provide real value to advocacy and activist campaigns. But that value is generally not directly tied to membership recruitment or donations. During the same years that Upwell struggled to develop a stable funding model within the ocean funding community, CrowdTangle flourished by offering its external analytics product to companies like PBS, Univision, MTV, and Major League Baseball. It simultaneously maintained contracts with dozens of nonprofit advocacy organizations, staying true to the values and vision of its founder. CrowdTangle developed a profitable business model based on its external analytics work, while Upwell looked to maintain charitable funding from foundations and major donors. CrowdTangle carved out a market niche as a for-profit business, while Upwell tried to subsist on consulting contracts to sustain the infrastructural services it was providing to the broader progressive communities. Without a grassroots supporter base, Upwell was left to the whim of progressive donors, while CrowdTangle expanded through its business contracts.

Social listening tools like Upwell and CrowdTangle can offer substantial value to activist organizations and causes that rest below the analytics floor. They dip into the sea of digital sentiment that is available through social media channels and help both to identify moments when a small, niche issue is attracting greater attention and allies who care about that issue. External analytics can help small organizations make sense of the fast-moving hybrid media system. But for internal growth and capacity-building, the analytics floor continues to be a limiting factor.

Figure 5.5 Share page optimized by ShareProgress

List-Pooling to Achieve Scale: ShareProgress.org

Sign a petition at Greenpeace, Sierra Club, Planned Parenthood, Credo Action, or more than 60 other advocacy websites and you'll find yourself immediately staring at a "share page" (figure 5.5). These share pages are designed to encourage social sharing through email, Facebook, and Twitter. They are critical for maximizing list growth and helping political messages to spread beyond a core activist base. And every one of these pages looks exactly the same.

This is not merely a case of imitation as the sincerest form of flattery. It's the product of a third-party vendor called ShareProgress. ShareProgress is run by technologist Jim Pugh, the former director of analytics & development at Organizing for America and former chief technology officer of RebuildtheDream.org. The organization defines its mission as "help[ing] progressive organizations achieve success through the use of data and technology. Innovations in these fields have made it possible to organize and campaign more effectively than ever before, but most groups don't have the knowledge or ability to take advantage of these advances. We help progressive organizations harness these innovations for their work."[11] Put more plainly, ShareProgress helps smaller organizations benefit from digital testing and analytics. It does this by running experiments that are broadly relevant within the

---

[11] http://www.shareprogress.org/about/ (accessed November 11, 2015).

progressive advocacy world and then drawing from its large list of nonprofit clients to create the necessary scale to run these experiments effectively. All the organizations that partner with ShareProgress then reap value from its findings.

ShareProgress is representative of a broader route around the problem posed by the analytics floor. By pooling the traffic to an expansive list of organizations, Pugh and his team can run a wide range of experiments and optimization tests that benefit all of the participating organizations. We see a similar pattern among technology vendors like Blue State Digital and NationBuilder, which offer software as a service to their advocacy and electoral clients and are able to incorporate user experience and feedback into the code base for future releases of the software. Likewise, Nathan Woodhull at ControlShift Labs supplies the distributed petition platform that is used by Coworker, Credo Action, Democracy for America, 350.org, and a number of international organizations. Woodhull's team is able to improve their product by experimenting and optimizing across multiple organizations. Wide adoption of his software increases the power of the toolset for all of the organizations involved.

While this list-pooling activity is valuable for small organizations, it is still a limited form of analytic activism. The problem is that, although third-party vendors like ShareProgress are hugely valuable for tactical optimization, and other third-party vendors can fashion reports that capture passive democratic feedback, they do not provide the flexibility or speed necessary for larger-scale computational management routines. ShareProgress increases social sharing for dozens of organizations, but it does not provide tangible strategic objects that can affect day-to-day decision making. Exporting data to ShareProgress means moving from a reliance on internal analytics to a reliance on external analytics. And that limits the range of what an activist organization can do with its data.

Coworker's approach to strategically targeted membership growth, Upwell's approach to big listening through external analytics, and ShareProgress's approach to list-pooling as a means of expanding the scale of digital experiments represent the three primary routes around the challenge posed by the analytics floor. The next set of examples reveal how organizations have navigated the second boundary condition, creating new metrics and incentives to expand into the analytics frontier.

Replacing List Growth: SumOfUs.org's New Metrics

Growthiness is just one metric that netroots organizations can focus on. It is easy to calculate, necessary for achieving scale, and particularly valuable to any organization attempting to rise above the analytics floor. But, as we saw previously in this chapter, it can also be a deceptive metric, particularly when it produces hollow list growth through the addition of new supporters who are unlikely to take future actions. Some netroots organizations have, in fact, found that "the most viral campaigns attract the least returning members."[12] For large-scale digital organizations, list growth simply isn't the right metric to focus on. Some of them have decided to replace it with an alternative metric.

Tara Harwood is the manager of analytics and data science at SumOfUs.org. SumOfUs (whose founder, Taren Stinebrickner-Kauffman, was quoted earlier) is one of the leading corporate campaign organizations in the world. Since SumOfUs's founding in 2011, it has rapidly achieved a global membership of more than 10 million while running aggressive campaigns targeting companies like Apple, United Airlines, and Monsanto. But if you visit SumOfUs's website, you will see no mention of the organization's total membership list. That's because Harwood has concluded that membership is a vanity metric. "In our case, looking at the number of mailable members lets us know that we are bringing people in, but doesn't tell us anything about whether we are truly building a movement to challenge corporate power. . . . To increase the power of our movement, we needed to shift to metrics that measure member engagement, not just acquisition."[13]

In 2014, under Harwood's direction, SumOfUs developed a new metric called MeRA (members returning for action). MeRA is defined as "the number of unique members who have taken an action other than their first one." This is an executive-level metric, calculated on a monthly basis and used by the organization's leadership to monitor the health of the organization. Rather than prioritizing campaigns that lead to list growth, SumOfUs prioritizes campaigns that lead to ongoing engagement from those on its supporter list. SumOfUs has also developed a workflow metric called ARRRG (action rate + reactivation rate + growth) for monitoring day-to-day campaign activities. Action rate is a measure of actions taken across the entire list. Reactivation rate is a measure of actions taken by existing members who have not taken action recently. Growth is a measure of new member acquisitions. The difference between ARRRG and MeRA is that MeRA is calculated retrospectively, at the end of the month. While MeRA is valuable for monthly and quarterly direction setting and review, as a strategic object it is ill-suited to the day-to-day organizational workflow of a SumOfUs campaigner—you cannot run an A/B test or compare two potential campaign options according to daily MeRA statistics. ARRRG provides a more useful strategic object for the day-to-day work of SumOfUs's digital campaigners.

[12] Interview notes, Tara Harwood, October 14, 2015.
[13] Interview notes, Tara Harwood, October 14, 2015.

MeRA and ARRRG are examples of the new tools that analytic activist organizations are developing, tools that stretch beyond standard practices and help expand the analytics frontier. Optimizing for growthiness is not the same as optimizing for effectiveness. This does not mean that analytic activist groups are destined to produce lightweight clicktivist campaign tactics. It simply means that these groups have to do additional work in order to develop metrics that track better with their definition of effectiveness. For Change.org, growthiness largely *is* equivalent to effectiveness. That's because the organization does not have a specific political mission; it simply wants to engage the most people it can. For Coworker, growthiness *in particular sectors* is also equivalent to effectiveness, because building membership density within an individual company or sector of the economy is a necessary precondition of deeper workplace organizing campaigns. For SumOfUs and its peer organizations, membership size is less important than what those members are willing and likely to *do*. So SumOfUs invents different metrics and tunes its algorithms and workflows toward MeRA instead of member growth.

Alongside measuring MeRA and ARRRG, Harwood leads an internal team at SumOfUs, called Optimise Prime.[14] Optimise Prime plays a role similar to that of the Analytics Whiteboard at 38 Degrees (discussed in chapter 1). They brainstorm and develop internal experiments that produce workable insights for the organization's campaign work. These experiments can include modifications to the website, changes to campaign messaging and framing, and novel strategic campaign efforts. By developing the right measurement schemes, Harwood and her team are able to run more valuable experiments, which in turn strengthen the organization's campaign endeavors.

Harwood and SumOfUs are not alone in their concern with vanity metrics in analytic activism. In 2015, Greenpeace Mobilization Lab and Citizen Engagement Lab commissioned a report titled "Beyond Vanity Metrics," which drew on the insights and experiences of campaign organizations, consultancies and incubators, technology vendors, and leading researchers to highlight the pitfalls of commonly used metrics (list size, petition signatures, open rates, website traffic, etc.) and move the netroots community toward savvier analytics practices (Holtz 2015).

Michael Silberman, director of Greenpeace Mobilization Lab, and Jackie Mahendra, director of strategic collaboration of Citizen Engagement Lab, summarize the findings of that report by highlighting four themes that emerge when an organization attempts to move beyond vanity metrics. First, they argue that "rates trump aggregates." The rate of membership engagement and the rate of

---

[14] Yes, like the Transformer. SumOfUs seems like a fun place to work.

membership growth tend to be more valuable indicators of organizational success than the total list size or total actions taken. Second, "tracking cohorts reveals valuable trends." Rather than treating the entire member list as a single unit, they recommend identifying specific subgroups that share a common characteristic, then performing experiments to see how these cohorts react. Third, "scoring reveals levels of engagement." Organizations are developing massive databases of second-party, internal analytic information about which members take which actions related to which issues. This data can lie fallow, or it can be converted into "engagement scores," which help indicate which members are most likely to engage in which ways. Fourth, "simplicity can be your friend." Analytics and algorithms are valuable only if they can be translated into workable insights for campaigners and organizers. Metrics should be designed to help organizations make decisions, and this often requires simplifying their outputs (Silberman and Mahendra 2015).

SumOfUs is primarily a campaign organization. It hires talented, creative, hard-working campaigners and empowers them to stir up trouble for corporations. SumOfUs primarily wants members who "open [emails], read, take action, donate, share, and participate in higher-bar actions," and it cares more about the actions they take than their total numbers.[15] This is, for the most part, an atomized, organization-to-member interaction model. SumOfUs does not envision or invest in a membership that actively deliberates, debates, or strategizes around campaign initiatives. In the typology developed earlier, it focuses on the campaigning and mobilizing modes of activism. What types of analytics do groups that focus on organizing make use of? To answer this question, let's turn to a digital activist group that has centered its membership model on organizing: 350.org.

350.org and Distributed Organizing

350.org is a digital climate justice organization with a unique lineage that in turn drives its membership model. Bill McKibben, a writer and professor who was among the first to alert the mass public to the threat of climate change (with his 1989 book, *The End of Nature*), and seven of his students at Middlebury College organized the Step It Up day of action in 2007 (see chapter 1). Step It Up used the Internet to organize more than 1,400 simultaneous protest events across the country. Rather than call for a single massive rally in Washington or New York City, the Middlebury team believed they could harness more public energy,

---

[15] Interview notes, Tara Harwood, October 14, 2015.

ignite more long-term activism, and capture more public attention (through multiplied local media coverage) by uniting thousands of simultaneous events under the same banner. Step It Up leveraged existing social and digital networks (through Facebook, for instance) as well as organizational networks of climate activists to plan these events; organizations like the Sierra Club, Greenpeace, MoveOn, and Energy Action Coalition all took on publicizing, promoting, and organizing the events (Fisher and Boekkooi 2010). The whole thing was coordinated through a simple website where visitors could find or create local events and pledge to participate. The rallying cry for Step It Up was climate scientist James Hansen's claim that the atmospheric concentration of carbon dioxide could not rise above 350 parts per million if the world wanted to avoid catastrophic global warming. After the event, McKibben and his team formed 350. org to move forward with this model of distributed climate activism.

As a result, 350.org has a strikingly different membership model than most netroots organizations. The sheer list size and growthiness that are common among petition-based mobilization efforts are almost entirely absent from 350's activism work (see Hestres 2014, 2015; Liacas 2015). Instead, 350 focuses on "high-bar" engagement tactics from the outset. Rather than building a large list through a Change.org-style petition, then encouraging those members to sign another petition, make a donation, email a legislator, and then (eventually, perhaps) attend an in-person event, 350.org immediately asks potential members to join a local group and get involved by planning local actions and events (see figure 5.6). Those local groups then wage climate campaigns in their own cities, towns, and states, and also come together for national and international protests, marches, and rallies.

I asked Phil Aroneanu, US managing director and cofounder of 350.org, what the organization looks for from its members. His response was, "In short, we want people who are ready to get out of their armchairs and take action in the streets, together. Beyond that, we want folks who are going to organize and mobilize their friends and family members, run local climate campaigns, and pitch in when we push campaigns out from the national level."[16]

This is an organizing-centric membership model. It has fostered a style of digital engagement that focuses much more on identifying, supporting, and coaching local leadership than on monitoring and promoting atomistic actions by the mass membership. In the organization's 2014 annual report, the metrics it focuses on are all related to the size and scale of the events it planned rather than on sheer list size or the number of online actions its members had taken. The organization's staff is strongly committed to building a culture of "trust and

---

[16] Personal communication, November 2, 2015.

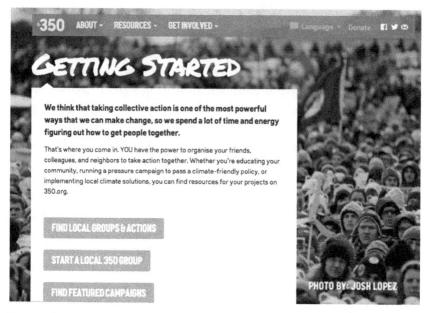

Figure 5.6 Screenshot of 350.org's "Getting Started" web page (November 3, 2015)

support" among its network of local leaders. This is both due to a belief that change needs to start at the local level (the old environmental slogan, "Think globally, act locally") and due to the requirements of its national- and global-scale events. Planning a series of Step It Up–style actions requires strong relationships between local leaders and the national organization. Planning an anti-Keystone XL civil disobedience event where thousands will risk arrest requires commitment and a shared identity (McAdam 1999). 350.org has a US-based staff of just 30 people.[17] It is far more efficient for those staffers to develop strong relationships with reliable volunteer leaders around the nation (and the globe!) than to independently try to set up thousands of simultaneous events several times per year. The types of campaign tactics that 350.org prefers favor an organizing-based membership strategy.

Interestingly, 350.org's website does include an open petition platform (campaigns.350.org). This platform was designed by Nathan Woodhull at ControlShift Labs, and it features the same optimized share page (through ShareProgress) that you would find at Coworker, Credo Action, and dozens of other sites. But where Coworker.org makes "start a campaign" the most prominent feature of its website, 350.org's website features a map of local groups that visitors can join. The petition tool is available to 350.org's activist community,

---

[17] Globally, 350.org has roughly 120 staffers.

but the organization's emphasis is on using its digital tools to funnel people toward offline activism.

While 350.org is a digital-native, netroots organization, its leadership does not directly perceive its work as analytics-heavy. This, I would argue, is because the organization has been working since its inception to address the challenges posed by the analytics frontier. 350.org does not focus on the types of outcome variables (list growth, fundraising totals, etc.) that electoral campaigns have traditionally optimized for. It also does not focus on the types of atomistic outcome variables most commonly employed by Internet-mediated issue generalist groups like MoveOn.org (passive democratic feedback for issue prioritization, fundraising, low-bar online actions). It instead has focused on what Tom Liacas (2015) calls "distributed action":

> Distributed action is an approach to movement-building that encourages self-starting local groups. Over the last 15 years, this strategy has grown in parallel with social networks, which now make it possible on a larger scale. . . . Most famously, it was the driving force behind the spontaneous spread of the Occupy Wall Street movement from a single New York protest to 951 cities. 350.org, for its part, has taken on the distributed action model by handing control of its digital platforms over to its followers, letting them build their own local chapters and even plan their own events.[18]

350.org is indeed engaging in analytic activism, and it is charting an essential part of the analytics frontier in the process. The organization employs digital tools to listen to its membership. It runs experiments, it measures success, and it crafts digital data into strategic objects that help guide strategic decision making. The difference between 350.org's "distributed actions" and Change.org's petition-based campaigns is based on which metrics the organizations assign value to. 350.org uses data to help identify which volunteers are showing leadership potential. It uses data to help assign its scarce resource (staff coaching and support) to the volunteer units that need it most. This makes 350.org different from the distributed Occupy Wall Street movement in an important way: OWS used distributed tools to help the movement spread, but it had no core leadership that was capable of monitoring the health of the movement, learning from the success or failure of movement tactics, or otherwise *digitally listening* to the outputs of those distributed tools. OWS was engaged in digitally enabled activism, but

---

[18] This strategy is similar to the one originally adopted by Democracy for America in the aftermath of the 2004 Howard Dean campaign, which I termed a "neo-federated" organizational model in my previous book (Karpf 2012, ch. 4).

it was not particularly engaged in analytic activism, because it lacked a central core that could convert analytics into strategic objects. 350.org partially shares OWS's distributed tactical repertoire, but it deploys that repertoire in a different way because of the feedback and learning it gains over time.

The Analytics Frontier for Governance: The AFL-CIO's Experiment in Governance Gamification

> Enter this site and the more you do to help a candidate, campaign,
> or cause, the more power you get to wield. The more doors you
> knock, conversations you have, the louder your voice. Loud enough
> to be heard all across America. You want some extra canvassers out
> in the streets of Milwaukee? Done. You want another ad put up in
> Reno, Nevada? It's up. How about some extra phone bankers in
> Orlando? Deal."
> —YouTube video, "Introducing RePurpose"

The single most ambitious response to the analytics frontier was a pilot project launched by the AFL-CIO's Workers Voice Political Action Committee (PAC) in the late stages of the 2012 election. The pilot project was called "RePurpose," and it represented a massive reorientation of the way an advocacy group interacts with, listens to, and incentivizes its members. The project operated only during the final six weeks of the 2012 election, so it serves more as a theoretical proof-of-concept than as a full-fledged case of analytic activism applied to governance. Still, the implications of this project are far-reaching enough that they are worth dwelling upon at length.

A YouTube video produced by Workers Voice PAC and headlined "RePurpose Tutorial" helpfully explains how RePurpose works:

> Our movement should be guided by the people building it. That belief is the founding principle of RePurpose. Here's how. Jesse volunteers at his local field office. And knocks on 50 doors for candidate Jones. Jesse turns in his walk packet and the next day receives an email letting him know he has earned 100 points in RePurpose. Jesse logs into RePurpose and looks at different ways he can redeem his points to direct the campaign's strategy and tactics to other volunteers. Jesse chooses to spend his points to sponsor a local phone bank for local candidate Smith. Next week, the campaign sets up Jesse's phone bank to make calls for candidate Smith. Sue and Steve make calls for candidate Smith and earn

points in RePurpose. RePurpose lets you make the decisions that help us win elections. It's time to get to work. Work connects us all.

This theme of "work" is particularly resonant for a labor PAC. The logic of this system is simple: The more productive time and energy you contribute to the success of the organization, the more voice you will have in determining its strategic direction. RePurpose is based on the underlying value proposition that work should be rewarded and workers should have a voice.

RePurpose is an innovative attempt at applying the logic of "gamification" to political campaign work and to connect the project's analytics to the activities that matter most to the organization's ultimate success. Gamification is defined as the act of adding "game mechanics" to non-game social interactions (think FourSquare/Swarm check-ins and badges, or upvoting and downvoting on Reddit, or Fitbit's Leaderboards). As Josh Lerner (2014, 4), executive director of the Participatory Budgeting Project, describes it in his book *Making Democracy Fun*, "Games are designed to be enjoyable, and democracy is not. Game designers work tirelessly to craft enjoyable experiences, drawing on the rich lessons of game design theory and practice. Designers of democratic processes are in fact largely unaware of these lessons." Most attempts at gamification in politics have focused on awarding points or digital "badges" to members who take part in repeated tasks (Pugh 2015). The Obama campaign, for instance, included some gamification features in its digital platform (my.BarackObama.com, nicknamed "MyBO"). Volunteers logged into MyBO could view a personalized analytics dashboard of their activity with the campaign, alongside a point system that encouraged them to aim for higher "scores."

The research on campaign gamification has produced mixed results so far. The problem, generally speaking, is that the introduction of points and credits tends to commodify the relationship between the organization and its members. If you make 100 phone calls for an advocacy group, and the group rewards you with a T-shirt, you might pause for a moment to wonder whether that T-shirt was worth all the work you just provided *for free*. Put another way, gamifying the work of social movements can coarsen the identity-based relationships that social movements are trying to strengthen. If politics is, as Max Weber put it, "a strong and slow boring of hard boards," then gamifying politics runs the risk of reminding committed partisans that there are more enjoyable things they could be doing with their time.

There is a key difference between the RePurpose experiment and other attempts to gamify politics, though: RePurpose is an attempt at *governance gamification*. Instead of rewarding volunteers with T-shirts, levels, or digital badges, Workers Voice PAC connected the point system to actual strategic resources within the organization. This makes it more akin to participatory budgeting practices, which Hollie Russon Gilman (2016, 3) credits for "engaging citizens to form new civic relationships and become meaningful participants in democracy." As Nicole Aro, the AFL-CIO's deputy digital director, explained it, "The theory of change behind this is that we will actually empower volunteers literally down to where we spend money. We hope that that will really help folks to feel empowered, and really incentivize them to come in and take ownership" (Stirland 2012).

In the six weeks leading up to the 2012 election, members of the AFL-CIO demonstrated exactly what was possible with such a system. Thousands of volunteers donated their RePurpose points to help direct AFL-CIO resources toward a burgeoning campaign to boycott American Crystal Sugar, which in turn pushed the organization to aggressively commit to this campaign priority.

RePurpose is perhaps best understood as a much more active and transparent form of the *passive democratic feedback* that MoveOn first developed a decade earlier. MoveOn and similar netroots organizations gauge the will of the membership by monitoring which issues, frames, and actions receive the most attention and activity. Passive democratic feedback allows digital activist groups to identify opinion signals from their issue public, without that public actively recognizing that they are engaging in the governance conversation. It is listening without conversation, and thus gathers valuable opinion traces in silence. RePurpose, instead, begins by identifying the types of *activist work* that the organization values most in its campaigning. It makes the value of that work public, through a transparent scoring system, and then it vocally asserts the principle that "the people who do the work of our movement should have a voice in leading it."[19] In effect, the transparent scoring and clear routes to governance authority make programs like RePurpose more active and more conversational. Members know that they are being tracked, they know what activities are valued, and they are given room to express their own perspectives on the direction of the organization.

The transparency of RePurpose also renders it a much more radical analytics intervention than SumofUs's MeRA and ARRRG systems. MeRA is an executive metric and ARRRG is a workflow metric. Both are campaigner-facing metrics meant to capture and reward the types of campaign activity that align with SumofUs's vision of power-building. But SumofUs's members never directly grapple with MeRA or ARRRG, while RePurpose points increase the capacity of active members to engage in the strategic direction-setting conversation. RePurpose makes public Workers Voice PAC's vision of power-building and invites supporters to actively participate in making that vision a reality.

---

[19] http://repurpose.workersvoice.org/how_it_works (accessed April 14, 2016).

It is too early to make any specific claims about the potential of governance gamification systems like RePurpose for activist organizations. There are hard technical challenges to implementing it at scale: How does a system like this get launched? How do core volunteers learn the system? What percentage of the budget should be devoted to gamified governance? What risks of manipulating (or "gaming") the system does the organization face, and how can an organization mitigate those risks?

Nonetheless, if there is one silver-bullet solution to the analytics frontier, it likely will be found through some version of governance gamification. Gamifying governance forces an organization to think clearly and transparently about what it wants from its members. Does it want them to mobilize, to donate, to campaign, to recruit their friends, or to organize? If the danger posed by the analytics frontier is that it will tempt activist organizations to settle for the metrics that are easiest to track, then governance gamification demands of those same organizations that they think hard about what activist activities they value, what metrics they can commit to prioritizing and monitoring, and then render these measures public, open to scrutiny and debate. If an activist organization can effectively navigate those challenges, governance gamification potentially helps send a clear signal of what the group values and creates positive rewards that foster leadership and organizational identity among the volunteers who share the same vision.

Conclusion

The analytics floor and the analytics frontier are theoretical guideposts. They are meant to help with sorting through the hype surrounding "big data" and "disruption." Put plainly, analytic activism is a powerful toolset for improving activist tactics, strategic decision making, membership feedback, and internal learning and innovation practices. The power of analytics increases with the size and scale of an organization's list, but only to the extent that the organization is building the right *kind* of list and asking supporters to do the right *kinds* of things. Analytic activism values growthiness, but it also requires a clear plan for what type of growth is required. Analytic activism tracks outcomes, so it also requires intentional planning to ensure that the right types of outcomes are being measured through the right metrics. None of this is settled, particularly because so much of the political analytics industry has been created through work in the conceptually simple electoral arena.

There is a normative danger in analytic activism, a fear that the data is leading activists astray. Its naive form is often voiced by op-eds and blog posts decrying clicktivism. Its more sophisticated form is found at activist conferences and in internal reports that discuss "the shrimp that we eat" and the dangers posed by "vanity metrics." The danger is that the focus on analytics in activism will unintentionally privilege the types of mobilizing and campaigning for which there is an abundance of data. It poses the threat of "mission drift" and the threat that the easy availability of analytics data—both external and internal—will potentially affect activists' sense of the possible.

In the final chapter of this book, I take this normative danger seriously and highlight the types of work necessary to avoid the warping influence that analytics, algorithms, and metrics can have on twenty-first-century social movements. The chapter highlights the major themes and findings of this book, while also paying particular attention to the *biases* of analytic activism—or what the data *doesn't* tell us.

6

What Is Left Undone

As we entered the twenty-first century, political scientist Steven Schier offered a provocative critique of modern interest group politics in his book, *By Invitation Only* (2000). The book draws a distinction between the mass mobilization that characterized nineteenth- and early-twentieth-century politics and the narrow "activation" that emerged during the late-twentieth-century industrial broadcast era.[1] His critique could easily have been aimed at present-day analytic activists. Schier writes:

> Activation strategies . . . mobilize strategic minorities while cloaking the effort in a misleading guise of popular rule. (15)
>
> The new technology lowers the costs of activation. Identifying supporters and communicating with them is easier than ever before in national politics. The technology is also widely available and transportable. One can arrange state-of-the-art communication from anywhere in the country. All this should stimulate group formation and the uses of activation. With ever more activators operating, competitively successful activation becomes more difficult, particularly when each individual candidate or organization has limited resources. Hence *activation involves narrow, precise targeting of the public in order to be successful.* Gone are the days when large partisan organizations could monopolize resources for mobilization and engage the general public broadly at election time. The new modus operandi involves slicing surgically into the public to bring out just the right segment to vote in an election or make a spiel to government. (30–31, emphasis added)
>
> Activation engenders a seemingly "spontaneous" voice in fact produced by elite, entrepreneurial calculation. The goal of activation is results, not discussion as an end in itself. (37)

[1] For the sake of clarity, I should note that what I and other contemporary researchers now refer to as "mobilization" is equivalent to what Schier labels "activation."

The story Schier is telling should be familiar to us now. Though he was taking aim at the interest groups and political campaigns of the 1990s, he could easily have been assessing the rise of big data, analytics, A/B testing, and microtargeting. Reduced to its essence, Schier's warning goes something like this: *New communications technologies yield greater efficiency. That greater efficiency has the potential to wreak havoc on our democracy. Beware.* And if there was cause for concern in the 1990s, then we should surely be petrified now. We have replaced beepers and 56K modems with iPhones and Wi-Fi. There is more data, everywhere, than ever before. And that data will only become richer and more sophisticated in the years to come. Much as when one rereads Neil Postman's broadside critique of the broadcast era, *Amusing Ourselves to Death* (1985),[2] one is left with the suspicion that Schier is raising the specter of critical social issues a decade or two before his time. (*If only* we could return to the broadcast distractions of the television age! *If only* we could go back to an activist politics of handwritten letters and protest marches!)

Returning to the days of torchlight processionals, handwritten letters, or the captive broadcast audience is not an option. We cannot wish away the problems of the digital media landscape, nor can we reclaim the spirit and insights of social movements past by replicating their tactics and rhetoric.[3] Much of the power of successful social movement tactics is based in an insightful reading of the present media system. And just as earlier social movement leaders developed a keen understanding of their media system, so too must we come to understand our own. The social movement tactics that were designed to exploit the industrial broadcast system are losing their bite in the hybrid media system. The tactics that thrive in the current moment are designed to leverage social media and networked publics (Barberá et al. 2015; Gonzalez-Bailon and Wang 2016; Freelon, McIlwain, and Clark 2016). They also benefit from the conditions for rigorous learning and experimentation that were previously much harder to create in the field. We no longer have to select tactics because they are the ones we've always used or because we recall that one time when they appeared to work so well. In the face of a tactical dilemma, the appropriate and available answer is now "Well, we'll test it."[4]

---

[2] Postman was worried about the distractions created by broadcast television. If only he had been around to see us put captions on cat photos.

[3] Even if we could replicate the movement structures and media systems of the past, we would surely be reminded that those same tactics, technologies, and organizational strategies were themselves subject to fierce criticism.

[4] This culture of testing extends beyond digital tactics. David Broockman and Joshua Kalla (2016) recently demonstrated the value of persuasive door-to-door conversations in reducing persistent transphobic prejudices. Door-to-door canvasses are about as analog of a political tactic as one can imagine. But the research, conducted through rigorous field experiments, nonetheless drew on the new culture of testing and experimentation that has led frontline activist organizations to start partnering with social scientists to measure the effectiveness of their tactics.

This is not to suggest that analytic activist tactics and strategies are without their limitations or that some elements of the industrial broadcast media system weren't helpful to activist causes. We are living through an era of extraordinary political polarization, wealth inequality, and government dysfunction. There are no easy solutions to the challenges that face activist movements. If the problems that motivate social justice activists were easy to solve, they would have been solved already. So the goal of this book has been to help understand the opportunities, challenges, and threats that activist practitioners face as we move forward.

I have taken care in this book to rebut the common charges of "clicktivism" and "slacktivism," on the one hand, and "spontaneous bottom-up online movements," on the other. Both these perspectives are rooted in imaginary ideals— either of what activism once was or of what we imagine activism ought to be. The difference between frivolous clicktivism and powerful digital activism generally depends on the broader strategic and organizational contexts where vision, learning, and leadership come into play. Data and analytics become useful and powerful only when treated as strategic objects. The hybrid media system offers new leverage points for social movement organizations, weakening some old political tactics and strengthening others. Apparently-spontaneous digital movements rely on an infrastructure of digital organizations (both petition sites like Change.org and social network sites like Twitter and Facebook) that have their own internal organizational logics. For exactly that reason, I have attempted throughout this book to take organizations seriously as an object of analysis.

But, in this final chapter, it seems appropriate to take up the mantle of Schier and other social critics. Analytic activism is built on new forms of listening. Indeed, the activist organizations described in this book are likely better at listening to their members and supporters than any organizations that came before them. But, as Micah Sifry (2014a) notes in *The Big Disconnect*, this style of activism is characterized by *listening without conversation*. It used to be hard to find out what 10,000 supporters thought of your organization's work. Hearing from them required two-way conversations. Now, many large advocacy organizations run daily A/B tests of this size before lunch. The new technologies associated with digital listening and the culture of testing have rendered listening processes much more efficient. But what are the potential unintended consequences of that new efficiency for our democracy? And what happens when these same practices are replicated and refashioned in the wider public arena?

This final chapter highlights four potential problems that arise from analytic activism: (1) the loss of beneficial inefficiencies, (2) listening without conversation, (3) perverse measurement incentives, and (4) analytic astroturf. I call each of these *potential* problems with a clear intention: They are challenges that can be avoided, through strategic planning and intentional design. Activist leaders and political technologists have agency. They can influence how this field develops. The Internet is not an inexorable force leading us toward justice or ruin. It is a still-developing suite of technologies that we co-create.

The chapter concludes with a discussion of the broader implications of this research for academics, for practitioners, and for informed citizens.

The Loss of Beneficial Inefficiencies (Or, You Can't Crowdfund a Training Department)

In the final chapter of my previous book, I warned of the threat posed by the loss of "beneficial inefficiencies" (Karpf 2012a, 169). Beneficial inefficiencies are valuable public goods that are incidental byproducts of the dominant communications regime and are lost or threatened during the shift to newer, more efficient communications technologies. As a simple example, consider the replacement of phone trees with listservs among civic associations: A phone tree is a slow, cumbersome means of reminding all members of an upcoming meeting. It also happens to be good for strengthening social ties among participants, which are a public good ("I'm calling to remind you of the upcoming meeting. Oh, and while we're on the phone, I should tell you about this new babysitter . . ."). Listservs are much more efficient tools for sending out reminders. With the rise of email, phone trees have largely been replaced by listservs. The byproduct social ties that the phone trees supported can be endangered in the process. They must be intentionally created by some other means. In the same vein, analytic activism leverages the new efficiencies of digital media to listen, test, learn, and strategize in new ways. And, likewise, the efficiency of digital listening at the heart of analytic activism threatens some beneficial inefficiencies in ways that ought to give us pause.

This book has taken political organizations as a central object of analysis. Digital listening tools gain power only when they are converted into strategic objects that affect the choices leaders make. As we saw in chapters 3 and 4, differences in mission, vision, and business model can lead analytic activist organizations toward completely different priorities and outcomes. And as we saw in chapter 5, the analytics floor and analytics frontier establish the current parameters of analytic activism and can threaten to warp an organization's mission and vision if it does not approach them with care and planning. By placing organizations at the center of our analysis, we must also concern ourselves with a set of organizational-maintenance questions (Moe 1991; Halpin 2014). Where do the resources that sustain these organizations—funding, motivated volunteers, and talented staff members—come from? What types of activity are rewarded and supported? What types are overlooked or undercut? Rather than looking at the grand sweep of digital affordances—the lowered transaction costs and many-to-many communication capacity of digital media (Bimber 2003; Shirky 2008a; Earl and Kimport 2011; Bennett and Segerberg 2013; Margetts et al. 2015)— we must adopt a more meso-level analysis. What types of activist activities and organizational funding models align well with social fundraising? What types of necessary infrastructure go unfunded as fundraising technologies change?

In particular, there is a cluster of organizations that provide critical "activist infrastructure" whose mission and vision are quite clear but whose business models appear terribly vulnerable in the crowdfunding era. I specifically mean groups like the New Organizing Institute (NOI), the Analyst Institute (AI), and Citizen Engagement Lab (CEL). NOI provides training for digital advocacy professionals. AI runs sophisticated experiments in the electoral and advocacy arenas. CEL acts as an incubator for digital advocacy groups, helping to spread operational knowledge and lower the technical barriers to launching a new nonprofit. All of these organizations are routinely celebrated as important network forums for digital advocacy professionals. None of them have large lists of dues-paying members, and none of them produce the types of impact that fit neatly into a pitch deck or Kickstarter page. And that means that their year-to-year operational budgets rely on the fickle interests of large institutional donors. It was clearer how these activist infrastructure organizations were funded in the era of large nonprofits with big, centralized budgets. In the current rush to celebrate and embrace mass crowdfunding, it is much less clear.

The ill fate of NOI is instructive. NOI was founded after the 2004 election by alumni of the Howard Dean and John Kerry digital teams. For a decade, it was arguably *the* central network forum responsible for training and supporting a new generation of online campaign professionals (see Karpf 2012a, 106–109). Its annual RootsCamp "unconference" grew from a few hundred scrappy activists in a church basement to a 3,000-person meeting at the Washington Convention Center. Its "boot camp" trainings produced many of the top digital campaign professionals working in progressive politics today. But despite NOI's sterling reputation, by 2014 it began to encounter substantial trouble convincing large donors to continue to support its mission. This led to a series of management problems that culminated in the complete implosion of the organization in February 2015 (McMorris-Santoro 2015). NOI's demise was not solely a failure of the donor community, but the management issues it encountered all stemmed from a $200,000 budget shortfall that strained relationships between the executive director and key staffers. In retrospect, it seems astonishing that such a small sum could undo a critical piece of activist infrastructure.

By comparison, recall an example from chapter 4. New Era Colorado, with the help of Upworthy.com (and some strong video editing), was able to crowdfund nearly $200,000 for its campaign against Xcel Energy. Indeed, crowdfunding platforms like Kickstarter.com, GoFundMe.com, and IndieGoGo.com have been used to raise millions of dollars to support victims of tragedies and fund innovative social ventures. In the aftermath of the Michael Brown shooting in Ferguson, Missouri, the *Huffington Post* likewise used crowdfunding to support a full-time reporter who would remain on the ground during the months that followed. Crowdfunding has often been cited as evidence of the power that digital communities now have to replace traditional political organizations (Lerner 2014; Margetts et al. 2015). Crowdfunding, from this perspective, increases the efficiency of social giving, allowing small donors to pool their donations and support specific, favored projects without going through a large organizational intermediary.

The most important difference between New Era Colorado's local ballot initiative campaign and NOI's annual operating budget is that the Xcel Energy fight is linked to a limited-duration campaign with a tangible outcome. Civic crowdfunding exhibits a bias in favor of these types of outcomes (Davies 2015). Large-donor philanthropy exhibits a bias in favor of "disruptive" new ideas that promise high social returns and long-term viability (Teles, Hurlburt, and Schmitt 2014). Activist infrastructure like the NOI rests precariously between these two trends. It lacks a mass membership base, it lacks public-facing campaign efforts, and it appears less and less "disruptive" with every passing year. While direct blame for NOI's collapse can be placed on a series of specific management failures, its financial problems highlight a troubling weakness in the broader ecology of twenty-first-century activist organizations. Given the current technologies that dominate political fundraising (crowdfunding and mass emails for small donations; slide decks and Silicon Valley–style pitches for large donations), it is unclear how social movements can support certain types of critical infrastructure over the medium and long term.

This is the most threatening area in which beneficial inefficiencies have melted away in the rush toward digitally networked social movements. Strong political institutions—labor organizations, civic organizations, and political parties—have the financial capacity to invest in long-term movement infrastructure. The combined operating budgets of NOI, AI, and CEL are approximately 1% of what the 2012 Obama campaign spent on advertising alone. Movement infrastructure is cheap when viewed in relation to other movement-wide budget items. But when we weaken those large political institutions, we also reduce their capacity to fund external infrastructure. When we replace these institutions with unpredictable crowdfunding mechanisms and the whims of individual wealthy benefactors, we reduce the funds available for the invisible movement-building work that is always quietly appreciated and never publicly celebrated.

The real danger in the "spontaneous, bottom-up online movements" perspective on digital politics is that it replicates this blindness to movement infrastructure. When we glamorize individual hashtags, crowdfunding success stories, and viral petitions, we replicate the myth that twenty-first-century social movements can succeed without overhead costs, without long-term strategic direction setting, and without training, learning, and reflection. Activism is a *craft* that is learned over time. Social movement activists need training and support. Field organizers need paychecks and health care. The work of winning sustained policy victories in 2016 still resembles Max Weber's (1919) description of the "strong and slow boring of hard boards." By focusing on activist *moments* instead of activist *movements*, scholars in the organizing-without-organizations tradition devalue political infrastructure. And that is a problem, because the activist movements that win are activist movements that learn, adapt, and grow over time. You can't crowdfund a sustainable training program. As analytic activism becomes more attuned to the whims and will of crowdfunders, either activist leaders will have to find alternative revenue streams for movement infrastructure, or they will witness the hollowing out and abandonment of that infrastructure, regardless of the public value it provides.

Listening Without Conversation: Building Activist Identities

The legendary organizer Cesar Chavez, when asked to describe the secret of organizing, explained, "I only know one way to organize, and that's to talk to one person, then another person, and then another." Organizing, in other words, is about relationship-building through intentional conversation.[5] But analytic activism relies on new forms of digital listening *without* conversation. The promise of listening without conversation is central to the value of big data and analytics: By gathering and analyzing digital trace data, we can gain insights into public behavior that previously were inaccessible. Nonprofits, researchers, governments, and corporations are all adapting digital listening techniques to their needs and interests. But can activists engage in organizing without engaging in authentic conversations? The greatest successes of analytic activist organizations have tended to be campaigning successes or mobilizing successes. The cases where analytics have been used for organizing are exceptionally rare.

This is the point Micah Sifry is making when he describes the problem with the "atomization" of digital politics. In *The Big Disconnect*, Sifry (2014a, 23) writes, "I've started to wonder if the bigger trend is atomization; a combination of 'let's watch it by ourselves' and 'let's respond to it by ourselves.' In the case

---

[5] For more on relational organizing, see Ganz 2009; Han 2014; and McKenna and Han 2015.

of KONY 2012, millions of people were temporarily transfixed by a powerful piece of propaganda . . . but that burst of concentrated attention failed to get most to do anything." Atomization likewise is the root of what troubles Schier about the "activation" practices he witnessed in the 1990s. Simple digital acts like signing a petition, retweeting or sharing a message, and making a micro-donation indeed qualify as acts of political participation (as argued by Yannis Theocharis 2015). But these acts of political speech often occur in isolation. John Ahlquist and Margaret Levi (2013) have written about how participation in a shared "community of fate" changes the perspectives and preferences of those involved. Standing together, chanting in unison, builds a feeling of psychic solidarity and shared identity that sitting alone, urgently retweeting, lacks. And this is a problem for those social movements that require more than just mass mobilization or innovative campaigning to be effective. Organizing transforms its participants and builds deep identity-based ties through shared conversation. Digital listening without conversation does not produce this same type of transformation.

As an extreme case, consider two very different ways of engaging with the Occupy movement circa 2011. Some people took part in the digital "crowd" that supported Occupy Wall Street. They shared, they liked, they retweeted, perhaps they even contributed a photo to WeArethe99Percent.tumblr.com. Participation in this digital crowd is something more than the passive spectatorship of the industrial broadcast era. The digital crowd spread Occupy's message beyond the boundaries of Zuccotti Park. It signaled to media organizations that Occupy deserved attention. It affected how the movement was framed to the broader public. This mainstream media coverage, in turn, held strategic value in temporarily forestalling police efforts to shut down the camps.

But we should be careful not to equate Occupy's online supporters with the Occupiers themselves (Karpf 2014c). Occupy's digital "crowd" constitutes a different entity than Occupy's in-person participants. Thousands took up physical residence at Occupy encampments around the United States and, later, around the world. The Occupiers worked to create alternative democratic structures. They demanded, through their occupation of public space, that issues of economic inequality and injustice no longer be ignored. Participating at an Occupy site was difficult, taxing, and sometimes dangerous. It was *hard*. And, as a result, it was also transformative for those who took part in it. Activists who took up residence in these camps developed new skills and forged a lasting collective identity. Digital activists who supported Occupy Wall Street online without disrupting their daily lives added value to the protests but *received* less value from the protests (Kavada 2015). Retweeting a message or contributing to a meme does not change a person the way constructing a shared living space or standing in solidarity amid the tear gas does.

Conversations, particularly when conducted among large groups, constitute work. And, what's more, they are work for *everyone involved*. They require the same commitment of minutes and hours from all participants. The work of digital listening falls primarily on the analysts, technologists, and strategists who are gathering and rendering the data accessible. It is atomistic: We watch alone, we take action alone, we even share alone. And when we *do* talk about the latest Upworthy video or Change.org petition, we do not hold those conversations through Upworthy or Change.org. We instead congregate in the very spaces where they can happen most easily: on our own Facebook walls and/or within our own existing social networks (online or offline). This can be effective activism and can help spread messages beyond traditional echo chambers, but it is not very effective organizing (Rohlinger and Bunnage 2015). And some of the valuable byproducts of organizing—the shared organizational bonds, social movement identities, and richer civic skills—are lost when activists harness the power of listening without engaging in the work of conversation.

We can see evidence of this in the 2008 and 2012 Obama for America (OFA) campaigns, as documented by Elizabeth McKenna and Hahrie Han (2015). OFA was exceptional both in its devotion to community organizing techniques and in its reliance on metrics. We can see the handiwork of Marshall Ganz in this commitment to relational organizing—many of OFA's key leaders studied under Ganz and recruited him to help design OFA's "Camp Obama" trainings for the 2008 campaign (McKenna and Han 2015, 56–59). This produced a tension that ought to, at this point, sound familiar to readers:

> More than a third of our respondents who worked or volunteered in 2012 noted that the campaign shifted too far toward a centralized system that emphasized national purpose at the expense of local action. Campaigns have clear goals they must meet; they have time constraints and a bottom-line goal of a winning vote share. . . . By 2012, some of our respondents reported that the focus on the number of door knocks, voter registration forms, and phone calls overshadowed the relational dimension of organizing that had set OFA apart. (McKenna and Han 170–171)

Relational organizing conversations were crucial for building a deep, devoted, skilled volunteer core. They also looked inefficient when viewed strictly through voter contact metrics, and that inefficiency created a tension between OFA's immediate mission and the community organizing values it espoused.

The tension between metrics-driven analytic activism and community organizing also becomes clear if we look at the job titles at major netroots political organizations. I first took note of this while attending an international meeting of netroots advocacy professionals: All of these digital activists referred to themselves as "campaigners" rather than "organizers."[6] Groups like SumOfUs.org, Change.org, MoveOn.org, and Progressive Change Campaign Committee hire digital campaigners, not digital organizers. With the occasional exception of "organizing director" (a title whose popularity has waxed and waned over the years), the organizations define their staff positions by campaign work and mobilization work rather than organizing work. These organizations hire campaigners and demand "strong writing skills for a popular audience."[7] They are committed to digital listening and experimentation. But that is a different culture than Chavez's "talking to one person, then another person, then another," and it produces different outcomes.

We should not rush to the conclusion that the campaigning and mobilizing trends in analytic activism are somehow causing the demise of an otherwise robust relational organizing tradition in US politics. As I discussed in my previous book, the era of cross-class federated membership organizations that built strong member-to-member ties ended more than forty years ago (Karpf 2012a, 26). It was replaced by an era of direct mail–based membership organizations that reduced membership to check writing and barely attempted to gauge member opinion. In fact, Kay Lehman Schlozman and her coauthors (2015) recently completed a study demonstrating that the universe of American political associations is increasingly composed of organizations with no members whatsoever! Listening without conversation is preferable to barely listening at all.

I firmly believe that we are democratically better off with organizations that listen to their members, experiment with new tactics, and attempt to seize opportunities to spread messages beyond their narrow echo chambers than we would be with the former status quo. But the culture of community organizing, rooted as it is in conversation, slow deliberation, and shared civic work, is not well matched to the digital listening, culture of testing, and scale that define analytic activism as it is currently practiced.

There are plenty of present-day social movements that *do* rely on community organizing techniques. Young immigration reform activists organizing through United We Dream have worked to give voice to undocumented Americans, changing the dynamics of the immigration debate in the process. Climate activists working through 350.org and similar groups have won a series of local victories, helping to build a market for clean energy solutions while the national and international political situations have remained sclerotic. Black Lives Matter activists have also turned moments of tragedy into a cohesive movement identity that is changing the politics of police violence in this country. All of these

---

[6] Field notes, January 7, 2013.

[7] http://front.moveon.org/careers/#.VoxOqpMrIxg (accessed April 14, 2016).

movements make use of digital communication tools. All of them are helping to expand the analytics frontier as they develop new technologies to aid them in their work. But they also tend to engage in different activist practices than have been discussed in this book. They lean less heavily on building large email lists, running routine experiments, and converting measures of digital sentiment into strategic objects than the leading analytic activist organizations. They operate out along the analytics frontier, and some voice a mistrust of analytics altogether.

It remains to be seen whether a focus on analytics and testing can be merged with a focus on conversation and activist identity-building. We may be headed toward a symbiotic future where analytic activism functions as a cavalry of sorts, coming to the aid of organizing-rich social movement organizations with expansive mobilization capacity when the campaign moment is ripe. Or we may be headed toward an integrated future where analytic activist organizations learn to more effectively measure, track, promote, and value conversation and identity-building. But we may instead be headed toward a competitive future in which the fundraising prowess of analytic activist organizations, combined with a lack of funder interest in supporting infrastructure, crowds out social movement organizations that rely on community organizing practices. It is this third future that Schier and Sifry warn us against. I would add that it is a future that activists, technologists, and informed citizens ought to collaboratively work to prevent.

Choose Wisely: Beware Perverse Measurement Incentives

There is another hidden danger in analytic activism: You have to be particularly intentional when choosing what decisions should be made solely on the basis of analytics and algorithms. Algorithms and analytics are a means of automating value judgments. If you focus on optimizing pageviews or list growth, you will come to prioritize very different issues and practices than if you optimize for members taking multiple actions or participating in offline protest events. You track different metrics to assess list growth, message reach, dollars raised, headlines earned, elected officials terrified, and members inspired. Some of these metrics are much easier to track than others. Analytics render an imperfect portrait of public sentiment. Using analytics for activism requires acknowledging and adapting to those imperfections. It also requires a detailed analysis of how your organization or movement expects to build the power, leverage, or capacity necessary to enact your shared vision.

Here the lazy journalistic trope that ascribes near-wizardly power to data scientists and technologists is particularly troubling, since it can lead decision makers to put the *wrong kind of faith* in digital listening.[8] The problem with blindly trusting the data, as we saw in chapter 2, is that there is a crucial difference between revealed preferences and metapreferences. Digital listening tools traffic in revealed preferences—what we click, what we share, what we do. The campaign tactics, issue topics, and message frames that are most *popular* are not necessarily the ones that are most *powerful*. In particular, organizations must beware of substituting popularity for importance. The growthiest issue is not necessarily the issue one should prioritize. The fundraising practices that produce the most immediate revenue might also build mistrust and spam-listing in the long term. Clickbait headlines that leave readers feeling tricked will eventually degrade your brand and reputation. Analytics reports can be fashioned into strategic objects that improve the quality of activist deliberation, or analytics and algorithms can be used to sidestep deliberation altogether.

Vanity metrics can hold a siren-song attraction. They can serve to boost the organization's image in the eyes of highly placed stakeholders—donors, bosses, and boards of directors—who do not understand the inner workings of digital listening but feel a generic need to remain "cutting-edge." For frontline communications staffers or online campaigners, focusing on vanity metrics can provide job security and justify their departmental budget ("All of our graphs go up and to the right!"). Additionally, vanity metrics may sometimes appear to be the only game in town (particularly for organizations stationed far beyond the analytics frontier). If an organization lacks the budget to invest in developing a new, customized system to track its ideal engagement metrics, it might indeed be sensible to conclude that some flawed data is better than no data at all.[9]

Particularly among advocacy and activist organizations that are large and complex enough to rise above the analytics floor, identifying the *right* metrics poses an additional problem. In large organizations with multiple stakeholders and long histories, there will frequently be multiple competing theories of how to best build power and achieve the organization's goals. Committing to a set of metrics and a culture of testing means making a decision about which behaviors to value, track, and reward. As we saw in chapter 5, this is far simpler for electoral campaigns (and for businesses) than it is for social movement organizations.

---

[8] This trope is solely the province of *lazy* journalists. There is plenty of excellent, insightful, critical reporting on digital media and politics. It tends to come from journalists who are committed to this beat and take the time to develop expertise. But there is also an endless supply of thinly sourced articles about how technology is about to disrupt politics any minute now. And it is within this brand of lazy journalism that we still routinely see data scientists described as though they can turn lead into gold.

[9] Indeed, from a Bayesian perspective it almost surely is. But only if that new, flawed data is treated as merely another flawed signal and weighted accordingly.

What is the *right* path to ending structural racism, addressing economic inequality, or pursuing climate justice? It is an important question that can have no conclusive answer. Making a decision about analytics requires wading through these difficult mission- and vision-related questions. In the absence of strategic clarity, it is much simpler to adopt whatever default industry metrics are readily available.

There is, however, a simple solution to the problems of vanity metrics and putting too much faith in the data: *Always be blending.* All of the leading analytic activist organizations have adopted a blended approach to analytics signals. They don't blindly follow the numbers, diverting their mission daily in pursuit of the most popular issue, most potent fundraiser, or most viral tactic. Instead, they maintain a healthy mix of alternative signals. They conduct weekly member surveys. They make phone calls and talk with their active volunteers. They ask hard questions of their coalition partners, and they don't assume that if there is a tension between campaigners' instincts and testing results, the data is either objective or infallible. They hire, train, and empower the right people, then trust those people's judgment. Analytics and the broader culture of testing, in other words, are a valuable additional input into strategic thinking. They are not a replacement for strategic thinking.

The challenge on the near horizon is that, as more organizations adopt the tools of analytic activism, they fail to adopt this blended approach to the data. Analytic activism requires strategic clarity, a healthy skepticism about where the data provides a biased picture, and a sense of what the data *cannot* tell you. When journalists, vendors, consultants, and scholars imbue big data with near-mystical qualities (Anderson 2008, for instance), they also foster the misuse of analytics and algorithms, with potentially disastrous consequences.

Analytic Astroturf?

This fourth and final problem arises not directly *from* analytic activism, but in parallel to it: The tools of analytic activism are not reserved for social movement leaders or nonprofit professionals. As I noted in chapter 1, analytic activism combines three key features: digital listening, a culture of testing, and scale. As we saw in chapter 2, much of the most valuable analytic activism is rooted in *internal* analytics—richer data that an organization can control, manipulate, and customize. It follows that many of the organizations that are best positioned at the intersection of digital listening, testing, scale, and rich internal analytics are themselves profit-making companies trying to establish and defend their place in the new digital marketplace. *The organizations with the greatest access to data are not scrappy activist groups.*

Companies like Uber, Airbnb, and FanDuel have massive customer databases, and they are starting to use them for political ends. We have recently begun to see examples of what happens when government regulators take an interest in the "disruptive" behavior of these companies. When New York City mayor Bill de Blasio threatened to cap the size of Uber's vehicle fleet, Uber responded by adding a "de Blasio's Uber" feature to its mobile interface ("No Cars—See Why"), which redirected users to a petition opposing the new rules (Walker 2015). Uber also hired David Plouffe, a former Obama strategist, to serve as its "strategic adviser." When San Francisco considered a ballot measure that would reign in Airbnb usage, the company ran traditional political ads, reached out to Airbnb users within the city, and recruited Airbnb hosts to write op-eds and act as the public face of their effort. The company boasts that it has "almost as many U.S. users as there are members of the National Rifle Association" (Brown 2015), including 17% of San Francisco's population.

Matthew Stempeck tracks cases like these through a Tumblr site, CompaniesMobilizingCustomers.tumblr.com. In an article for the *Harvard Business Review*, Stempeck (2015) writes, "Leading technology companies are increasingly soliciting their users to take political action on their behalf to defend controversial business models from regulation, support new programs, and promote their moral values in active political battles. . . . We're entering a brave new world where the creators of technology platforms can activate billions of users to specific political action of their choosing. We're being introduced to a new lever of corporate influence on democracy." The cases are quickly multiplying. Just as the Obama campaign adopted rigorous A/B testing practices through cross-pollination with the tech industry (Kreiss 2016), the tech industry is now beginning to mimic the mobilization and campaign practices of analytic activism.

Corporations adopting a veneer of grassroots activism is nothing new. As Ed Walker documents in *Grassroots for Hire* (2014), there is a large industry of public affairs consultants who specialize in creating and mobilizing grassroots constituencies to speak out in favor of preferred corporate policies. Walker argues that only some of these consultants are engaging in true "astroturf" (fake grassroots) campaigning. Astroturf campaigns involve making fraudulent claims about grassroots support, paying people to pretend they are volunteer supporters, and/or hiding the role that companies are playing in the campaign. For the most part, he argues, public affairs consultants are simply further spreading the "grassroots from the top down" engagement techniques that were developed by advocacy professionals over the years. It turns out that these engagement techniques can be used just as effectively by their corporate opponents.

It is quite likely that we will see further expansion of this corporate spinoff of analytic activism in the coming years. The customer mobilization practiced by Uber and Airbnb has many surface similarities to the activism discussed throughout this book. These companies have already embraced the culture of testing and digital listening practices. They are achieving massive scale as part of their core business model. And they are turning to strategic advisers and consultants to teach them how to wage a defensive issue advocacy campaign. What is missing from these corporate campaigns is the commitment to civic goals and the ongoing attention to political power-building. It is commodified activism, organized in short-term bursts to support the company's bottom line. But this commodified activism can be quite effective, particularly in response to short-term threats. To paraphrase Melvin Kranzberg (1986), the tools of analytic activism are neither good nor bad, and they most certainly are not neutral.

The particular cause for concern here is the additional informational asymmetry that digital companies like Uber, Facebook, Amazon, and Google have over their political competitors. By virtue of their business models, these companies will *always* have greater access to data than their opponents do. They will also enjoy a massive engineering advantage, with highly skilled, well-paid employees whose sole purpose is to develop specialized internal analytics and algorithms. Alongside this data advantage come new forms of leverage and power that exceed the advantage corporations have historically held by virtue of their financial position.

And this is particularly true as we move toward an increasingly data-rich Internet of Things (Howard 2015). Within the next decade, tens of billions of devices will be connected to the Internet. Cars, phones, coffee makers, and thermostats will all be digitally connected. Analytic activist organizations will seek to develop new strategies and tactics that respond to the new opportunities presented by the Internet of Things. But compared with the companies that have first- or second-party control of the data itself, they will likely find themselves ill-positioned and outflanked. Facebook and Amazon can be wonderful tools for analytic activists, so long as those activists do not become a threat to Facebook and Amazon.

Nonetheless, proponents of analytic activism can find solace in the knowledge that politics outside of elections is not simply a game of raw numbers. An online petition can be many things, including an entry point into an ongoing activist community. Though the digital media juggernauts will always have more data than the activists and advocates, they will also only rarely be committed to galvanizing supporters and building the skills and capacities for political action. Digital public affairs consultants may become masters of the well-timed A/B test, but they will never be pioneers along the analytics frontier. Long-term, large-scale activist and advocacy campaigns benefit committed organizations that have a culture of learning and experimentation. If analytic astroturf becomes increasingly prominent, that will further spur the need for innovations among analytic activists.

Whether you are an academic, an activist, or a concerned citizen, each of these four problems should color your perception of analytic activism. Digital listening provides a powerful set of tools and helps large-scale advocacy organizations adapt to the nimble media environment that is still in the process of emerging. But the tools of analytics have biases and flaws; they can get better or worse over time.

Let me not end on such a sour note, though. This book is mostly about exciting new possibilities among twenty-first-century activist organizations. It is about what we can do today that we could not do before and about the new directions in which activist leaders are beginning to move. As such, I ask readers' patience as I indulge myself by offering what I hope three audiences—academics, activists, and citizens—will take away from this book.

Implications for Academics

This book provides a distinctly different perspective on analytics, digital listening, and Internet politics than most of the scholarly treatments in the field. And this is rooted in a central contradiction that we face in the era of big data. On the one hand, we now have access to massive datasets that provide fascinating new windows on political behavior. On the other hand, these massive datasets are saddled with their own hidden biases. Online political behavior does not rise up spontaneously. It does not reflect the will of the masses, finally come to light. Instead, it refracts the public will through an apparatus of algorithmic weighting and organizational maintenance that demands study in its own right. But the data we have easily at hand does little to reveal the workings of the apparatus producing it.

One of the great dangers of the digital moment we currently are living through is that the discipline as a whole will succumb to a particularly virulent form of availability bias. It is easy to gather data for Twitter studies. It is harder to navigate the Facebook terms of service, and even harder still to cobble together a comprehensive email dataset. As a result, both academic journals and academic conferences feature mountains of Twitter papers, molehills written about Facebook, and an awkward silence regarding email. We study the kinds of social media that we can access, regardless of their relative importance in political life.

The most important implication that this book hopefully holds for academics lies in the way it approaches political organizations. Put succinctly, organizations still *matter* for digital politics. The current wave of political communication and social movement research that glorifies hashtag activism and celebrates the seemingly spontaneous nature of online political action has managed to studiously avert its gaze from the work of digital political organizations. In so doing, it has reified the "spontaneous, bottom-up movements" perspective while avoiding all evidence that might contradict or complicate the theory. It is indeed true that anyone can post a political message online today that has the *potential* to turn into a viral moment or viral movement. But we should not suppose that this viral potential renders organizations unimportant. Many contemporary political science and political communication researchers have chosen to study digital speech while ignoring digital listening by designing empirical studies that have no room to evaluate listening practices.

I am not by any means alone in my assertion that organizations and practitioners matter. There is an important minority tradition in political communication that, building on insights from Science and Technology Studies, works to embed research in the lived experiences and messy realities of the newsroom (Boczkowski 2004, 2010; Anderson 2013a; Usher 2014), the electoral campaign (Howard 2005; Kreiss 2012; Nielsen 2012; McKenna and Han 2015; Baldwin-Philippi 2015), and the advocacy organization (Bimber, Flanagin, and Stohl 2012; Chadwick 2013; Costanza-Chock 2014; Powers 2014; Han 2014). Researchers like Caroline Lee (2014) and Edward Walker (2014) have likewise produced groundbreaking scholarship that starts by treating the work of deliberative democracy professionals and public engagement professionals as deserving of serious, methodical examination. But ours remains a minority tradition, particularly when compared with the sheer volume of studies that attempt to draw grand conclusions about online political behavior from whatever datasets prove most accessible during a single election or a single social movement episode.

Analytic activism is not the whole of online political mobilization. It does not comprise the majority of online political behavior. But if we narrow our attention to the long-term, large-scale social movement work that has always been critical to achieving lasting policy successes and altering the balance of power, then the digital listening behavior I document in this book becomes a particularly vital area of study. Analytic activism produces new tactics and strategies, new organizational learning routines, and new avenues for mass political engagement. Activist organizations today are adapting their strategies to the hybrid media landscape. They are developing new tactical repertoires in the hope of building the kinds of traction and leverage for digital-era contentious politics that the marches and sit-ins of the 1960s found in the broadcast media environment. If we want to understand how movements learn, grow, adapt, and succeed, we have to take these organizations seriously. It is not enough to study digital trace data as an alternative to surveys and content analysis. We must also attend to the messy, flawed, incomplete organizational logics that incorporate this data into strategic deliberation.

Implications for Practitioners

There are two points that I hope activists, mobilizers, campaigners, and organizers will take away from this book. There is a tension between the two, but it is my hope that it will prove to be a dynamic, productive tension.

First, I hope readers will take away a sense of the things that advocacy organizations can do with analytics that they could not do before. Activists have always marshaled existing media technologies to try to exert influence over their targets. Whether these were broadsheets and pamphlets, press releases and rallies, or retweets and Vine clips, the power and effectiveness of activist tactics have always been rooted in the logics of the broader media system—and we have entered a moment where the media system has become decidedly hybridized. Old media logics and routines are changing, old institutions are adapting, and new institutions are rising to prominence. Digital listening and the culture of testing allow large activist groups to develop novel engagement practices and pressure tactics. Analytic activism creates new feedback loops that facilitate learning and experimentation. We are mired in a long, messy, exciting moment of creativity and failure and new possibilities and lost beneficial inefficiencies. This is chaos for established activist tactics that were developed for the industrial broadcast era and no longer quite fit with the emerging media system. It can be a productive chaos, though. The activist organizations that succeed and develop power will likely be those that listen, experiment, fail, and learn. Analytic activism provides a new toolkit that we are only beginning to explore.

But, second, I hope readers will take away a *tempered* enthusiasm for analytic activism. It is both easy and dangerous to put too much faith in the data. Digital listening is not a miracle cure for the maladies of social movements past. Analytics cannot actually predict the future. Experimentation mostly creates marginal increases in the power of individual tactics; it does not create unstoppable political juggernauts overnight. Organizations like Change.org, MoveOn. org, and Upworthy.com have used analytics to build new institutions that provide an infrastructure on which twenty-first-century political battles will be fought. But, at best, they are bending the arc of history a handful of degrees further toward justice. They do not always win, and their victories are rarely more than partial. What they have accomplished is worth studying and understanding, but it also is not nearly *enough*.

There is a lot that advocates and activists can learn through analytic activism and digital listening. But analytics should always be treated as a valuable but flawed signal. The data is never perfect. The future is never immutable. Strategy is messy work, as it always has been. There is still ample room for leadership and vision, conversation and debate. Analytics reports and experiments should always be used to enhance, not replace, strategic debates.

I hope that activists will walk away from this book with new questions about where digital listening is most useful to their work, about which long-held assumptions they should now test, and about what the data they are gathering is and is not useful for. I hope the book has made clear that analytic activist tools can lead organizations in many different directions, depending on their mission, vision, and funding model. I am also hopeful that readers will take away the belief that the best approach when trying to gauge public sentiment or opinion is to blend multiple imperfect signals rather than to treat any one signal (polls, focus groups, personal anecdotes, or digital metrics) as a complete answer.

Finally, particularly for younger activists who have picked up this book to learn how to start a digital movement from scratch, I hope to have imparted the value of scale and stability. Hashtagged movements can be a useful entry point, but every successful social movement must eventually build leadership and governance capacities that allow it to deliberate, fail, learn, and adapt. Analytic activism becomes increasingly valuable as you increase your size and scale. Find the people who share your passion and your vision. Work closely with them. Listen.

Implications for Citizens

What about those readers who have approached this book as concerned citizens? What message should they take away? Well, you know now that you are being listened to online. Your actions leave digital footprints and trails. Those trails tell a story, and many actors—governments, advocates, technologists, and corporations—are analyzing those trails. But so what? Is analytic activism good or bad? Should we celebrate it or bemoan it? As it would be for any proper scholar, my answer is perhaps frustratingly nuanced. As I often tell my students, the short answer to any worthwhile question is always, "Well, it's complicated."

But I suppose an appropriate final point to leave you with concerns the gap between digital listening and digital conversation. It relates to a phenomenon that I have often termed the "Field of Dreams Fallacy."

The Field of Dreams Fallacy ("If you build it, they will come") undermines many civic technology and political technology initiatives. Too often, a starry-eyed activist or technologist will come to believe that our political system is broken and can be fixed through a new digital website, platform, or app.[10] She will draw up an epic slide deck and approach foundations and investors with the idea

---

[10] Civic technologist Joshua Tauberer (2015) mirrors my own thoughts on this matter, writing, "If there was an idea that could 'fix' democracy, it would have been thought-up already."

that there is a *technological solution* to the ills of twenty-first-century democracy. By providing citizens with better information, or making it easier for them to make their voice heard, or giving them a platform for engaging more easily in politics, we can finally build a better tomorrow and upgrade democracy. Sometimes these new proposals get funded, and these websites and platforms get built. And that is when the technologist or activist encounters a harsh lesson: The lowered transaction costs of the digital media environment tend to *reveal* people's existing preferences, not substitute new preferences. Most members of the mass public do not engage with politics because they do not want to engage with politics. They aren't disengaged because politics is too hard; they are disengaged because politics is too boring, too frustrating, or too dispiriting.

The Field of Dreams Fallacy is a downer.[11] It is also the shorthand explanation I provide for the fact that so many efforts to use the Internet to facilitate bottom-up citizen protest movements flounder and fail. Organizing is hard work. Deliberative democracy is few people's idea of a good time. People have learned for generations that politics is frustrating and terrible and best avoided whenever possible. And this, indeed, may be one reason why analytic activism features so much more digital listening than digital conversation. Listening is easy; conversation is harder.

But the Field of Dreams Fallacy is right only until we make it wrong. If you worry that twenty-first-century activism is filled with too much listening and not enough conversation, then start conversing more! One benefit of becoming an active citizen is that, in a quiet mass crowd, the person who begins to speak immediately becomes the loudest in the room. If we demand conversation, if we value deeper participation, then those preferences and values will leave digital footprints and trails as well. Analytic activism detects the behavior of those who choose to make their voice heard. Not so long ago, advocates, activists, and organizations were not listening. They are listening now. So find what you want to say, and speak up.

---

[11] I am no fun at parties.

Bibliography

350.org. (2014). 2014 Annual Report. http://350.org/2014-report/.

Abebe, N. (2014, March 23). Watching Team Upworthy Work Is Enough to Make You a Cynic. Or Lose Your Cynicism. Or Both. Or Neither. *New York Magazine*. http://nymag.com/daily/intelligencer/2014/03/upworthy-team-explains-its-success.html.

Ahlquist, J. S., and Levi, M. (2013). *In the Interest of Others: Organizations and Social Activism*. Princeton, NJ: Princeton University Press.

Alexander, J. C. (2010). *The Performance of Politics: Obama's Victory and the Democratic Struggle for Power*. New York: Oxford University Press.

Alinsky, S. (1971). *Rules for Radicals*. New York: Random House.

Ananny, M. (2016). Toward an Ethics of Algorithms: Convening, Observation, Probability, and Timeliness. *Science, Technology, & Human Values*, 41(1), 93–117. doi: 10.1177/0162243915606523.

Anderson, C. (2008). The End of Theory: The Data Deluge Makes the Scientific Method Obsolete. *Wired*, 16(7). http://www.wired.com/2008/06/pb-theory/.

Anderson, C., Bell, E., and Shirky, C. (2014, December 3). Post Industrial Journalism: Adapting to the Present. *Tow Center for Digital Journalism*. http://towcenter.org/research/post-industrial-journalism-adapting-to-the-present-2/.

Anderson, C. W. (2011). Between Creative and Quantified Audiences: Web Metrics and Changing Patterns of Newswork in Local US Newsrooms. *Journalism*, 12(5), 550–566.

Anderson, C. W. (2013a). *Rebuilding the News: Metropolitan Journalism in the Digital Age*. Philadelphia: Temple University Press.

Anderson, C. W. (2013b). What Aggregators Do: Towards a Networked Concept of Journalistic Expertise in the Digital Age. *Journalism*, 14(8), 1008–1023.

Andrews, K. T. (2004). *Freedom Is a Constant Struggle: The Mississippi Civil Rights Movement and Its Legacy*. Chicago: University of Chicago Press.

Andrews, K. T., and Edwards, B. 2004. Advocacy Organizations in the U.S. Political Process. *Annual Review of Sociology*, 30, 479–506.

Anstead, N., and O'Loughlin, B. (2015). Social Media Analysis and Public Opinion: The 2010 UK General Election. *Journal of Computer-Mediated Communication*, 20(2), 204–220. doi:10.1111/jcc4.12102.

Arceneaux, K., and Johnson, M. (2013). *Changing Minds or Changing Channels? Partisan News in an Age of Choice*. Chicago: University of Chicago Press.

Ariely, D. (2010). You Are What You Measure. *Harvard Business Review*, June 2010. https://hbr.org/2010/06/column-you-are-what-you-measure.

Baldwin-Philippi, J. (2015). *Using Technology, Building Democracy: Digital Campaigning and the Construction of Citizenship*. New York: Oxford University Press.

Baldwin-Philippi, J. (2016). The Cult(ure) of Analytics in 2014. In J. A. Hendricks and D. Schill (Eds.), *Communication and Midterm Elections: Media, Message, and Mobilization* (25–42). Basingstoke: Palgrave Macmillan.

Balkin, J. M. (2016). Information Fiduciaries and the First Amendment. Social Science Research Network working paper. http://papers.ssrn.com/sol3/papers.cfm?abstract_id=2675270.

Barberá, P., Wang, N., Bonneau, R., Jost, J. T., Nagler, J., Tucker, J., and González-Bailón, S. (2015). The Critical Periphery in the Growth of Social Protests. *PLoS ONE, 10*(11). doi: 10.1371/journal.pone.0143611.

Barthel, M., Shearer, E., Gottfried, J., and Mitchell, A. (2015, July 14). The Evolving Role of News on Twitter and Facebook. *Pew Research Center.* http://www.journalism.org/2015/07/14/the-evolving-role-of-news-on-twitter-and-facebook/.

Bastos, M. T., and Mercea, D. (2015). Serial Activists: Political Twitter Beyond Influentials and the Twittertariat. *New Media & Society,* May 2015. doi: 10.1177/1461444815584764.

Bastos, M. T., and Mercea, D. (2016). Being a Serial Transnational Activist. *Journal of Computer-Mediated Communication, 21,* 140–155.

Baumgartner, F. R., and Jones, B. D. (1993). *Agendas and Instability in American Politics.* Chicago: University of Chicago Press.

Benkler, Y. (2006). *The Wealth of Networks: How Social Production Transforms Markets and Freedom.* New Haven, CT: Yale University Press.

Benkler, Y., Roberts, H., Faris, R., Solow-Niederman, A., and Etling, B. (2015). Social Mobilization and the Networked Public Sphere: Mapping the SOPA–PIPA Debate. *Political Communication, 32*(4), 594–624.

Bennett, W. L., and Segerberg, A. (2013). *The Logic of Connective Action: Digital Media and the Personalization of Contentious Politics.* New York: Cambridge University Press.

Bennett, W. L., Lawrence, R. G., and Livingston, S. (2008). *When the Press Fails: Political Power and the News Media from Iraq to Katrina.* Chicago: University of Chicago Press.

Berger, J., and Milkman, K. L. (2012). What Makes Online Content Viral? *Journal of Marketing Research, 49*(2), 192–205. http://dx.doi.org/10.1509/jmr.10.0353.

Berman, A. (2015a). *Give Us the Ballot: The Modern Struggle for Voting Rights in America.* New York: Farrar, Straus and Giroux.

Berman, A. (2015b, July 28). How the 2000 Election in Florida Led to a New Wave of Voter Disenfranchisement. *The Nation.* http://www.thenation.com/article/how-the-2000-election-in-florida-led-to-a-new-wave-of-voter-disenfranchisement/.

Bernays, E. (1947). The Engineering of Consent. *The Annals of the American Academy of Political and Social Science, 250,* 113–120.

Bimber, B. (2003). *Information and American Democracy: Technology in the Evolution of Political Power.* New York: Cambridge University Press.

Bimber, B., and Davis, R. (2003). *Campaigning Online: The Internet in U.S. Elections.* New York: Oxford University Press.

Bimber, B., Flanagin, A., and Stohl, C. (2012). *Collective Action in Organizations: Interaction and Engagement in an Era of Technological Change.* New York: Cambridge University Press.

Bluestein, A. (2013, August 5). How Ben Rattray's Change.org Became a Viral Consumer Watchdog. *Fast Company.* http://www.fastcompany.com/3014809/change-org-petitions-ben-rattray.

Blumer, H. (1948). Public Opinion and Public Opinion Polling. *American Sociological Review, 13*(5), 542–549.

Boczkowski, P. J. (2004). *Digitizing the News: Innovation in Online Newspapers.* Cambridge, MA: MIT Press.

Boczkowski, P. J. (2010). *News at Work: Imitation in an Age of Information Abundance.* Chicago: University of Chicago Press.

Bode, L. (2012). Facebooking It to the Polls: A Study in Online Social Networking and Political Behavior. *Journal of Information Technology & Politics, 9*(4), 352–369. doi:10.1080/19331681.2012.709045.

Bond, R. M., Fariss, C. J., Jones, J. J., Kramer, A. D. I., Marlow, C., Settle, J. E., and Fowler, J. H. (2012). A 61-Million-Person Experiment in Social Influence and Political Mobilization. *Nature, 489*, 295–298. doi:10.1038/nature11421.

boyd, danah. (2014). *It's Complicated: The Social Lives of Networked Teens*. New Haven: Yale University Press.

Bradford, H. (2014, October 16). Starbucks to Finally Let Employees Show Their Tattoos. *Huffington Post*. http://www.huffingtonpost.com/2014/10/16/starbucks-tattoos-policy-work_n_5999746.html.

Brewer, J. (2014, June). The Problem with Petitions: Working with Leaders, Not Just at Them. Keynote speech presented at Personal Democracy Forum 2014, New York. https://www.youtube.com/watch?v=a_KJoJsSUEg.

Broockman, D., and Kalla, J. (2016). Durably Reducing Transphobia: A Field Experiment on Door-to-Door Canvassing. *Science, 352*(6282), 220–224. doi: 10.1126/science.aad9713.

Brown, K. V. (2015). Meet the Apptivists: The Volunteer Lobbyists Helping Keep Airbnb, Uber, and Other Startups Alive. *Fusion*. http://fusion.net/story/232769/airbnb-and-uber-users-are-reshaping-politics/.

Brunton, F. (2013). *Spam: A Shadow History of the Internet*. Cambridge, MA: MIT Press.

Campbell, D. T. (1979). Assessing the Impact of Planned Social Change. *Evaluation and Program Planning, 2*(1), 67–90. http://dx.doi.org/10.1016/0149-7189(79)90048-X.

Carlson, M. (2015). When News Sites Go Native: Redefining the Advertising–Editorial Divide in Response to Native Advertising. *Journalism, 16*(7), 849–865. doi: 10.1177/1464884914545441.

Carnell, T. (producer), and Perota, J. (director). (2014). *Last Week Tonight with John Oliver*, Episode 1.5 [Video]. HBO.

Carpenter, D. (2003). The Petition as a Recruitment Device: Evidence from the Abolitionists' Congressional Campaign. Working paper. http://people.hmdc.harvard.edu/~dcarpent/petition-recruit-20040112.pdf.

Carpenter, D. (2015, May). Recruitment by Petition: American Antislavery, French Protestantism, English Suppression. Paper presented at the Conference on Special Interests in American Politics, University of Michigan, Ann Arbor.

Carr, D. (2010). Plentiful Content, So Cheap. *New York Times*. http://www.nytimes.com/2010/02/08/business/media/08carr.html?8dpc&_r=0.

Castells, M. (2009). *Communication Power*. New York: Oxford University Press.

Castells, M. (2012). *Networks of Outrage and Hope: Social Movements in the Internet Age*. Malden, MA: Polity Press.

Center for Media Justice, ColorofChange.org, and Data & Society. (2015). The Digital Culture Shift: From Scale to Power. *Center for Media Justice*. http://centerformediajustice.org/digital-culture-shift-from-scale-to-power/.

Chadwick, A. (2013). *The Hybrid Media System: Politics and Power*. New York: Oxford University Press.

Chadwick, A., and Dennis, J. (2016). Social Media, Professional Media, and Mobilization in Contemporary Britain: Explaining the Strengths and Weaknesses of the Citizens' Movement 38 Degrees. *Political Studies*, 1–19. Online First: doi: 10.1177/0032321716631350.

Christian, B. (2012). Test Everything: Notes on the A/B Revolution. *Wired*. http://www.wired.com/2012/05/test-everything-notes-on-the-ab-revolution/.

Clemens, E. S. (1997). *The People's Lobby: Organizational Innovation and the Rise of Interest Group Politics in the United States, 1890–1925*. Chicago: University of Chicago Press.

Coleman, G. (2014). *Hacker, Hoaxer, Whistleblower, Spy*. New York: Verso.

Compton, M. (2013, September 27). We the People Is Two Years Old. [Blog post], *WhiteHouse.gov*. https://www.whitehouse.gov/blog/2013/09/27/we-people-two-years-old.

Costanza-Chock, S. (2014). *Out of the Shadows, into the Streets! Transmedia Organizing and the Immigrant Rights Movement*. Cambridge, MA: MIT Press.

Couldry, N., and van Dijck, J. (2015). Researching Social Media as if the Social Mattered. *Social Media + Society, 1*(2). doi:10.1177/2056305115604174.

Crawford, S. (2013). *Captive Audience: The Telecom Industry and Monopoly Power in the New Gilded Age.* New Haven, CT: Yale University Press.

Critchfield, S. (2013, June). The Big Data Secret That No One's Talking About—Yet. Keynote speech presented at Personal Democracy Forum 2013, New York. https://www.youtube.com/watch?v=9wEBf6QRzec.

Critchfield, S. (2015, July 9). Case Study: Upworthy's Most Viral Video of All-Time. [Blog post], *Sara Critchfield.* http://saracritchfield.com/2015/07/09/upworthys-most-viral-video-of-all-time/.

Cushman, J. (2011, February 24). What We Can't Teach: Courage and Commitment in Campaigns. [Blog post], *New Organizing.* http://www.leadership-development-initiative.org/blog/2011/03/18/joy-cushmans-fabulous-article-2.

Cutts, M. (2011, January 21). Google Search and Search Engine Spam. [Blog post], *Google Official Blog.* https://googleblog.blogspot.com/2011/01/google-search-and-search-engine-spam.html.

Dahl, R. A. (1957). The Concept of Power. *Behavioral Science, 2*(3), 201–215. doi:10.1002/bs.3830020303.

Davies, R. (2015). Three Provocations for Civic Crowdfunding. *Information, Communication & Society, 18*(3), 342–355. doi:10.1080/1369118X.2014.989878.

Dayan, D., and Katz, E. (1992). *Media Events: The Live Broadcasting of History.* Cambridge, MA: Harvard University Press.

Dearborn, R. (2013, March 14). Quick and Dirty: The Minimum Viable Campaign. *Lean Impact.* http://leanimpact.org/the-minimum-viable-product-campaign/.

Dearborn, R. (2015, January 12). Bittersweet News: Upwell Is Shutting Down. *Upwell.* http://www.upwell.us/bittersweet-news-upwell-shutting-down.

DeGeneres, E. (Producer). (2011). *The Ellen DeGeneres Show,* Episode dated February 17, 2011 [Video]. Warner Bros. Television Distribution.

DeNardis, L. (2009). *Protocol Politics: The Globalization of Internet Governance.* Cambridge, MA: MIT Press.

DeSilver, D. (2014, February 20). American Unions Membership Declines as Public Support Fluctuates. *Pew Research Center.* http://www.pewresearch.org/fact-tank/2014/02/20/for-american-unions-membership-trails-far-behind-public-support/.

Diakopoulos, N. (2015). Algorithmic Accountability: Journalistic Investigation of Computational Power Structures. *Digital Journalism, 3*(3), 398–415. doi: 10.1080/21670811.2014.976411.

Dixit, A. K., Skeath, S., & Reiley, D. H., Jr. (2014). *Games of Strategy* (4th ed.). New York: W. W. Norton.

DLD. (2014). *A New Way to Meaningful Content (Eli Pariser, Jochen Wegner)* [Video]. Digital-Life-Design: Digital-Life-Design Conference. https://www.youtube.com/watch?v=onv2emeve8g.

Duhigg, C. (2012, February 16). How Companies Learn Your Secrets. *New York Times.* http://www.nytimes.com/2012/02/19/magazine/shopping-habits.html?_r=1.

Earl, J., and Kimport, K. (2011). *Digitally Enabled Social Change.* Cambridge, MA: MIT Press.

Entman, R. M. (1993). Framing: Toward Clarification of a Fractured Paradigm. *Journal of Communication, 43*(4), 51–58. doi:10.1111/j.1460-2466.1993.tb01304.x.

Epstein, R., and Robertson, R. E. (2015). The Search Engine Manipulation Effect (SEME) and Its Possible Impact on the Outcomes Of Elections. *PNAS, 112*(33). doi:10.1073/pnas.1419828112.

Erikson, R. S., and Wlezien, C. (2012). *The Timeline of Presidential Elections: How Campaigns Do (and Do Not) Matter.* Chicago: University of Chicago Press.

Eyal, H. (2016). Digital Fit as a Leg-Up for Nongovernmental Organizations' Media and Political Success. *Political Communication, 33*(1), 118–135. doi: 10.1080/10584609.2015.1011294.

Fenno, R. (1978). *Home Style: House Members in Their Districts.* New York: Little, Brown.

Ferrara, E., Varol, O., Davis, C., Menczer, F., & Flammini, A. (2014). The Rise of Social Bots. Working paper. http://arxiv.org/abs/1407.5225.

Finley, K. (2013, September 26). Meet Change.org, the Google of Modern Politics. *Wired*. http://www.wired.com/wiredenterprise/2013/09/change-org/all/.

Fisher, D. R. and Boekkooi, M. (2010). Mobilizing Friends and Strangers: Understanding the Role of the Internet in the Step It Up Day of Action. *Information, Communication & Society, 13*(2), 193–208. doi:10.1080/13691180902878385.

Fligstein, N., and McAdam, D. (2012). *A Theory of Fields*. New York: Oxford University Press.

Forrest, A., and Montanez, L. (2012, November). Engineering Virality. Slideshow presented at D.C. Week 2012, Washington, DC. http://www.slideshare.net/Upworthy/engineering-virality-dc-week-2012.

Fraade, J. (2014, June 9). Upworthy's Unworthy Politics. *Al Jazeera America*. http://america.aljazeera.com/opinions/2014/6/upworthy-politicsclickbaitlifestyle.html.

Freelon, D., McIlwain, C. D., & Clark, M. D. (2016, February). *Beyond the Hashtags: #Ferguson, #Blacklivesmatter, and the Online Struggle for Offline Justice*. Center for Media & Social Impact. Washington, DC: American University School of Communication.

Fung, A., and Shkabatur, J. (2015). Viral Engagement: Fast, Cheap, and Broad, but Good for Democracy? In D. Allen and J. S. Light (Eds.), *From Voice to Influence: Understanding Citizenship in a Digital Age* (155–177). Chicago: University of Chicago Press.

Gamson, W. A. (1975). *The Strategy of Social Protest*. Belmont, CA: Wadsworth.

Gamson, W. A., and Wolfsfeld, G. (1993). Movements and Media as Interacting Systems. *Annals of the American Academy of Political and Social Science, 528*, 114–125.

Gans, H. (2004). *Deciding What's News: A Study of CBS Evening News, NBC Nightly News, Newsweek and Time*. Evanston, IL: Northwestern University Press.

Ganz, M. (2009). *Why David Sometimes Wins: Leadership, Organization, and Strategy in the California Farm Worker Movement*. New York: Oxford University Press.

Gast, P., Botelho, G., & Sayers, D. M. (2013, May 24). Boy Scouts to Allow Gay Youths to Join. *CNN*. http://www.cnn.com/2013/05/23/us/boy-scouts-sexual-orientation/.

Gerbaudo, P. (2012). *Tweets and the Streets*. New York: Palgrave Macmillan.

Gillespie, T. (2011). Can an Algorithm Be Wrong? Twitter Trends, the Specter of Censorship, and Our Faith in the Algorithms Around Us. [Blog post], *Culture Digitally*. http://culturedigitally.org/2011/10/can-an-algorithm-be-wrong/.

Gillespie, T. (2014). The Relevance of Algorithms. In T. Gillespie, P. J. Boczkowski, and K. A. Foot (Eds.), *Media Technologies: Essays on Communication, Materiality, and Society* (167–193). Cambridge, MA: MIT Press.

Gillespie, T., Boczkowski, P. J., & Foot, K. A. (Eds.). (2014). *Media Technologies: Essays on Communication, Materiality, and Society*. Cambridge, MA: MIT Press.

Gilman, H. R. (2016). *Democracy Reinvented: Participatory Budgeting and Civic Innovation in America*. Washington, DC: Brookings Institution Press.

Gitelman, L. (Ed.). (2013). *Raw Data Is an Oxymoron*. Cambridge, MA: MIT Press.

Gitlin, T. (1980). *The Whole World Is Watching: Mass Media in the Making and Unmaking of the New Left*. Berkeley: University of California Press.

Gitlin, T. (2012). *Occupy Nation: The Roots, the Spirit, and the Promise of Occupy Wall Street*. New York: It Books.

Gladwell, M. (2010, October 4). Small Change: Why the Revolution Will Not Be Tweeted. *The New Yorker*. http://www.newyorker.com/reporting/2010/10/04/101004fa_fact_gladwell?currentPage=all.

González-Bailón, S., and Wang, N. (2016). Networked Discontent: The Anatomy of Protest Campaigns in Social Media. *Social Networks, 44*, 95–104. doi: 10.1016/j.socnet.2015.07.003.

Goodhart, C. (1981). Problems of Monetary Management: The U.K. Experience. In A. S. Courakis (Ed.), *Inflation, Depression, and Economic Policy in the West* (111–144). New York: Rowman & Littlefield.

Gottlieb, J. (2015). Protest News Framing Cycle: How *The New York Times* Covered Occupy Wall Street. *International Journal of Communication, 9*, 231–253.

Gould-Wartofsky, M. A. (2015). *The Occupiers: The Making of the 99 Percent Movement.* New York: Oxford University Press.

Graeff, E., Stempech, M., & Zuckerman, E. (2014). The Battle for "Trayvon Martin": Mapping a Media Controversy Online and Off-Line. *First Monday, 19*(2). http://firstmonday.org/article/view/4947/3821.

Green, D., & Gerber, A. (2000). The Effects of Canvassing, Telephone Calls, and Direct Mail on Voter Turnout: A Field Experiment. *American Political Science Review, 94*(3), 653–663.

Grim, R. (2012, October 22). Change.org Changing: Site to Drop Progressive Litmus Test for Campaigns, Say Internal Documents. *Huffington Post.* http://www.huffingtonpost.com/2012/10/22/changeorg-corporate-gop-campaigns-internal-documents_n_1987985.html.

Hadden, J. (2015). *Networks in Contention: The Divisive Politics of Climate Change.* New York: Cambridge University Press.

Haile, T. (2014, March 9). What You Think You Know about the Web Is Wrong. *Time.* http://time.com/12933/what-you-think-you-know-about-the-web-is-wrong/.

Hall, N. (2016). *Displacement, Development, and Climate Change: International Organizations Moving Beyond Their Mandates.* New York: Routledge.

Hallahan, K., Holtzhausen, D., van Ruler, B., Verčič, D., and Sriramesh, K. (2007). Defining Strategic Communication. *International Journal of Strategic Communication, 1*(1), 3–35. doi: 10.1080/15531180701285244.

Halpin, D. (2014). *The Organization of Political Interest Groups: Designing Advocacy.* New York: Routledge Press.

Halupka, M. (2016). The Rise of Information Activism: How to Bridge Dualisms and Reconceptualise Political Participation. *Information, Communication & Society, 19*(10), 1487–1503.

Han, H. (2014). *How Organizations Develop Activists: Civic Associations and Leadership in the 21st Century.* New York: Oxford University Press.

Herbst, S. (1993). *Numbered Voices: How Opinion Polling Has Shaped American Politics.* Chicago: University of Chicago Press.

Herbst, S. (1998). *Reading Public Opinion: How Political Actors View the Democratic Process.* New York: Cambridge University Press.

Herrman, J. (2015, June 17). Platform Patched. *The Awl.* http://www.theawl.com/2015/06/platform-patched.

Hersh, E. (2015). *Hacking the Electorate: How Campaigns Perceive Voters.* New York: Cambridge University Press.

Hestres, L. E. (2014). Preaching to the Choir: Internet-Mediated Advocacy, Issue Public Mobilization, and Climate Change. *New Media & Society, 16*(2), 323–339. doi:10.1177/1461444813480361.

Hestres, L. E. (2015). Climate Change Advocacy Online: Theories of Change, Target Audiences, and Online Strategy. *Environmental Politics, 24*(2), 193–211. doi:10.1080/09644016.2015.992600.

Hillygus, D. D., and Shields, T. G. (2008). *The Persuadable Voter: Wedge Issues in Presidential Campaigns.* Princeton, NJ: Princeton University Press.

Hindman, M. (2005). The Real Lessons of Howard Dean: Reflections on the First Digital Campaign. *Perspectives on Politics, 3*(1), 121–128.

Hindman, M. (2008). *The Myth of Digital Democracy.* Princeton, NJ: Princeton University Press.

Hindman, M. (Forthcoming). *The Industrial Internet.* Princeton, NJ: Princeton University Press.

Hirschman, A. O. (1984). Against Parsimony: Three Easy Ways of Complicating Some Categories of Economic Discourse. *Bulletin of the American Academy of Arts and Sciences, 37*(8), 11–28.

Holbrook, T. M. (1996). *Do Campaigns Matter?* Thousand Oaks, CA: Sage.

Holst, L. (2015, October 7). Coworker.org Founder Jess Kutch: "We're Talking to the President on Wednesday (and You Can, Too)." [Blog post], *WhiteHouse.gov.* https://www.whitehouse.gov/blog/2015/10/07/email-founder-coworkerorg-jess-kutch.

Holtz, C. (2014). *Grassroots-Led Campaigns: Lessons from the New Frontier of People-Powered Campaigning Platforms and Programs*. Citizen Engagement Laboratory and Mobilisation Lab at Greenpeace report. http://www.mobilisationlab.org/wp-content/uploads/2014/01/MobLab-Grassroots-led-Campaigns-Report_FINAL.pdf.

Holtz, C. (2015). *Beyond Vanity Metrics: Toward Better Measurement of Member Engagement*. Citizen Engagement Laboratory and Mobilisation Lab at Greenpeace report. http://www.mobilisationlab.org/wp-content/uploads/2015/04/Beyond-Vanity-Metrics_FINAL.pdf.

Hopkins, D. J. (2013). The Exaggerated Life of Death Panels: The Limits of Framing Effects in the 2009–2012 Health Care Debate. Social Science Research Network working paper. http://ssrn.com/abstract=2163769.

Howard, A. (2014, July 25). Congress Passes Bill to Make Unlocking Cellphones Legal, Shining New Sunlight on White House E-Petitions. [Blog post], *E Pluribus Unum*. http://e-pluribusunum.com/2014/07/25/congress-passes-bill-unlocking-cellphones-legal-whitehouse-epetitions/.

Howard, A. (2015, July 29). White House Responds to Remaining "We The People" E-Petitions. *Huffington Post* http://www.huffingtonpost.com/entry/white-house-clears-the-backlog-of-we-the-people-epetitions_55b788dde4b0074ba5a6165a?xfde7b9.

Howard, P. N. (2005). *New Media Campaigns and the Managed Citizen*. New York: Cambridge University Press.

Howard, P. N. (2006). *New Media Campaigns and the Managed Citizen*. New York: Cambridge University Press.

Howard, P. N. (2012, August 16). Let's Nationalize Facebook. *Slate*. http://www.slate.com/articles/technology/future_tense/2012/08/facebook_should_be_nationalized_to_protect_user_rights_.html.

Howard, P. N. (2015). *Pax Technica: How the Internet of Things May Set Us Free or Lock Us Up*. New Haven, CT: Yale University Press.

Issenberg, S. (2012). *The Victory Lab: The Secret Science of Winning Campaigns*. New York: Crown Books.

Jacobs, L. R., and Shapiro, R. Y. (2000). *Politicians Don't Pander: Political Manipulation and the Loss of Democratic Responsiveness*. Chicago: University of Chicago Press.

Jamieson, K. H., and Cappella, J. N. (2008). *Echo Chamber: Rush Limbaugh and the Conservative Media Establishment*. New York: Oxford University Press.

Jenkins, H., Ford, S., and Green, J. (2013). *Spreadable Media: Creating Value and Meaning in a Networked Culture*. New York: New York University Press.

Karpf, D. (2009, April). Advocacy Group Involvement in the 2008 Democratic Presidential Primary: The New Generation Arrives. Paper presented at the Midwest Political Science Association Annual Meeting, Chicago. https://davekarpf.files.wordpress.com/2009/03/mpsa-2010-paper.pdf.

Karpf, D. (2010). Online Political Mobilization from the Advocacy Group's Perspective: Looking Beyond Clicktivism. *Policy & Internet*, 2(4). http://www.psocommons.org/policyandinternet/vol2/iss4/art2/.

Karpf, D. (2012a). *The MoveOn Effect: The Unexpected Transformation of American Political Advocacy*. New York: Oxford University Press.

Karpf, D. (2012b.) Social Science Research Methods in Internet Time. *Information, Communication & Society*, 15(5), 636–661. http://dx.doi.org/10.1080/1369118X.2012.665468.

Karpf, D. (2012c, June 19). Change.org and the Dilemmas of Success. *TechPresident*. http://techpresident.com/news/22396/op-ed-changeorg-and-dilemmas-success.

Karpf, D. (2012d). Americans Elect: They Built It, and Nobody Came. *Techpresident*. http://techpresident.com/news/22148/op-ed-americans-elect-they-built-it-and-nobody-came.

Karpf, D. (2013a, May 4). E-Government and Its Limitations: Assessing the True Demand Curve for Citizen Public Participation. *Selected Papers of Internet Research*, 14. http://spir.aoir.org/index.php/spir/article/view/791.

Karpf, D. (2013b, November 4). Netroots Goes Global. *The Nation*. http://www.thenation.com/article/176700/netroots-goes-global.

Karpf, D. (2014a, June 16). The Deliverability Sinkhole. [Blog post], *Shouting Loudly*. http://www.shoutingloudly.com/2014/06/16/the-deliverability-sinkhole/.

Karpf, D. (2014b, June 20). How the White House's We The People E-Petition Site Became a Virtual Ghost-Town. *TechPresident*. http://techpresident.com/news/25144/how-white-houses-we-people-e-petition-site-became-virtual-ghost-town.

Karpf, D. (2014c). Comment on "Organization in the Crowd: Peer Production in Large-Scale Networked Protests." *Information, Communication & Society, 17*(2), 261–263. doi:10.1080/1369118X.2013.868020.

Karpf, D. (2015, August 21). No, Politico, Google Can't Rig the 2016 Election (without Trying REALLY Hard, at Least). [Blog Post], *Shouting Loudly*. http://www.shoutingloudly.com/2015/08/21/no-politico-google-cant-rig-the-2016-election-without-trying-really-hard-at-least/.

Katz, J., Barris, M., and Jain, A. (2013). *The Social Media President: Barack Obama and the Politics of Digital Engagement*. New York: Palgrave Macmillan.

Kavada, A. (2012). Engagement, Bonding, and Identity Across Multiple Platforms: Avaaz on Facebook, YouTube, and MySpace. *MedieKultur: Journal of Media and Communication Research, 52*, 28–48.

Kavada, A. (2015). Creating the Collective: Social Media, the Occupy Movement and Its Constitution as a Collective Actor. *Information, Communication & Society, 18*(8) 872–886. ISSN 1369–118X.

Kelly, K. J. (2015, July 23). Demand Media Looking to Sell Off eHow, Cracked. *New York Post*. http://nypost.com/2015/07/23/demand-media-looking-to-sell-off-ehow-cracked/.

Kessler, S. (2015, January 23). The Secret Tool that Upworthy, Buzzfeed, and Everyone Else Is Using to Win Facebook. *Fast Company*. http://www.fastcompany.com/3040951/the-secret-tool-that-upworthy-buzzfeed-and-everyone-else-is-using-to-win-facebook.

Key, V. O. (1961). *Public Opinion and American Democracy*. New York: Knopf.

Kingdon, J. W. (1984). *Agendas, Alternatives, and Public Policies*. Boston: Little, Brown.

Kirchner, L. (2011, January 27). Demand Media IPO Valued Higher than the NYT. *Columbia Journalism Review*. http://www.cjr.org/the_news_frontier/demand_media_ipo_valued_higher.php.

Klein, Ezra. (2013, December 10). Does Upworthy Prove Media Outlets Are Hurting Themselves by Publishing So Much Content? *Washington Post*. http://www.washingtonpost.com/blogs/wonkblog/wp/2013/12/10/does-upworthy-prove-media-outlets-are-hurting-themselves-by-publishing-so-much-content/.

Kling, R. (1991). Computerization and Social Transformation. *Science, Technology, & Human Values, 16*(3), 342–367.

Koechley, P., and Pariser, E. (2014, April 1). Our Mission Is Huge: Here's How We're Building the Business to Support It. [Blog post], *Upworthy Insider*. http://tmblr.co/Z1g28v1BozZMS.

Kolari, P., Java, A., Finin, T., Oates, T., & Joshi, A. (2006). Detecting Spam Blogs: A Machine Learning Approach. *Proceedings of the National Conference on Artificial Intelligence, 21*(2), 1351–1356.

Kramer, A. D. I., Guillory, J. E., & Hancock, J. T. (2014). Experimental Evidence of Massive-Scale Emotional Contagion Through Social Networks. *PNAS, 111*(24), 8788–8790. doi:10.1073/pnas.1320040111.

Kranzberg, M. (1986). Technology and History: "Kranzberg's Laws." *Technology and Culture, 27*(3), 544–560. doi:10.2307/3105385.

Kreiss, D. (2012). *Taking Our Country Back: The Crafting of Networked Politics from Howard Dean to Barack Obama*. New York: Oxford University Press.

Kreiss, D. (2016). *Prototype Politics*. New York: Oxford University Press.

Kristofferson, K., White, K., and Peloza, J. (2014). The Nature of Slacktivism: How the Social Observability of an Initial Act of Token Support Affects Subsequent Prosocial Action. *Journal of Consumer Research, 40*(6), 1149–1166.

Kutch, J. (2015, June). Labor Codes: The Power of Employee-Led Online Organizing. Keynote speech presented at Personal Democracy Forum 2015, New York. https://personaldemocracy.com/media/labor-codes-power-employee-led-online-organizing presented at

LaFrance, A. (2015). Raiders of the Lost Web. *The Atlantic*. http://www.theatlantic.com/technology/archive/2015/10/raiders-of-the-lost-web/409210/.

Lang, K., and Lang, G. E. (1953). The Unique Perspective of Television and Its Effect: A Pilot Study. *American Sociological Review, 18*(1), 3–12.

Lapowsky, I. (2013, October 23). Change.org Launches Portal for Congress. *Inc.* www.inc.com/issie-lapowski/change-portal-for-congress.html.

La Raja, R. J. (2013). Richer Parties, Better Politics? Party-Centered Campaign Finance Laws and American Democracy. *Forum: A Journal of Applied Research in Contemporary Politics, 11*(3), 313–338.

Lazer, D., Kennedy, R., King, G., and Vespignani, A. (2014). The Parable of Google Flu: Traps in Big Data Analysis. *Science, 343*(6176), 1203–1205. doi:10.1126/science.1248506.

Lee, C. (2014). *Do-It-Yourself Democracy: The Rise of the Public Engagement Industry*. New York: Oxford University Press.

Lee, T. (2002). *Mobilizing Public Opinion: Black Insurgency and Racial Attitudes in the Civil Rights Era*. Chicago: University of Chicago Press.

Lehmann, N. (2013, April 15). When the Earth Moved. *The New Yorker*. http://www.newyorker.com/magazine/2013/04/15/when-the-earth-moved.

Leiserowitz, A., Maibach, E., Roser-Renouf, C., Feinberg, G. and Howe, P. (2013). Global Warming's Six Americas. September 2012, Yale University and George Mason University. New Haven, CT: Yale Project on Climate Change Communication. http://environment.yale.edu/climate/publications/Six-Americas-September-2012.

Lerner, J. A. (2014). *Making Democracy Fun: How Game Design Can Empower Citizens and Transform Politics*. Cambridge, MA: MIT Press.

Lewis, K., Gray, K., and Meierhenrich, J. (2014). The Structure of Online Activism. *Sociological Science*. https://www.sociologicalscience.com/structure-online-activism/.

Liacas, T. (2015, November). Innovations in Networked Movement Building: Distributed Activism as Practiced by 350.org and Hollaback! Working paper presented at the Social Media, Activism, and Organisations Symposium 2015, London. http://www.academia.edu/17670880/Innovations_in_networked_movement_building_Distributed_activism_as_practiced_by_350.org_and_Hollaback_.

Lichtblau, E. (2015, May 2). F.E.C. Can't Curb 2016 Election Abuse, Commission Chief Says. *New York Times*. http://www.nytimes.com/2015/05/03/us/politics/fec-cant-curb-2016-election-abuse-commission-chief-says.html?_r=1.

Lippmann, W. (1922). *Public Opinion*. New York: Harcourt, Brace.

Lippmann, W. (1925). *The Phantom Public*. New York: Macmillan.

Lowenstein, F. (2014, June 23). Why You Should Pay Attention to Upworthy Measuring Engagement in "Attention Minutes." *Columbia Journalism Review*. http://www.cjr.org/behind_the_news/upworthy_attention_minutes.php.

MacKinnon, R. (2012). *Consent of the Networked: The Worldwide Struggle for Internet Freedom*. New York: Basic Books.

Madrigal, A. C. (2013, December 12). Welcome to the Internet of Thingies: 61.5% of Web Traffic Is Not Human. *The Atlantic*. http://www.theatlantic.com/technology/archive/2013/12/welcome-to-the-internet-of-thingies-615-of-web-traffic-is-not-human/282309/.

Manheim, J. B. (1991). *All of the People, All the Time: Strategic Communication and American Politics*. New York: M.E. Sharpe.

Mansbridge, J. (1983). *Beyond Adversary Democracy*. Chicago: University of Chicago Press.

Mansbridge, J. (1986). *Why We Lost the ERA*. Chicago: University of Chicago Press.

March, E. (2015, June 25). 5 Incredibly Delicious Chain Restaurants You Should Never, Ever Eat at and 1 You Should but Can't. *Upworthy*. https://www.upworthy.com/5-incredibly-delicious-chain-restaurants-you-should-never-ever-eat-at-and-1-you-should-but-cant?c=hpstream.

Margetts, H., John, P., Hale, S., and Reissfelder, S. (2015a). Leadership without Leaders? Starters and Followers in Online Collective Action. *Political Studies, 63*(2), 278–299.

Margetts, H., John, P., Hale, S., and Yasseri, T. (2015b). *Political Turbulence: How Social Media Shape Collective Action*. Princeton, NJ: Princeton University Press.

Masket, S., Sides, J., and Vavreck, L. (2016). The Ground Game in the 2012 Presidential Election. *Political Communication*, 33(2), 169–187. doi: 10.1080/10584609.2015.1029657.

Mayer-Schönberger, V. (2009). *Delete: The Virtue of Forgetting in the Digital Age*. Princeton, NJ: Princeton University Press.

Mayer-Schönberger, V., and Cukier, K. (2013). *Big Data: A Revolution That Will Transform How We Live, Work and Think*. Boston: Houghton Mifflin Harcourt.

McAdam, D. (1999). *Political Process and the Development of Black Insurgency, 1930-1970* (2d ed.). Chicago: University of Chicago Press.

McChesney, R. W., and Pickard, V. (2011). *Will the Last Reporter Please Turn out the Lights? The Collapse of Journalism and What Can Be Done To Fix It*. New York: New Press.

McDonald, S. N. (2014, June 4). John Oliver's Net Neutrality Rant May Have Caused FCC Site Crash. *Washington Post*. https://www.washingtonpost.com/news/morning-mix/wp/2014/06/04/john-olivers-net-neutrality-rant-may-have-caused-fcc-site-crash/.

McKenna, E., and Han, H. (2015). *Groundbreakers: How Obama's 2.2 Million Volunteers Transformed Campaigning in America*. New York: Oxford University Press.

McKibben, B. (1989). *The End of Nature*. New York: Random House.

McMorris-Santoro, E. (2015, February 10). Liberal Organizing Group Implodes in One Tumultuous Afternoon. *Buzzfeed*. http://www.buzzfeed.com/evanmcsan/new-organizing-institute-implodes#.byZMBVDLm.

Meltzer, E. (2013, November 5). Boulder Utility Clears Hurdle as Voters Reject Xcel-Backed Question 310. *Daily Camera*. http://www.dailycamera.com/boulder-election-news/ci_24459325/boulder-ballot-issue-310-2e-municipalization.

Messing, S., and Westwood, S. (2014). Selective Exposure in the Age of Social Media: Endorsements Trump Partisan Source Affiliation When Selecting News Online. *Communication Research*, 41(8), 1042–1063.

Miller, E. (2010.) How Not to Run an A/B Test. [Blog post], *EvanMiller*. http://www.evanmiller.org/how-not-to-run-an-ab-test.html.

Moe, T. (1991). Politics and the Theory of Organization. *Journal of Law, Economics, & Organization*, 7 (special issue), 106–129. http://jleo.oxfordjournals.org/content/7/special_issue/106.extract.

Morozov, E. (2010, October). Two Views on the Internet and Democratization. Keynote speech presented at Personal Democracy Forum-Europe 2010, Barcelona. https://www.youtube.com/watch?v=RFgWQz__Azo.

Nahon, K., and Hemsley, J. (2013). *Going Viral*. Malden, MA: Polity Press.

New Era Colorado. (2013, September 3). We Just Became Upworthy [Facebook post]. https://www.facebook.com/NewEraColorado/posts/10152181437673206.

Newman, N. (2015). Executive Summary and Key Findings of the 2015 Report. *Digital News Report 2015*. Reuters Institute for the Study of Journalism. http://www.digitalnewsreport.org/survey/2015/executive-summary-and-key-findings-2015/.

Nickerson, D. W., and Rogers, T. (2014). Political Campaigns and Big Data. *Journal of Economic Perspectives*, 28(2), 51–74. http://www.aeaweb.org/articles.php?doi=10.1257/jep.28.2.51.

Nielsen, R. K. (2012). *Ground Wars: Personalized Communication in Political Campaigns*. Princeton, NJ: Princeton University Press.

O'Donovan, C. (2014, February 6). You Won't Believe Upworthy's New Way of Measuring Audience Engagement until You Read It. *Nieman Lab*. http://www.niemanlab.org/2014/02/upworthy-has-a-new-way-of-measuring-engagement/.

O'Neil, C. (2015, June). Weapons of Math Destruction. Keynote speech presented at Personal Democracy Forum 2015, New York. https://www.youtube.com/watch?v=gdCJYsKlX_Y.

Papacharissi, Z. (2014). *Affective Publics: Sentiment, Technology, and Politics*. New York: Oxford University Press.

Pariser, E. (2011a, March). Beware Online "Filter Bubbles." Talk presented at TED, Long Beach, CA. http://www.ted.com/talks/eli_pariser_beware_online_filter_bubbles.

Pariser, E. (2011b). *The Filter Bubble: How the New Personalized Web Is Changing What We Read and How We Think*. New York: Penguin Press.

Pariser, E. (2013, June). The Truth Needs Better Marketing. Talk presented at TEDxPoynter-Institute, St. Petersburg, FL. https://www.youtube.com/watch?v=-WvhFXxORis&list=PLs RNoUx8w3rP8wFnKBmT5Biq5VBBmFX-2.

Pasquale, F. (2015). *The Black Box Society: The Secret Algorithms That Control Money and Information.* Cambridge, MA: Harvard University Press.

Petre, C. (2015, May 7). The Traffic Factories: Metrics at Chartbeat, Gawker Media, and The New York Times. *Tow Center for Digital Journalism.* http://towcenter.org/research/traffic-factories/.

Petre, C. (Forthcoming). Managing Metrics: The Containment, Disclosure, and Sanctioning of Audience Data at the *New York Times.* Working paper.

Polletta, F. (2002). *Freedom Is an Endless Meeting: Democracy in American Social Movements.* Chicago: University of Chicago Press.

Postman, N. (1985). *Amusing Ourselves to Death: Public Discourse in the Age of Show Business.* New York: Viking Adult.

Powers, M. (2014). The Structural Organization of NGO Publicity: Explaining Divergent Publicity Strategies at Humanitarian and Human Rights Organizations. *International Journal of Communication, 8.* http://ijoc.org/index.php/ijoc/article/view/2517.

Powers, M. (2015). The New Boots on the Ground: NGOs in the Changing Landscape of International News. *Journalism,* January 2015. doi: 10.1177/1464884914568077.

Prior, M. (2007). *Post-Broadcast Democracy: How Media Choice Increases Inequality in Political Involvement and Polarizes Elections.* Princeton, NJ: Princeton University Press.

Pugh, J. (2015, October 2). How Nonprofits Can Increase Engagement Through Gamification. *Huffington Post.* http://www.huffingtonpost.com/jim-pugh/nonprofits-engagement-gaming_b_8215248.html.

Rattray, B. (2011, June). How Hyperlocal Online Organizing Is Disrupting Traditional Advocacy. Keynote speech presented at Personal Democracy Forum 2011. https://www.youtube.com/watch?v=WV2XK46LkQE.

Rattray, B. (2012, October 25). The Case for Change. *Huffington Post.* http://www.huffington-post.com/ben-rattray/the-case-for-change_b_2018554.html.

Rattray, B. (2013, June). The Next Generation of People-Powered Movements. Keynote speech presented at Personal Democracy Forum 2013. https://www.youtube.com/watch?v=38j2fp5O5po.

Ries, E. (2011). *The Lean Startup: How Today's Entrepreneurs Use Continuous Innovation to Create Radically Successful Businesses.* New York: Crown.

Roberts, D. (2015, November 8). What Critics of the Keystone Campaign Misunderstand about Climate Activism. *Vox.* http://www.vox.com/2015/11/8/9690654/keystone-climate-activism.

Roeder, E. (2012, December 5). I Am Not Big Brother. *New York Times.* http://www.nytimes.com/2012/12/06/opinion/i-am-not-big-brother.html?_r=0.

Rohlinger, D. A., and Bunnage, L. A. (2015). Connecting People To Politics over Time? Internet Communication Technology and Retention in MoveOn.org and the Florida Tea Party Movement. *Information, Communication, & Society,* 18(5), 539–552.

Romanesko, J. (2013, December 3). Gawker Boss: We Got Overtaken by Buzzfeed and Smarmy Upworthy Is Nipping at Our Heels. [Blog post], *JimRomenesko.* http://jimromenesko.com/2013/12/03/gawker-boss-we-got-overtaken-by-buzzfeed-and-smarmy-upworthy-is-nipping-at-our-heels/.

Rosales, L. (2015, August 18). Demand Media Closing Austin Office, Staff Surprised to Lose Their Jobs. *American Genius.* http://theamericangenius.com/business-news/demand-media-closing-austin-office-roughly-100-surprised-to-lose-their-jobs-what-happened/.

Rosen, J. (2009, December 16). Jay Rosen Interviews Demand Media: Are Content Farms "Demonic"? *Readwrite.* http://readwrite.com/2009/12/16/jay_rosen_vs_demand_media_are_content_farms_demoni.

Roth, D. (2009). The Answer Factory: Demand Media and the Fast, Disposable, and Profitable as Hell Media Model. *Wired, 17.* http://www.wired.com/2009/10/ff_demandmedia/.

Rudder, C. (2014). We Experiment on Human Beings! [Blog post], *OkCupid*. http://blog.okcupid.com/index.php/we-experiment-on-human-beings/.

Schier, S. (2000). *By Invitation Only: The Rise of Exclusive Politics in the United States*. Pittsburgh: University of Pittsburgh Press.

Schlozman, K. L., Jones, P. E., You, H. Y., Burch, T., Verba, S., and Brady, H. E. (2015). Organizations and the Democratic Representation of Interests: What Does It Mean When Those Organizations Have No Members? *Perspectives on Politics, 13*(4), 1017–1029. doi: 10.1017/S1537592715002285.

Schneier, B. (2015). *Data and Goliath: The Hidden Battles to Collect Your Data and Control Your World*. New York: W. W. Norton.

Schudson, M. (1998). *The Good Citizen: A History of American Civic Life*. New York: Free Press.

Schudson, M., and Downie, L. (2009). The Reconstruction of American Journalism. *Columbia Journalism Review*, November/December 2009. http://www.cjr.org/reconstruction/the_reconstruction_of_american.php.

Scocca, T. (2013, December 5). On Smarm. *Gawker*. http://gawker.com/on-smarm-1476594977.

Sen, A. (1977). Rational Fools: A Critique of the Behavioral Foundations of Economic Theory. *Philosophy and Public Affairs, 6*(4), 317–344.

Shaiko, R. (1993). Greenpeace U.S.A.: Something Old, New, Borrowed. *Annals of the American Academy of Political and Social Science, 528*, 88–100.

ShareProgress. (2015). About Shareprogress. http://www.shareprogress.org/about/.

Sheppard, K. (2014, January 9). 100 Local Anti-Fracking Activists Receive Grants from MoveOn. *Huffington Post*. http://www.huffingtonpost.com/2014/01/09/moveon-fracking-activists_n_4568439.html.

Shields, M. (2014, February 6). Upworthy Touts New Metric. *Adweek*. http://www.adweek.com/news/advertising-branding/upworthy-touts-new-metric-155516.

Shirky, C. (2008a). *Here Comes Everybody: The Power of Organizing Without Organizations*. New York: Penguin Books.

Shirky, C. (2008b, March 16). Newspapers and Thinking the Unthinkable. *Edge*. https://edge.org/conversation/clay_shirky-newspapers-and-thinking-the-unthinkable.

Shontell, A. (2012, November 5). How to Create the Fastest Growing Media Company in the World. *Business Insider*. http://www.businessinsider.com/upworthy-how-to-create-a-fast-growing-media-company-2012-11.

Shulman, S. (2009). The Case Against Mass E-mails: Perverse Incentives and Low Quality Public Participation in U.S. Federal Rulemaking. *Policy & Internet, 1*(1), 23–53.

Sides, J., and Vavreck, L. (2014a, January 21). Obama's Not-So-Big Data. *Pacific Standard*. http://www.psmag.com/books-and-culture/obamas-big-data-inconclusive-results-political-campaigns-72687.

Sides, J., and Vavreck, L. (2014b). *The Gamble: Choice and Chance in the 2012 Presidential Election*. Princeton, NJ: Princeton University Press.

Sifry, M.L. (2013, September 4). You Can't A/B Test Your Response to Syria. [Blog post], *Techpresident*. http://techpresident.com/news/24316/you-cant-ab-test-your-response-syria.

Sifry, M. L. (2014a). *The Big Disconnect: Why the Internet Hasn't Transformed Politics (Yet)*. New York: O/R Books.

Sifry, M. L. (2014b, July 3). Why Facebook's "Voter Megaphone" Is the Real Manipulation to Worry about. *TechPresident*. http://techpresident.com/news/25165/why-facebooks-voter-megaphone-real-manipulation-worry-about.

Silberman, M., and Mahendra, J. (2015, June 8). Moving Beyond Vanity Metrics. *Stanford Social Innovation Review*. http://ssir.org/articles/entry/moving_beyond_vanity_metrics.

Siroker, D., and Koomen, P. (2013). *A/B Testing: The Most Powerful Way to Turn Clicks into Customers*. Hoboken, NJ: Wiley Books.

Skocpol, T. (2003). *Diminished Democracy: From Membership to Management in American Civic Life*. Norman: University of Oklahoma Press.

Skocpol, T. (2013, February). Naming the Problem: What It Will Take to Counter Extremism and Engage Americans in the Fight against Global Warming. Paper prepared for the Symposium on the Politics of America's Fight Against Global Warming, Cambridge, MA. http://www.scholarsstrategynetwork.org/sites/default/files/skocpol_captrade_report_january_2013_0.pdf.

Sobel Fitts, A. (2014, May 1). The King of Content. *Columbia Journalism Review.* http://www.cjr.org/feature/the_king_of_content.php.

Sobel Fitts, A. (2015). The New Importance of "Social Listening" Tools. *Columbia Journalism Review,* July/August 2015. http://www.cjr.org/analysis/the_new_importance_of_social_listening_tools.php.

Starr, P. (2009, March 4). Goodbye to the Age of Newspapers (Hello to a New Era of Corruption). *New Republic.* http://www.newrepublic.com/article/goodbye-the-age-newspapers-hello-new-era-corruption.

Stempeck, M. (2015, August 11). Are Uber and Facebook Turning Users into Lobbyists? *Harvard Business Review.* https://hbr.org/2015/08/are-uber-and-facebook-turning-users-into-lobbyists.

Stinebrickner-Kauffman, T. (2013, June). You Know Nothing, Campaigners. Keynote speech presented at Personal Democracy Forum 2013, New York. https://personaldemocracy.com/media/you-know-nothing-campaigners.

Stirland, S. L. (2012, September 18). With "RePurpose," AFL-CIO Invites Supporters to Join in Playing Politics. *TechPresident.* http://techpresident.com/news/22873/afl-cio-super-pac-playing-politics.

Stromer-Galley, J. (2014). *Presidential Campaigning in the Internet Age.* New York: Oxford University Press.

Stroud, N. J., Muddiman, A., and Scacco, J. (2013, November). Framing Comments in Social Media. Paper presented at the National Communication Association, Political Communication Division, Washington, DC. http://engagingnewsproject.org/research/social-media-buttons/.

Sunstein, C. (2001). *Republic.com.* Princeton, NJ: Princeton University Press.

Sunstein, C. (2007). *Republic.com 2.0.* Princeton, NJ: Princeton University Press.

SXSW. (2014). *Do Algorithms Dream of Viral Content?* (full session) | *Interactive 2014* | *SXSW* [Video]. https://www.youtube.com/watch?v=QEso8VSA0d0.

Tanzer, M. (2014, June 19). The Page View Just Won't Die. *Buzzfeed.* http://www.buzzfeed.com/mylestanzer/why-wont-the-page-view-just-die-already#.geeX5K7Wg.

Tau, B. (2014, August 16). How the Media Discovered Ferguson. *Politico.* http://www.politico.com/story/2014/08/how-the-media-discovered-ferguson-110072.html.

Tauberer, J. (2015, November 22). So You Want to Reform Democracy. [Blog post], *Medium.* https://medium.com/@joshuatauberer/so-you-want-to-reform-democracy-7f3b1ef10597#.i4xiap9tq.

Teles, S., Hurlburt, H., and Schmitt, M. (2014). Philanthropy in a Time of Polarization. *Stanford Social Innovation Review, 12*(3).

Terkel, A., and Grim, R. (2012, December 5). MoveOn Moving On: Progressive Powerhouse Launches Radical Strategic Overhaul. *HuffingtonPost.* http://www.huffingtonpost.com/2012/12/04/moveon-changes_n_2240238.html.

The Iowa House v Zach Wahls and His Moms. (2011, February 4). Democracy in America Blog, *The Economist.* http://www.economist.com/blogs/democracyinamerica/2011/02/politics_and_morality_gay_marriage.

Theocharis, Y. (2015). The Conceptualization of Digitally Networked Participation. *Social Media + Society, 1*(2). doi:10.1177/2056305115610140.

Thorson, K., and Wells, C. (2015). Curated Flows: A Framework for Mapping Media Exposure in the Digital Age. *Communication Theory, 26*(3), 309–328, doi:10.1111/comt.12087.

Tufekci, Z. (2012, November 16). Beware the Smart Campaign. *New York Times.* http://www.nytimes.com/2012/11/17/opinion/beware-the-big-data-campaign.html?_r=0.

Tufekci, Z. (2014a). Engineering the Public: Big Data, Surveillance, and Computational Politics. *First Monday, 19*(7). http://dx.doi.org/10.5210/fm.v19i7.4901.

Tufekci, Z. (2014b). Facebook and Engineering the Public. *Medium*. https://medium.com/message/engineering-the-public-289c91390225#.xglesgs54.

Tufecki, Z. (2014c, August 14). What Happens to #Ferguson Affects Ferguson: Net Neutrality, Algorithmic Filtering and Ferguson. *Medium*. https://medium.com/message/ferguson-is-also-a-net-neutrality-issue-6d2f3db51eb0#.dqliaxgkd.

Turow, J. (2011). *The Daily You: How the New Advertising Industry Is Defining Your Identity and Your Worth*. New Haven, CT: Yale University Press.

Tversky, A., and Kahneman, D. (1981). The Framing of Decisions and the Psychology of Choice. *Science, 211*(4481), 453–458. http://www.jstor.org/stable/1685855.

Upworthy. (2014a, January 9). The Most Upworthy Topics of 2013. [Blog post], *Upworthy Insider*. http://tmblr.co/Z1g28v13n2xeh.

Upworthy. (2014b, Feb. 6). What Uniques and Pageviews Leave Out (and Why We're Measuring Attention Minutes Instead). [Blog post], *Upworthy Insider*. http://tmblr.co/Z1g28v16bnaaE.

Upworthy. (2014c, Mar. 10). The Most Important Topics Of 2014, According to You. [Blog post], *Upworthy Insider*. http://tmblr.co/Z1g28v19mkD65.

Upworthy. (2014d, June 13). The Most We've Ever Said about Curation at Upworthy. [Blog post]. *Upworthy Insider*. http://tmblr.co/Z1g28v1IaQnW1.

Upworthy. (2014e). What It Really Means to Be an Earthling. *Upworthy*. https://www.upworthy.com/what-it-really-means-to-be-an-earthling.

Upworthy. (2014f). Ellen, Katy Perry, and a Hockey Player Walk into an Ad and Shatter a Ridiculous Argument. *Upworthy*. https://www.upworthy.com/ellen-katy-perry-and-a-hockey-player-walk-into-an-ad-and-shatter-a-ridiculous-argument.

Upworthy. (2015). *Upworthy Editorial Vision* [Slideshow]. *Linkedin*. http://www.slideshare.net/UpworthyAdmin/july-8-2015-upworthy-editorial-vision.

Usher, N. (2014). *Making News at the New York Times*. Ann Arbor: University of Michigan Press.

Vaidhyanathan, S. (2011). *The Googlization of Everything (and Why We Should Worry)*. Berkeley: University of California Press.

Van Dijck, J. (2013). *The Culture of Connectivity: A Critical History of Social Media*. New York: Oxford University Press.

Van Laer, J., and van Aelst, P. (2010). Internet and Social Movement Action Repertoires. *Information, Communication & Society, 13*(8), 1146–1171. doi: 10.1080/13691181003628307.

Vromen, A., and Coleman, W. (2013). Online Campaigning Organizations and Storytelling Strategies: GetUp! in Australia. *Policy & Internet, 5*(1), 76–100.

Waldman, K. (2014, May 22). For Love or Money. *Slate*. http://www.slate.com/articles/health_and_science/science/2014/05/upworthy_audience_reach_and_business_success_morality_clicktivism_and_the.html.

Walker, E. (2014). *Grassroots for Hire: Public Affairs Consultants in American Democracy*. New York: Cambridge University Press.

Walker, E., Martin, A., and McCarthy, J. (2008). Confronting the State, the Corporation, and the Academy: The Influence of Institutional Targets on Social Movement Repertoires. *American Journal of Sociology, 114*(1), 35–76.

Walker, E. T. (2015, August 6). The Uber-ization of Activism. *New York Times*. http://www.nytimes.com/2015/08/07/opinion/the-uber-ization-of-activism.html?_r=0.

Weber, M. (1919). Politics as a Vocation. In H. H. Gerth and C. Wright Mills (Eds. and trans.), *Max Weber* (27). New York: Free Press.

Weidinger, R. (2013). When Sharks Attack, Jump into the Water. Keynote speech presented at Personal Democracy Forum 2013, New York. https://personaldemocracy.com/media/when-sharks-attack-jump-water.

Weidinger, R., Dearborn, R., Fitzgerald, M., Dugas, S., Mulvaney, K., and Bravo, B. (2013). Upwell Pilot Report. *Upwell*. http://www.upwell.us/upwells-pilot-report-aka-165-pages-awesomeness.

Wells, C. (2015). *The Civic Organization and the Digital Citizen: Communicating Engagement in a Networked Age*. New York: Oxford University Press.

White, M. (2011, July 13). #OccupyWallStreet. *Adbusters*. https://www.adbusters.org/blogs/adbusters-blog/occupywallstreet.html.

White, M. (2010, August 12). Clicktivism Is Ruining Leftist Activism. *The Guardian Online*. http://www.guardian.co.uk/commentisfree/2010/aug/12/clicktivism-ruining-leftist-activism.

Williams, B. A., and Delli Carpini, M. X. (2011). *After Broadcast News: Media Regimes, Democracy, and the New Information Environment*. New York: Cambridge University Press.

Wojcieszak, M. (2010). "Don't talk to me": Effects of Ideologically Homogeneous Online Groups and Politically Dissimilar Offline Ties on Extremism. *New Media & Society, 12*(4), 637–655.

Wojcieszak, M., Bimber, B., Feldman, L., & Stroud, N. J. (2015). Partisan News and Political Participation: Exploring Mediated Relationships. *Political Communication*, 1–20. doi:10.1080/10584609.2015.1051608.

Woolley, S. C. (2016). Automating Power: Social Bot Interference in Global Politics. *First Monday, 21*(4). http://dx.doi.org/10.5210/fm.v21i4.6161.

Workers' Voice PAC (2012a). *Introducing RePurpose* [Video]. https://www.youtube.com/watch?v=9Cs4A7zO3C8.

Workers' Voice PAC (2012b). *RePurpose Tutorial* [Video]. https://www.youtube.com/watch?v=Te08hHdSBe8.

Workers' Voice PAC (2016). About RePurpose. *WorkersVoice*. http://repurpose.workersvoice.org/how_it_works.

Wright, S. (2012). Assessing (e-)Democratic Innovations: "Democratic Goods" and Downing Street E-petitions. *Journal of Information Technology and Politics, 9*(4), 453–470.

Wright, S. (2015a). Populism and Downing Street E-petitions: Connective Action, Hybridity, and the Changing Nature of Organizing. *Political Communication, 32*(3), 414–433. doi:10.1080/10584609.2014.958256.

Wright, S. (2015b). "Success" and Online Political Participation: The Case of Downing Street E-petitions. *Information, Communication & Society*, 1–15. doi:10.1080/1369118X.2015.1080285.

Wu, T. (2010). *The Master Switch: The Rise and Fall of Information Empires*. New York: Vintage Press.

Yeselson, R. (2013). Fortress Unionism. *Democracy, 29*(Summer 2013), 68–81.

Zaller, J. (1992). *The Nature and Origin of Mass Opinion*. New York: Cambridge University Press.

Zittrain, J. (2008). *The Future of the Internet (And How to Stop It)*. New Haven, CT: Yale University Press.

Zuiderveen Borgesius, F. J., Trilling, D., Möller, J., Bodó, B., de Vreese, C. H., and Helberger, N. (2016). Should We Worry about Filter Bubbles? *Internet Policy Review, 5*(1). doi: 10.14763/2016.1.401.

Index